GOD'S NAME IN VAIN

M. Carey - OP
LL. Lewis 2008

D0121604

God's Name in Vain

The Wrongs and Rights of Religion in Politics

STEPHEN L. CARTER

BASIC
BOOKS

A Member of the Perseus Books Group

Scripture taken from the Holy Bible, New International Version®. Copyright © 1973, 1978, 1984 by International Bible Society. Used by permission of Zondervan Publishing House. All rights reserved.

Copyright © 2000 by Stephen L. Carter

Published by Basic Books,
A Member of the Perseus Books Group

All rights reserved. Printed in the United States of America. No part of this book may be reproduced in any manner whatsoever without written permission except in the case of brief quotations embodied in critical articles and reviews. For information, address Basic Books, 10 East 53rd Street, New York, NY 10022-5299.

Library of Congress Cataloging-in-Publication Data
Carter, Stephen L., 1954
  God's name in vain : the wrongs and rights of religion in politics
Stephen L. Carter.
     p. cm.
Includes bibliographical references and index.
ISBN 0-465-00887-9
1. Religion and politics.   2. Religion and state.   I. Title.
BL65.P7 C37 2000
322'.1'0973–dc21   00-033741
                                                                          CIP

Designed by Rachel Hegarty

FIRST PAPERBACK EDITION

For Fred Harris

". . . and some to be pastors and teachers."

(Eph. 4:11)

TABLE OF CONTENTS

ACKNOWLEDGMENTS

Testing one's scholarly ideas through repeated presentations to learned but skeptical audiences is an important part of academic tradition, but one that is rapidly disappearing, as more and more scholars share their ideas, if at all, only with those who are likely to agree with them. I have tried hard, despite the occasional psychic cost, to behave otherwise. Thus, the major themes of Part I formed the core of the Zabriskie Lectures, which I delivered at the Virginia Theological Seminary in the fall of 1998, and of the Payton Lectures, which I delivered at Fuller Theological Seminary in the spring of 2000. Other parts of the book have been the subject of lectures, panels, or workshops at the following institutions, among others: the Association of American Law Schools, the Aspen Institute, Boalt Hall (the law school of the University of California at Berkeley), Boston College Law School, Catholic University Law School (a conference sponsored jointly with Howard University Law School), the Chautauqua Institute, DePaul University Law School, the Georgetown Law Center, Hamline University Law School, Middlebury College, Union University, the University of Chicago Divinity School, the University of Minnesota Law School, the University of Texas at Austin, the Yale Medical School, and the Yale Law School. I am grateful, as always, for the comments and questions, whether disparaging or supportive, on these occasions. A reader or listener can pay a writer or speaker no greater compliment than to take the work seriously enough to offer a thoughtful disagreement.

I am also grateful for the generous support of the dean of the Yale Law School, Tony Kronman, and for the assistance of a group of remarkable students who have contributed research assistance to this project (and its many subprojects) over the past several years, including Amy Campbell, Cary Berkeley Kaye, Janine Kim, Davis Oliver, Nicole Pierre, and Nathaniel Zylstra.

For thoughtful comments on various parts of the draft, I am particularly indebted to Akhil Amar, Jack Balkin, Jon Butler, Ronald Feenstra, Robert K. Johnston, Lewis Smedes, and the faculty, students, and guests of the Virginia Theological Seminary and the Fuller Theological Seminary.

Finally, I wish to express my love and gratitude to my family: my children, Leah and Andrew, who have grown into fine young people despite their father's penchant to be off in his study writing at odd moments throughout the day, and my wife, Enola G. Aird, a rebellious and conscientious mother, a playful and marvelously contrarian Christian intellectual force who lives the instruction of Romans 12:2, and the earthly inspiration and best editor of all my work. God has blessed me beyond what I deserve, and I am ever grateful for his love and grace.

S. L. C.
Cheshire, Connecticut

GOD'S NAME IN VAIN

Introduction:
The Politics of Disbelief

THIS BOOK ARGUES TWO INTERRELATED THESES: First, that there is nothing wrong, and much right, with the robust participation of the nation's many religious voices in debates over matters of public moment. Second, that religions—although not democracy—will almost always lose their best, most spiritual selves when they choose to be involved in the partisan, electoral side of American politics.

The book is inspired by my love of God and love of my country, and my fear that millions of Americans, across the religious and political spectrum, have lost sight of the proper relationship between religion and politics.[1] On one side are those who treat the merest scintilla of religion in our public and political life as an offense against the American idea. On the other are those who believe it to be the responsibility of government to use its power to enforce as law the moral truths of their religion. The tension between these two wrong ideas is ruining our democracy, and threatens to ruin many of our religious traditions as well.

For example: As I sat down to write this introduction, the nation was in the midst of a silly brouhaha over whether or not presidential candidates should tell us about their religious views, which several prospective nominees had recently done. One side worried aloud about the "injection" of religion into politics and cautioned against the development of a Christian litmus test for those seeking the White House. The other insisted that faith was often an important part of character and that character is what politics—or, at least, governance—should really be about. Both sides, in good American fashion, subsequently set about impugning the motives, the integrity, and, in the end, the fundamental Americanness of the other. From the way people talked about the issue, one would be excused for thinking that only two possibilities existed: Either we would have a public square so religion-drenched that nobody would ever talk about anything else, or we would have a public square so carefully sterilized of God-talk that people to whom faith was important would be forced to adopt the chilly and (to them) often meaningless language of secular liberalism or to abandon politics altogether.

As so often in these debates that inspire us to nasty flights of polemical fancy, both sides were right. Both sides were also wrong. By trying to understand why each side was right, and why each side was wrong, we can come to a richer vision of the relationship between religion and politics. In order to work our way to this richer vision, however, we will have to avoid the usual bias of arguments of this kind—the bias that begins with the state and asks how religion fits into the politics that are a democracy's life's blood. If we start out thinking about the needs of the state, we have already relegated religion to an inferior position. Many citizens, however, believe that God wants us to put our faith in him and obedience to him ahead of everything else. Any argument that thinks about the state before it thinks about religion can scarcely be persuasive, or even plausible, to citizens for whom their connection to God is of first importance. Instead, we will begin with religion—with Micah's famous question, *What does the Lord require?* (Mic. 6:8). Only by looking at politics through the lens of faith, rather than faith through the lens of politics, will we be able to comprehend the nature and resilience (and the sensible limits) of the involvement of overtly religious organizations and individuals in our public life.

Comprehending this involvement is of first importance, and not only because talk show hosts find it an exciting subject for gab. It is important because America itself is at risk. The nation, whether ready to acknowledge it or not, faces a crisis of legitimacy. The more that the nation chooses to secularize the principal contact points between government and people—not only the public schools, but little things, like names and numbers and symbols, and big things, like taxes and marriage and, ultimately, politics itself—the more it will persuade many religious people that a culture war has indeed been declared, and not by the Right. Many people of deep religious commitment, especially but not exclusively evangelical Christians, look at the nation today and see a place that is run in ways that make it harder for them to practice their religion, and harder for them to pass it on to their children. One can scarcely be surprised if they therefore feel driven to the fringes of politics . . . or if they feel driven to the point of thinking that the nation is actively at war against them.

Rousseau taught the West that a government at war with its people loses its legitimacy, and he was perhaps talking fact as much as he was theory. If the state is going to interfere with the ability of the religious to build a religious world in which to live, we can hardly expect those religious people not to try to use politics as a way of building a world more to their liking. And for all the common complaints about the efforts of the religious to impose their views on others, and thus interfere with their freedoms, the point of view of many of the religious is the mirror image, that they are losing their religious freedoms as the majority, or, often, the minority, imposes its views upon them—views about the nature of moral authority, views about sex, views about procreation, views, in short, about the way the world should be. Much of the screaming about why religion should not be in politics is really an effort to evade the debate the religious are demanding: *Why are your views better than ours?* At a certain point, if we build too high the walls that are intended to keep religion out of politics, we will face religious people who will storm the barricades and declare the government no longer legitimate, because of its insistence on creating a single set of meanings, a single understanding of life, that everyone must share.

I suspect that I will be storming too.

I should make my biases clear. I write not only as a Christian but as one who is far more devoted to the survival of my faith—and of religion generally—than to the survival of any state in particular, including the United States of America. I love this nation, with all its weaknesses and occasional horrors, and I cannot imagine living in another one. But my mind is not so clouded with the vapors of patriotism that I place my country before my God. If the country were to force me to a choice—and, increasingly, this nation tends to do that to many religious people—I would unhesitatingly, if not without some sadness for my country, choose my God.

It is easy to paint people who put God first as dangerous fanatics, but, from the point of view of the believer, the fanatic is the one so certain that the state is right that he is willing to use law to interfere with religious belief. To take a simple example, I am not sure why it is more "fanatical" for parents to tell their children that the creation story in Genesis is literally true than for the public schools to tell the same children, required by law to attend, that the religion of their parents is literally false.[2] Or why it is more "fanatical" to criticize the culture for not reflecting a particular religious view on, say, the role of women than to criticize a religion for not reflecting the culture's views on the same thing. In short, the danger, if there is one, is mutual.

I hasten to add that one need not be a Christian, or be religious at all, to engage with and, I hope, profit from the stories I will tell. Indeed, as I argue in the book's penultimate chapter, one of the most vital (if often neglected) tasks of the religious voice in America is standing up for the religious freedom of all believers. We must never become a nation that propounds an official religion or suggests that some religions are more American than others. At the same time, one of the official religions we must never propound is the religion of secularism, the suggestion that there is something un-American about trying to live life in a way that puts God first. Quite the contrary: Preserving the ability of the faithful to put God first is precisely the purpose for which freedom of religion must exist.

One might generalize the point this way: To be earnestly religious is, at minimum, to believe in an obligation to the Divine that is prior to any merely constructed human obligations. Because we live in a country in which there is a healthy degree of religious freedom, we might suppose that these conflicts are few. But this is not so. The points of conflict are growing, growing fast, and that rapid growth is the principal cause of the upsurge over the past three decades of involvement in politics by traditional religionists, especially Christian evangelicals. A nation that truly values religious freedom—indeed, as we shall see in Chapter 5, a nation that truly values the constitutional separation of church and state—must welcome the religious voice into its political counsels. To do otherwise is one sure way to accomplish the task of alienating the religious from democracy, for it places official imprimatur on the cultural message that religion is an inferior human activity.

It is peculiar and sad, as the nation strides into a new century, that we continue to find so many Americans who agree with this message: that religion, on balance, does more harm than good, and certainly has no place in our politics. Fortunately, the fear that religions might have too much influence in America's public life arises principally among political, legal, and media elites. Few Americans agree.[3] And that is a very good thing. In the nineteenth century, that message would have sabotaged the abolitionist movement, which was led by Christian evangelicals whose fiery and unapologetically biblical sermons ultimately moved a nation. (See Chapter 6.) In the early years of the twentieth century, the religious voice was prominent in the fight to obtain some minimal protection for the industrial worker, including wage and hour laws and the right to organize unions. (See Chapter 7.) And without the clear, forceful, and deeply Christian preaching of Martin Luther King Jr. and many other clergy, the civil rights movement would have been unimaginable. (See Chapter 2.)

Indeed, I shall argue that, in the absence of the religious voice, American politics itself becomes unimaginable. An early-twentieth-century Social Gospel preacher whom we will meet in Chapter 7 told his flock, in the midst of the battle for the right of labor to organize, that morality, in religious terms, is nothing but the actual practice of one's religious faith. Religion is what we profess and morality is what it moves us to do. Politics needs morality, which means that politics needs religion. In a nation grown increasingly materialistic and increasingly involved in urging satisfaction of desire as the proper subject of both the market and politics, the religious voice, at its best, is perhaps the only remaining force that can call us to something higher and better than thinking constantly about our own selves, our own wants, our own rights. Politics without religion must necessarily be, in today's America, the politics of *me*.*

But if it is crucial to allow the religious voice in politics, it is also crucial for religionists to understand the risks and limits of political involvement. A religion that becomes too settled in the secular political sphere, happily amassing influence and using it, is likely to lose its best and most spiritual self, as has happened to established churches all over Europe, which nowadays find themselves virtually without a voice—small wonder, as they have relied on man rather than God for their sustenance. In consequence, they have redefined their role, trying to please humans instead of pleasing God. The same has happened to many of the churches of what has been called the "de facto establishment" of the nineteenth and early twentieth centuries.[4] Most of these once powerful denominations of the so-called Protestant mainline have reduced their teachings, in the fine phrase of the theologian Stanley Hauerwas, to "God is nice so we should be nice, too."[5] And, as we shall see in Chapter 3, the same has happened to many of today's organizations of conservative Christianity, so delighted with their political prominence that they have decided to try to keep it, resulting in a predictable softening of the hard, clear, Bible-based message that led to their prominence in the first place.

I previously wrote about some aspects of this challenge in my 1993 book *The Culture of Disbelief: How American Law and Politics Trivialize Religious Devotion*. There I argued, and I still believe, that many forces in our culture send messages that religion is a relatively unimportant human activity, an oddity, a hobby perhaps, like making model airplanes—in short, not a fit oc-

---

*This is not to deny that politics with religion can sometimes also be the politics of *me*, in this age when so many churches seem intent on preaching the gospel of self-satisfaction. I return to this point in the Afterword.

cupation for intelligent, public-spirited adults. This proposition, I contended, aside from being ridiculous, also had a profoundly alienating effect on millions of Americans of deep religious faith who have grown understandably unhappy about political and legal cultures that seem to them repeatedly to mock what gives their lives greatest meaning. Indeed, it would not be an overstatement to say that those cultural ideas, including an extreme and dangerous version of the otherwise laudable separation of church and state, helped to create the coalition of conservative political organizations nowadays sometimes described as the "Religious Right." If we want to have democratic government, I insisted, everybody must be allowed to play.

Many readers of *The Culture of Disbelief* urged me to take on a basic question that the earlier book left for another day: If religion is to be actively involved in politics, what is the proper form of that involvement? In proposing an answer, the current book presents two very simple and interrelated theses. The first is that religion and politics mix poorly. The second is that religion and politics mix well. The two theses are at first blush contradictory. But the apparent contradiction vanishes when we understand the multiple meanings of the word *politics*.

Secular politics is a very dangerous place for institutions concerned with spiritual matters that transcend ordinary human striving. Thus, the second theme of this book: Yes, religions can and sometimes must be politically active—but they must be extraordinarily cautious about how they do it, because too much politics can destroy them. In particular, electoral politics has been a difficult and often harmful location for religionists to try to make a stand against the culture. Possessing an honored voice that sometimes prevails is not the same as regularly exercising actual secular power to tell people, at a point of a gun, what they must do. Religion, which should be in love with witness and persuasion, has all too often in history allowed itself to be seduced by the lure of temporal power, a passionate but dysfunctional and even immoral love affair that has led to much human misery and has been destructive as well of true faith.

This is not to say that all efforts to enforce religious truth through the coercive power of law are bad. The abolitionists sought to do precisely that, and they prevailed, and that is a good thing. The preachers who fought for labor, for women's rights, for an end to segregation, all prevailed, and those were good things too. As so often, the difficulty is finding the balance—a task this book is designed to aid. There was much truth to the antimaterialist preaching of the First Great Awakening in the eighteenth century, when politics—and engagement with the world generally—was described as a contagion likely to corrupt those who entered it. The religious ideal, according to this theory, was a life lived apart from culture, working to earn one's bread but never to accumulate wealth, attending principally to preparation for personal salvation. As we shall see in Chapter 8, many early architects of the conservative political coalition sometimes described as the Religious Right, depressed by the nation's shoulder-shrugging reaction to the Monica Lewinsky scandal, have changed their minds and returned to the eighteenth-century Christian ideal, urging evangelicals to disengage from the culture generally and, in particular, to stay away from politics.

For most religious believers, however, disengagement is not an option. Those who think their only task is to prepare themselves and their families for the next world nevertheless often discover that they must engage with this world in order to obtain the cultural space for their preparation. Politics, often, will be one of the tools for preserving the space. And religionists who believe they have an obligation to engage the culture in order to work for the betterment of God's creation will presumably continue to do just that. Religion, in short, will be in politics. It cannot reasonably be kept out.

My purpose in this book is to defend that political involvement from its critics, but also to set out some sensible limits, as well as to offer examples of principled and prophetic religious activism. But those limits, I will argue, should rarely be enforced by the state: For the most part, religions should be free to accept or reject such limits as I propose. I will argue in Chapter 5, for example, that the Internal Revenue Service should not have the power to penalize religions for what is preached from the pulpit, a power it currently possesses; but to challenge the power is not the same thing as saying that preachers *should* endorse candidates for electoral office, one of the activities that the IRS punishes. I believe, and I shall argue in Chapter 3, that preachers *should not* endorse political candidates. But I also believe in the freedom of religion, and the freedom of religious speech particularly, so my view on the proper limits of preaching should not be enacted into law, and neither should anybody else's. The matter is one for the prayerful discernment of each religious tradition as it struggles to be faithful to God's will in a sinful world.

Most of all, I worry that we are on the verge of developing an antireligious politics in America, as though religious expressions in our public debates should be greeted not merely with derision but with hostility. But a politics without religion is empty of meaning. Jim Wallis, the founder of *Sojourners* magazine has argued that America needs a "new politics" built on

"the spiritual resources of our best moral and religious traditions."[6] Ralph
Reed, the former executive director of the Christian Coalition, has made
essentially the same point.[7] With such broad agreement across the political
spectrum, I am confident that we can yet turn our politics, and thus our nation, in the direction that the Spirit wants it to go.

This introduction has outlined the argument presented in Part I of the
book, entitled Religion's Sphere, which consists of seven chapters, using
contemporary and historical examples to illustrate ways in which religion
and politics do and do not mesh well. Part II of the book, entitled Religion's Voice, surveys several current issues (but not necessarily the ones
that might immediately come to mind) where the religious voice, if listened
to without preconceptions, might make vital contributions to our national
debates. The Afterword speculates on the future of religion in politics—and
the future of politics in religion.

The title of this book is inspired by a C. S. Lewis essay entitled "Meditation on the Third Commandment."[8] The reasons for that inspiration will
become clear in Chapter 3, although they are implied in Chapters 1 and 2.
The discovery of what the Third Commandment actually says I leave, as
Lewis did, as an exercise for the reader. All I will say here is that I take its
text very seriously, as I believe most Christians and Jews do. But I also
know how easy it is, flushed with the desire to make things right, to ignore
what the commandment commands. This book, then, might best be
viewed as a gentle and loving reminder.

PART I

Religion's Sphere

1

Chattering About the Lord

RELIGION HAS BEEN INSEPARABLE from American politics for as long as America has had politics, and will likely remain inseparable as long as Americans remain religious. Yet every generation seems to think it has discovered something new. Take presidential elections as an example. Early in the year 2000, when an internecine battle erupted in the Republican Party over the role of religious conservatives in the nomination process, astonished reporters told television audiences that nothing like this had ever happened before. Not since 1992, they might have added, when the religion-ful Republican convention raised precisely the same eyebrows. Or not since 1980, when candidate Ronald Reagan told the Religious Roundtable, a conservative evangelical group, "You cannot endorse me, but I endorse you." Not since 1976, when an outpouring of evangelical votes, many of them from first-time voters, ruined the Republican Party's Southern strategy and helped put Democrat Jimmy Carter in the White House. Or not since 1960, when candidate John F. Kennedy rushed to a convention of evangelical preachers in Houston to assure them that he, a Roman Catholic, would not do the Pope's bidding if elected. (In our celebration of the Kennedy moment, we tend to forget that the bidding that worried the evangelicals most was the Catholic Church's forceful opposition to racial segregation.)

The reporters, if inclined to do a little digging, could have gone back further. Back to the 1950s, perhaps, when Dwight Eisenhower assured the whole nation that belief in God was the first principle of Americanism. Back to Theodore Roosevelt, who said that the President should go to church regularly to set an example for the nation. Back to William McKinley, who ran a campaign showing how he was a better Protestant than William Jennings Bryan, and fought a holy war to prove it. Back to Abraham Lincoln, who announced in his Second Inaugural Address that the

Civil War was, in effect, a war over which side's reading of the Bible was right. Even all the way back to Thomas Jefferson, who spent much of his 1800 election campaign denying charges that he was an atheist.

Our current controversies, then, are nothing new for America. Only our failure of memory makes them seem peculiar. And that act of forgetting is a great danger to our democracy, for if we do not understand the historical relationship between religion and politics, we will never be able to make sense of the way our politics both accommodates and domesticates the impulse of believers to improve the world. In America, we have long separated the institutional church from the institutional state, a sensible idea, but we have never separated religion from politics, and we are unlikely to start any time soon.

Consider a single historical example, this one not involving an election. In 1854, a group of New England clergymen set off a firestorm when they sent a petition to the Senate demanding an immediate end to the practice of chattel slavery. The pro-slavery senators, citing the separation of church and state, argued that the petition should not even be received, that ordained ministers could not so much as discuss issues of public moment with the government.* But the preachers, not the senators, won the day. They won by refusing to shut up, by insisting on the relevance of God's Word in a broken world, and by persuading so many of their fellow citizens of the justice of their cause that the nation was willing to fight a war over it. The preachers understood a simple fact about America that the defenders of slavery did not (or at least pretended not to)—a fact just as true today as it was a century and a half ago: Most Americans want to talk about God. We have always done it. We do not seem ready to stop.

In truth, there is probably no country in the Western world where people use God's name quite as much, or quite as publicly, or for quite as many purposes, as we Americans do—the Third Commandment notwithstanding. Few candidates for office are able to end their speeches without asking God to bless their audience, or the nation, or the great work we are undertaking, but everybody is sure that the other side is insincere. Conservatives often claim God as one of their own. And not just conservatives. At a speaking engagement a couple of years ago, I received the following written question from the audience: "God wants us to change, so God is a liberal, right?" Athletes thank God, often on television, after scoring the winning touchdown, because, like politicians, they like to think God is on

---

*For more on this story, see Chapter 5.

their side. Churches erect huge billboards and take out ads in the paper. Arguments over God's gender make the news magazines. God's will is cited as a reason to be against gay rights. And a reason to be for them. God is said not to tolerate poverty. Or abortion. Or nuclear weapons. We Americans search for God constantly, in as many places as possible. Pantheists insist that a part of God exists in everything. New Agers proclaim that God is found within.

Lots of people take the Lord's name in vain—by cursing, for example, which still bothers some of us, although it is nowadays considered a little quaint, or even prudish, to take offense. (Goodness knows, few screenwriters know how to construct dialogue without it.) Some people solemnly swear to tell the truth, so help them God, and then solemnly lie. Casual interjections are rampant: "What in the name of God?" and "Oh, my God!" being two favorites. We mention God's name on our currency, in the Pledge of Allegiance, in some of our national songs. Advertisers see all this and decide how to profit from it. (Remember the friar in the old Xerox commercials? What about Hebrew National's marvelous old slogan—"We answer to a higher authority"—which at least possessed the virtue of sincerity?)

The media, too, are fascinated by God, although I often wish the media were a little bit more fascinated, so that journalists would get their facts right. In the winter of 2000, during one of the presidential debates, I cringed when a reporter asked the candidates a question using the terms "fundamentalist" and "evangelical" as though they were interchangeable, which many otherwise well-educated people seem to believe. But a media that does not understand (or care about) such distinctions will be equally unable to understand why, in his presidential campaigns, the Reverend Pat Robertson ran worse among fundamentalists than among white voters generally[1]—a fact that was left largely unreported, perhaps because even journalists who heard about it were unable to make sense of it. On the other hand, journalists tend to do a very good job at reporting on the simple and exciting fact that Americans, despite the massive cultural changes wrought by the forces of economics and technology, refuse to stop believing in God,[2] and refuse to stop talking about him.

Everybody who wants to change America, and everybody who wants not to, understands the nation's love affair with God's name, which is why everybody invokes it.

My writing on the subject of law and religion has me on everybody's mailing list. Scarcely a week goes by that I do not find in my mailbox at Yale a pamphlet or press release or even a book from some organization with a clear political goal, explaining why God is on the side of its cause. Because the great majority of Americans profess Christianity, the pamphlets are usually based on the Bible. It is an old and honored American game, played on all points of the political spectrum, and sometimes the players are sincere. "God-talk," the social theorists call it, and its resilience in a nation many prefer to regard as secular continues to amaze them, as, in an earlier era, it amazed William James[3] and Max Weber,[4] both of whom analyzed religion with the dispassionate tools of social science and concluded that it obviously met certain human needs, even if the whole thing was, in the end, a little silly. Many of today's philosophers and social scientists continue to think all this God stuff is a little odd—but that does not slow it down, nor has it ever.

The matter is surprisingly simple: People who believe in God talk about God. People who believe God is central to their lives may not easily be persuaded to cast God aside when they happen to step into the realm of politics. Although it may be frustrating to many observers—and I among the frustrated—that candidates for office, across the political spectrum, seem constantly on the hunt for potential clergy support, we can hardly wish or theorize the practice away. Whether in 1860, when southern pastors lined up for Stephen Douglas and against Abraham Lincoln and the religious orthodoxy they feared he would impose on the nation in the name of the abolition of slavery, or in 1896, when the Social Gospel preachers in New York City campaigned openly for the election to the mayoralty of a progressive writer named Henry George, or in 1976, when an outpouring of evangelical support helped make Jimmy Carter president, or four years later, when many of the same evangelicals turned to Ronald Reagan—year after year, in election after election, candidates understand that faith matters to people and so, using the name of the Lord—sometimes sincerely, sometimes in vain, sometimes both—politicians go out among the faithful and ask for their votes.

And therein hangs a tale.

II

On September 11, 1998, in the midst of the Monica Lewinsky mess—at a moment when, hard though it may be to remember, the foundations of Bill Clinton's presidency seemed to be crumbling—the President addressed the

annual National Prayer Breakfast. He told the assembled clergy, and a national television audience, that he was profoundly sorry for the wrongs he
had done. "There is no clever way," he intoned, "to say that I have sinned."

We Americans are, as ever, the wonder of Europe. A commentary in the
Times Literary Supplement professed mystification: "Confession of sin occurs
within communities of faith or between believers and God. For a church
member, one presumes, a confession should be made to God, to a clerical
intermediary, or to the community of faith or to the congregation." The
puzzled commentary continued: "The Constitution makes no provision for
a referendum: 'Forgive/Excommunicate: Click on One.'"[5] In other words,
even granting that the President had sinned against God, why was he asking forgiveness of the American people?

President Clinton, of course, did send a letter to his home congregation,
Immanuel Baptist Church in Little Rock. The contents of the letter, the
White House sensibly announced, were a private matter. But he did more:
In offering his contrition to the public as a sacrifice, he proclaimed that he
needed our forgiveness, too. And he was correct. He may not have needed
it theologically, but he certainly needed it politically.

And that is the point of the story: He needed it politically. That is, President Clinton, in order to survive the scandal, had to find a way to translate the requirements of his faith into the requirements of politics, and vice
versa. The American public, the body politic that, as the *Times* pointed out,
entirely lacks the authority to vote on forgiveness, nevertheless is fully possessed of the authority to confer it. The matter is so simple that we tend to
forget it. If most voters forgive a politician for his misdeeds, the politician
stands forgiven . . . politically forgiven, that is. And if voters refuse? If they
prefer, as the *Times* would have it, to excommunicate? Then the miscreant
teeters, and sometimes falls. History is full of lessons. Bill Clinton holds his
balance and Richard Nixon does not. How moralists or theologians might
evaluate their relative wrongs is entirely a moot point. All that finally matters in politics—and this is the fact President Clinton well understood!—all
that finally matters is the verdict of the public.

But why go to the public, as President Clinton did, with the language of
faith? Why stand behind a lectern in the White House and speak of sin and
forgiveness?

One answer that is easy, and wrong, is that we Americans are a forgiving people. We are not. Some politicians survive scandal, others are destroyed.[6] We as a people have been swept up all through our history by
passionate love affairs with the technologies of unforgiveness—capital pun-

ishment, for one, and a mighty, avenging military, for another. We like
to imagine ourselves as willing to forgive, and imagination is a powerful
tool in helping us be what we think we should; but our actions are often
otherwise.

Another answer, one that dances about the edge of the truth, is that we
are a religious people, and that all our major religions counsel forgiveness,
at least of the penitent. Thus, for the President of the United States to stand
before the nation, the whole of the American people, and from that platform to express his contrition and beg forgiveness, might resonate deeply
with the felt religious convictions of most of us. In other words, listening to
his apologies, we might well sense, deep within us, a welling up of our connection to the Divine, as though God Himself were urging us to forgive.
We would then be taking the President's words of contrition to mean what
he said they meant; not as some political ploy, but as a direct appeal to our
religious convictions. And it would be those convictions, not the President's
speech alone, that would lead us to forgive.

But there, once more, the analysis ultimately fails. There is nothing in the
theology of the nation's traditional faiths to suggest that forgiveness moves
us immediately past the need for any punishment.[7] In other words, the fact
that the public forgives the President does not tell us what should have happened next. The view of most Americans was that what should have happened next was . . . well, nothing. And here we see the true significance of
religion and of the use of God's name in our partisan political wars. Religion
is, too often, no more than a tool for helping us get what we want. I refer here
not to President Clinton but to the voters. The message the polls sent to
Washington was, evidently, simple: "We have forgiven him. Now get back to
doing our business." This message, which the President's supporters cheered,
actually is theologically somewhat odd. Moral crises, the message says,
should be set aside when our personal needs and desires are at stake. That
so many Clinton supporters quoted (or sometimes misquoted) the Gospel
passage about those without sin throwing the first stone only adds to the oddity. The use of the passage was surely a trope. The real message from the
public, then, was probably more like this: "The President has now mentioned
God. We, too, have mentioned God. Therefore, we are at least as godly as
you. So give us what we want."

And there lies the difficulty when God-talk mixes with the partisan side
of politics: More than likely, for too many people with causes to push and
desires to fulfill, the name of God will collapse into a mere rhetorical device. Instead of maintaining the sacred character guaranteed by the Third

Commandment, God's name becomes a tool, a trope, a ticket to get us where we want to go.

III

After the National Prayer Breakfast, the President's supporters cheered his public show of contrition and announced that the time had come to get on with the nation's business. His critics were less sure. Several of them fired off a public letter, entitled "Declaration Concerning Religion, Ethics, and the Crisis in the Clinton Presidency." The signers of the declaration warned about "the distortion that can come by association with presidential power in events such as the Presidential Prayer Breakfast of September 11, 1998." Why? Because, among other reasons, "the religious community is in danger of being called upon to provide authentication for a politically motivated and incomplete repentance that seeks to avert serious consequences for wrongful acts." Pastoral counseling sessions, the signatories conceded, were fine, but with a caveat: "[W]e fear that announcing such meetings to convince the public of the President's sincerity compromises the integrity of religion."[8]

There was more—much more—to the declaration, and we will return to it later in the book. But let us, for the moment, stick with this first set of ... well, of charges. Note that the declaration actually offers two separate warnings: first, that religionists should be wary of the corrupting influence of too close an association with the power of the presidency and, second, that religious integrity may be compromised by public announcements by religious leaders. Both cautions are of a form long known to Christianity: Politics profanes. One might even go so far as to suggest that the tilt of the declaration is distinctively Calvinist. After all, the partisan politics of a democratic society, with its difficulties, illusions, and compromises, is the method by which humans have chosen to run a significant part of the world. To avoid politics, then, is to avoid a chunk of the world, as though the world itself is, as John Calvin taught, a place of depravity and temptation.

Which of course it is.

So, putting to one side any question of partisanship, the argument of the declaration was anchored deeply in the often turbulent waters of the Christian tradition. Ever since the Protestant Reformation, Christians have been trying to find ways to protect the faith from the vicissitudes of life in political culture. True, some early Protestants embraced the idea that the laws of the state should be designed according to God's Word, and many Christians, maybe most, believe it to this day, but there is a sharp and important difference between the religious person who sees himself as the shaper of the law (because he is, like other citizens of a democratic nation, able to influence the course of governance) and the religious person who sees himself as a political insider, who seeks, in the phrase immortalized by the Reverend Jesse Jackson in the 1980s, a seat at the big table. There is a larger difference still—a veritable gulf, trackless and inconceivably vast—between the citizen, even the influential insider, on the one hand and, on the other, the lawgiver.

None of this means that Clinton was necessarily wrong in his public invocation of the symbols of Christian faith, or that the clergy who encouraged him were necessarily acting in a fashion inconsistent with their proper role. Such matters are, as the theologian Lewis Smedes has pointed out in explaining his refusal to sign the declaration, the imponderables of the situation. We cannot know the answers. We can think or suspect, but we cannot know. Was Clinton sincere? We cannot know. Smedes argues that none of us are ever quite pure in our repenting, even if our impurity amounts to pride "at what a splendid penitent I am." Were the clergy being used? We cannot know. Says Smedes: "It is possible to be *useful to* even this President without being *used by* him."[9]

Yet Smedes's response does not go quite to the heart of the declaration—the nonpartisan heart. For the very fact that the answers are imponderable, that we cannot know, is part of the challenge that faces religion when it brushes too close to politics. Several years ago, I sat on a panel in Miami with a journalist who kept insisting that Pat Robertson's Christianity was a sham. I did not agree—but that is not the point of the story. The point is that she seemed to think that her claim, if true, would refute his message. Actually, it wouldn't. Her argument, like all ad hominem attacks, rested on the erroneous assumption that if you discredit the messenger you discredit the message. Yet what was striking about her charges is that the audience seemed interested. They wanted to know why she thought Robertson was a fake. He was in the same situation as Clinton, albeit from the other side of the table: He was so close to politics that people were willing to wonder.

Ronald Reagan may have made more religious references in his speeches than any other president in history. But critics immediately jumped on such interesting facts as his failure to attend church regularly, or his divorce and remarriage, which many of his evangelical supporters preached, in other contexts, was a grievous sin. Does this mean that he was not sincerely religious?

Another imponderable. We simply cannot know. What we can say is that the admixture of politics and religion turned out, in Reagan's case too, to be volatile: If a politician paints himself as a religious hero, there will be plenty of observers ready to point to his feet of clay.

When you touch politics, it touches you back. Politics is a dirty business at its best, and it leaves few of its participants unsullied. The religious enjoy no special immunity. On the contrary—the religious face special risks. When the transcendent language of faith is dragged down into the arena of democracy, it usually winds up battered and twisted. Repentance and forgiveness are beautiful words, deeply resonant in the world's great religious traditions, but who can say what they mean anymore, now that politicians have seized on them for partisan advantage? That far, the declaration is precisely on the mark. But little of the fault is Bill Clinton's. The fault lies in the enthusiasm that draws the religious, like a vortex, toward the center of power. People, even religious people, who have ideas they think are good want other people to think they are good ideas, too; and, in the American fashion, people, even religious people, who have ideas they think are very good will look for political support.

Why? Because the religious, like everybody else, are tempted by politics. Seduced by its efficiency. By its potential. By the good it can do. And, it must be added, by the sheer delight of being, or believing oneself to be ... at the center of things. Who wants to be a voice crying in the wilderness when we can be witnesses testifying before Congress? Who wants to be a prophet without honor in his own land when White House breakfasts are available? Who wants to store up treasures in heaven when there are elections to be won here on earth?

If history has taught us anything, it is that religions that fall too deeply in love with the art of politics lose their souls—very fast. Look at the medieval Catholic Church, with its desperate and impossible ideal of building a "total society," in return for which it approved all manner of misconduct by emperors and princes.[10] Look at the fundamentalist Islamic regime in Iran. Look at any nation where religious leaders, having touched the levers of power, have refused to let them go; and so have become, not religious, but political. Critics of religious involvement in politics are fond of cataloguing all the wrongs done by institutional religions holding too great a share of temporal power.[11] But these lists and registries miss the point. The wrongs that religious regimes have done are not worse than the wrongs that secular regimes have done; they are, all through history, just about the same. The difference is that we expect more from the religious, or at least we should. At minimum, we should expect the religious not to join everybody else in the headlong rush to gather enough votes to tell everybody else what to do. Humanity needs someone to stand apart from politics, apart even from culture, to call us to righteousness without regard to political advantage.

Which is not to say that religion should stay out of our public debates over the important issues that divide us. My thesis is simply that religion, when it engages in the public life of the nation, must do so with some care.

IV

Over the years, many scholars, journalists, and activists have tried to craft rules for the participation of the religious in politics, and nearly all the efforts have foundered on the same uneasy shoals. The arguments, almost invariably, are made from the point of view of the state. That is, the critics assume the existence of the state and ask how some religion, or all religions, fit that model. And because they begin with the state, these critics, in the end, reason in a way that cannot be persuasive to people for whom an understanding of God's Will is at the center of all questions of morality.

Many objections are offered to the raising of religious voices in our political debates. Let us begin by dismissing the clunkers. First, as we will see in chapters to come, there is nothing un-American, undemocratic, or even particularly strange about religious activism and religious language in politics. The great social movement of the nineteenth century—the abolition of slavery—and the great social movement of the twentieth—the abolition of legal racial segregation—were both nurtured in churches, publicly justified in religious language, and unapologetically inspired by the Word of God. (We too often tend to forget that many of the mass protests that gave the civil rights movement so much of its vitality were organized by the Southern *Christian* Leadership Conference, run by the *Reverend* Martin Luther King Jr.)

Second, the First Amendment, and the wall of separation it supposedly erects between church and state, have no effect whatsoever on the consciences or voices of individual citizens as they seek to influence what government does in their names, and have only minimal effect—and maybe none—on the words or arguments that elected officials are entitled to offer in support of the policies they approve. In other words, the fact that a supporter of a bill happens to mention God does not make the bill unconstitutional. (The separation of church and state was a favorite theme of pro-slavery politicians seeking to put a brake on abolitionism.)

Third, history does not teach us (contrary to what is frequently claimed today) that the power of religion is uniquely dangerous among human endeavors, more likely to result in oppression and injustice than secular ideologies. The ideological wars of the twentieth century have killed more people than all history's religious wars rolled together. What history really teaches us is that humans holding authority over other humans are dangerous. Religious humans have not historically exercised this power more oppressively than other humans have.

Besides, any account of the history is incomplete unless it also mentions many of the gifts that religion has bestowed upon Western-style democracy. The idea of dissent arguably originated with the prophets of Israel, who arose in an era when rulers were presumed to be godlike and thus were not susceptible to ordinary criticism.[12] The idea of freedom, as Orlando Patterson has demonstrated, turns out to be a distinctively Christian idea in Western practice.[13] Even the idea that concrete law, as against arbitrary will, is the proper means of directing the exercise of government power, was popularized by Christianity—albeit sometimes in unhealthy ways.

And, fourth, there is no reason (other than bias) to suppose that religionists are, by the nature of their beliefs, significantly more dogmatic than anybody else. Despite the image often seen in the media and in the academy of religion as creating a mind so securely locked that reason finds no crevice through which to slip inside, it is not clear that any of the Western religions have ever taken this form. David Hume certainly believed that faith and reason were invariably at war, but he was wrong. One may place Hume in his context and understand his concern, for he wrote his *Dialogue* at a time when the Reformed Church was trying, through the use of violent force, to stifle dissent. But on what foundation has contemporary culture constructed the remarkable idea that an antipathy to reason is natural to religion? It is difficult to find a persuasive argument.

In his 1998 encyclical entitled *Faith and Reason,* Pope John Paul II pointed out that it is relativism, not religion, that defies reason. For reason, as serious philosophers even now understand, requires a kind of faith—a faith in the possibility of persuading our fellow human beings of the error of their ways, or the truth of ours. Moreover, many critics of religion write as though the historian Nathan O. Hatch's remarkable book, *The Democratization of American Christianity,* had never been published. Hatch demonstrates that the success of the early American republic persuaded citizens that they could think for themselves across a variety of matters—most notably the matter of religion. Sects that were hierarchical and dogmatic in Europe surrendered most of that character upon reaching these shores. Thus the most successful sermons of the early nineteenth century featured "the Jeffersonian notion that people should shake off all servile prejudice and learn to prove things for themselves."[14]

Those four objections are, as I said, the clunkers. Now let us consider the two serious objections to religious involvement in politics—the objections that are the subject of this book.

The first objection I have already mentioned. I have in mind the following difficulty: When a religious community becomes too regularly involved in politics, the community loses touch with its own best self and risks losing the power, and the obligation, to engage in witness from afar, to stand outside the corridors of power and call those within to righteousness. I shall call this the *Integrity Objection*.

The second objection, which I shall call the *Electoral Objection*, is this: When a religion decides to involve itself in the partisan side of politics, in supporting one candidate or party over another, it not only runs a high risk of error; it also, inevitably, winds up softening its message, compromising doctrine to make it more palatable to a public that might remain unpersuaded by the Word unadulterated. These two objections must be taken seriously by the religious, and will be the principal subjects of the first part of this book.*

This chapter opened with a discussion of the "Declaration Concerning Religion, Ethics, and the Crisis in the Clinton Presidency." Revisiting the declaration now, it is easy to see that the signers might have been worried about both objections. The Integrity Objection is raised by the fear that the language and symbols of faith are being misappropriated for political purposes and thus, literally, are losing their integrity. The Electoral Objection is raised by the fear that the purposes are not only political but actually partisan, as though religion has a side in the conflict. And the fact that some critics of the declaration believed the declaration itself to be subject to the same objections, only helps make the point: Religion will be at its weakest when it seems—even *seems!*—to be about partisan political advantage rather than offering answers to the great and difficult moral questions of the day.

Both of these objections apply as strongly to conservatives as to liberals, to Republicans as to Democrats. At the present moment, there is prob-

---

*The reader may be ready to object that I seem to be prescribing a general rule to apply to all religions. As I hope will become clear in the chapters to come, I am doing no such thing.

ably more reason for conservatives than liberals to be wary, for it is the Right rather than the Left that has lately evolved influential political organizations designed to bring religious values to bear on the stirring issues of the day. (In the 1960s it was the other way around.) To participate in dialogue is one thing. Too many religious groups, however, want to influence electoral politics—a danger not to politics or democracy but to faith.

Of course, to be involved in public dialogue without becoming involved in partisan politics will require a delicate balancing act, for it is very easy to stumble. Let us turn to the next chapter to begin to understand how it might be done.

2

The Religious Resistance
of Fannie Lou Hamer

FROM THE TRADITIONAL CHRISTIAN POINT OF view—and certainly from the point of view of many other faiths—religion is not merely an aspect of life, to be divided from its other parts. Belief in God is a totality. One reason so many evangelicals support classroom prayer in the public schools is their uneasiness with declaring an important part of their children's lives nonreligious. One can dispute the solution and still honor the instinct behind it: To the faithful, there is no part of the day that is outside of God's view. To be sure, very few religionists anywhere in the world live lives quite as faithful as they believe they should. But our religious faith helps most of us to see the road we should be traveling, even if our human weakness often makes us travel it poorly.

Human life is characterized by the search for meaning. Unlike other animals, we humans seem almost wired to believe in the idea of the telos—that there is, to each thing, a purpose it must fulfill. Although many people have decided that God-talk is nonsense, most humans still believe that we are somehow connected to something transcendent, something larger and wiser than we are. Thus religions, too, provide meanings to their adherents, meanings of a deep and transcendent sort.[1] What is religion, after all, but a narrative a people tells itself about its relationship with God, usually over an extended period of time?[2] And if the narrative is truly about the meaning God assigns to the world, the follower of the religion, if truly faithful, can hardly select a different meaning simply because the state says so. That is why deeply religious visions always seem radical: If Religionist believes that God's love does not allow some human beings to enslave others, no amount of teaching by the merely mortal agency of the state should cause

Religionist to change. Quite the contrary: Religionist, if she believes that the state is committing great evil, has little choice but to try to get the state to change. As I am using the term, the "radicalism" of a religious position is independent of where Religionist finds herself on the political spectrum. Thus, Religionist may appear equally radical whether she is trying to end segregation, abolish nuclear weapons, put a stop to abortion, or fight for a more equitable distribution of the nation's wealth. Her radicalism arises because her understanding of the very meaning of the world differs, often sharply, from the understanding of the dominant culture.

The trouble is that the state and the religions are in competition to explain to their people the meaning of the world.[3] When the meanings provided by the one differ from the meanings provided by the other, it is natural that the one on the losing end will do what it can to become a winner. In today's mass-produced world, characterized by the intrusion into every household of the materialist interpretation of reality, religions often are just overwhelmed, which leads some of them to change and many of them to die.[4] But more subtle tools are available in the assault on religious meaning. Indeed, all through history, the state has tried to domesticate religion, sometimes by force, simply eliminating dissenting faiths; sometimes through the device of creating an official, "established" church; sometimes—as in the twentieth-century American experience—through the device of reducing the power of religion by confining its freedom within a state-granted, state-defined, and state-controlled structure of constitutional rights.[5]

Religion, however, is no idle bystander. If the state tries to domesticate religion, its most powerful competitor in the creation of meaning, authentic religion tries simultaneously to subvert the state. Liberalism (as a political theory, not a contemporary political movement) sees this as one of religion's dangers. Actually it is one of religion's virtues. Liberalism tends toward hegemony. Not content to serve as a theory of organization of the state, it has grown into a theory of organization of private institutions in the state. If the state itself cannot discriminate among its citizens on the basis of race or sex or religion, then private institutions, it seems, should not do so either. One need not support any of these forms of discrimination to see the obvious conceptual difficulty: A theory that developed in order to explain the organization of the state itself (from which there is no simple exit for dissenters or subjects of discrimination) becomes a theory about the organization of everything. And that, I think, is the true source of the supposed conflict between liberal theory on one side and religion on the other. Religion resists. Let us think about that.

II

A good place to begin is with a fascinating anecdote about Fannie Lou Hamer, founder and guiding spirit of the Mississippi Freedom Democratic Party. In the summer of 1964, the MFDP waged a challenge to the credentials of the lily-white Mississippi slate of delegates to the Democratic National Convention, a slate chosen by the lily-white Mississippi Democratic Party. The MFDP offered an integrated slate of delegates, many of whom, like Mrs. Hamer herself, had tried to register to vote, and been punished for it. The controversy terrified President Lyndon Johnson, who wanted no blot on the celebration of his nomination. So he sent his vice-president-in-waiting, Hubert Humphrey, to visit Mrs. Hamer, with orders to buy her off.

Humphrey, believing that he was undertaking a political negotiation, asked Fannie Lou Hamer what she wanted.

Mrs. Hamer, a devout evangelical Christian, responded: "[T]he beginning of a New Kingdom right here on earth."

Humphrey, evidently stunned, explained that his political future was on the line if he could not close a deal with her to end the credentials challenge. He apparently wanted her to understand that his nomination would create a strong voice for racial equality at the highest levels of the White House, reason enough to compromise. Fannie Lou Hamer, who had survived beating and torture in a Mississippi jail for insisting on her constitutional rights, was unimpressed. In *God's Long Summer*, his splendid book on religion in the civil rights movement, the theologian Charles Marsh quotes her reply: "Senator Humphrey, I know lots of people in Mississippi who have lost their jobs for trying to register to vote. I had to leave the plantation where I worked in Sunflower County. Now if you lose this job of vice president because you do what is right, because you help MFDP, everything will be all right. God will take care of you."

This alone must have been hard on Senator Humphrey, who had fought for civil rights long before it became fashionable in the Democratic Party. But Mrs. Hamer was relentless: "But if you take [the vice presidential nomination] this way, why, you will never be able to do any good for civil rights, for poor people, for peace or any of those things you talk about. Senator Humphrey, I'm gonna pray to Jesus for you."

And that, according to Marsh, was the end of the Johnson administration's negotiation with Hamer.[6]

I begin with this story because it contains much that is useful in understanding both the appropriate and important role for religious voices in public debate over issues of moment, and the ways in which those voices can be distorted or corrupted or even destroyed if they join too readily and too completely with mortal humans seeking partisan political advantage. The main point is simple. Humphrey wanted to talk about policy (ending racial discrimination). Hamer wanted to talk about religion (establishment of the Kingdom). Does this mean that they were talking past each other, their arguments mutually incomprehensible? Not necessarily. Their negotiation, after all, took place at the Democratic National Convention. This suggests that each believed, quite reasonably, that the conversation was really about politics.

What difference does this make? The answer is simple: Any conversation about politics is also a conversation about coercion. A conversation about politics is either about what people should be forced to do, or forced not to do (law); or about who should do the forcing (elections). In that sense, a conversation about politics is a conversation about the highest trust a democracy can bestow. Humphrey wanted Mrs. Hamer to agree that he and Lyndon Johnson should be entrusted with the power to do the forcing; by mentioning civil rights, he was suggesting what it was that he and Johnson were willing to force people to do. That Hubert Humphrey and Fannie Lou Hamer could not reach agreement teaches us little that is interesting about politics, but it teaches us something good, not something bad, about religion . . . or, at least, about Mrs. Hamer's religion.

Hamer sought justice. Humphrey sought electoral victory (with justice as a possible, but not certain, side effect). And *that* is why the negotiation failed. Hamer knew or sensed what is missed by too many religionists who have the opportunity for political influence: There is a sharp distinction between knowing what needs to be done and choosing the people to do it. Especially when the decision is about governance, so that the people who will do it will be entrusted with the coercive, potentially violent authority to make law. The prophetic religious voice, calling the world to account, pointing us in the direction of God's will, is a very different voice from the one that tries to tell us who should be in charge.

The biblical prophets rarely called upon the nation to choose new leaders. Instead, they called upon the leaders themselves to change their hearts, often predicting doom if they did not. Consider, for example, the well-known story of David and Bathsheba from 2 Samuel, chapters 11 and 12. King David desired Bathsheba, the wife of Uriah. David sent for her, they slept together, and Bathsheba became pregnant. David then arranged for Uriah to die in battle so that he would be free to marry Bathsheba, which, in due course, he did. The Lord sent the prophet Nathan to call David to account–not to force him to resign, not to urge Israel to rise up against him, but to work changes in David's own heart, so that he would see his own sin and repent.[7] As a result of his repentance, he achieved the greatness that was his destiny.

Many of the great prophets of Israel called upon the kings to return to the ways of the Lord in the manner of their governance. The Lord sent Jeremiah to the palace of the king of Judah to command him to stop doing evil (Jer. 22:1–7). The prophet predicted punishment if the king ignored him, but still offered him the chance to repent, to change his ways, so that he might continue to rule. Even in the dramatic tale of Hosea and his unfaithful wife Gomer (said to symbolize God's relationship with the people of Israel, and, perhaps, with all of us), the children are commanded to drive Gomer out of the house–but the purpose of the divine command is not to get rid of her but to persuade her to change her ways, after which she is welcome in the house again (Hos. 2–3).

The point is that the prophets were not calling for new rulers–they were calling upon the current rulers to rule differently. Good kings are better than bad ones, but the bad ones always had the chance to become good. The prophets had no authority over the kings and wanted none. They spoke the words the Lord told them to, explaining to the rulers what policies the rulers should be pursuing, but that was the limit of their involvement. Even when (as they usually did) the prophets predicted the downfall of kings who ignored God's message, the prophets did not themselves take a hand in that downfall. They did not organize revolutions or search for new princes to replace the old. The prophets were like Fannie Lou Hamer: essentially indifferent to the *identity* of the rulers but very concerned that the rulers ruled right. Mrs. Hamer did not much care whether Johnson and Humphrey were elected. She cared whether justice was done.

And what was, for Mrs. Hamer, the measure of justice? Quite simply, how close the country moved to living according to God's commands. In that respect, too, she was like the prophets. Indeed, the very idea that God's will is both different from and higher than the will of fellow humans, even humans with the power to create binding law, is one of the signal contributions of Judaism to civilization. In the Jewish tradition, the idea of this difference is illustrated by the prophets calling Israel to account for failing to adhere to the will of God. Christianity, founded as a prophetic religion, squandered much of this wisdom during its thousand-year effort to meld the spiritual and temporal powers into one.

Postmodern theologians often describe religion as subversive of the culture it inhabits.[8] As long as religion avoids the temptation to join its authority to the authority of the state, it can indeed play a subversive role, because it focuses the attention of the believer on a source of moral understanding that transcends both the authority of positive law and the authority of human moral systems. In other words, religion can be subversive no matter what it teaches, as long as what it teaches carries the believer beyond the world of ordinary concerns and into the world of the divine. The follower of Religion **R** is simply different from his fellow citizen who is not a follower of Religion **R.** A devout Christian will not see the world the same way as a devout Muslim, who will not see the world the same way as a devout Jew, who will not see the world the same way as a devout Hindu. And, within these broad and often vague religious categories, the differences multiply. A believing Shiite understands life differently than a believing Sunni, a believing Roman Catholic differently than a believing Southern Baptist. These differences are not trivial. They are not "just" about spirituality. They are about life.

A religion that makes no difference in the life of the believer is not really worthy of the name. The difference religion makes—the way in which believers deviate from the cultural norm—is the measure of its subversive power. At its best, religion in its subversive mode provides the believer with a transcendent reason to question the power of the state and the messages of the culture. That is the reason that the state will always try to domesticate religion: to avoid being subverted.

This is no new insight, and it is not meant as a judgment. Any state will try to control the forces that might upend it, because a state, as though organic, will do whatever it must to survive. Religion is a potential threat to that survival. The domestication of religion is the process through which the state tries to move religion from a position in which it threatens the state to a position in which it supports the state. And that was the purpose of Hubert Humphrey's negotiation with Fannie Lou Hamer—to move her from a relatively radical position, in which she threatened his political prospects, to a domesticated position, in which she became a supporter. For there is a lesson every politician knows that too many religionists involved in politics forget: Once you take sides in an electoral contest, you are stuck with your candidate, warts and all. If it turns out that your candidate actually holds positions antithetical to your religion—well, if you want to be serious about your politics, you ignore or explain away or even lie about this inconvenient fact. Hamer, to her credit, refused to become a supporter; but, as we shall shortly see, that is very far from the end of the story.

III

The religious voice at its more pure is the voice of the witness. The witness comes to "bear witness," as the Bible puts it (e.g., John 1:8): to reveal to others the truth that the witness has seen. The truth may be the central truth of a tradition, or it may be the prophetic truth of God's will: *This is what the Lord requires.* The voice of the witness, to be sure, is subject to critical evaluation: Is the witness genuine, or crazy, or a fraud? Has she a stake in the outcome? Does our tradition share her vision? But one must not confuse the need to evaluate the message the witness brings with the importance of welcoming messengers. For it is always possible, as has been the experience of many traditions, that we will, by listening, come to change, as the witness teaches us something we did not know.

What is this competition really about, this battle between the insiders who run the state (and perhaps the culture) and the prophetic outsiders who are moved by their faith to call the insiders to account? It is a battle about the meaning of our very existence. In the unfortunate language that the late twentieth century is bequeathing to the twenty-first, however, it has become the common habit in public discourse to refer to religious voices as though they were a threat to democracy. This is, of course, quite silly. A democracy that lacks the moral force of religious understanding is likely to be a democracy without purpose, in which politicians promise to allow citizens simply to satisfy their own wants, whether for money, power, or sex, with little regard for the needs of others; in which the measure of success in war is how small a sacrifice the nation's citizens are called upon to make, as the enemy's dead, including civilians, pile up, unmourned, at least by Americans—they are, after all, merely the enemy; in which the worst off are allowed to languish and often die in their segregated urban prisons, while the elite live in safe high-rises and safer suburbs. And if that description sounds much like the America we actually have, either religion is being insufficiently prophetic or a selfish society has decided not to listen—or both.

Religion, at its best, is subversive: So much we have already seen. Religion resists. It often resists, in particular, the values of the dominant culture.

It resists because religious people sometimes feel called by God to stand for something different than what everybody else believes, no matter how radical the vision they are pressing might seem to others. Consider, for example, the following wisdom, from a sermon by one Alfred Wesley Wishart, minister of the Fountain Street Baptist Church in Grand Rapids, Michigan, delivered in 1921, at a time when the Social Gospel movement was gathering steam:

> Our industrial operations involve religious issues, first, because all industrial operations are the activities of human beings. Men cannot act without motives, more or less conscious. They have purposes; they are acting upon some principle, good or bad; their activities are more or less conscious activities directed toward certain ends. They want certain things and they proceed to get those things. So the question of motive in daily toil, whether it is in the mine, on the sea, on the farm, in the bank, or in the factory, the question of motive cannot be eliminated from economic activity, and the question of motives has to do with the question of religion.[9]

Human motive: That, for Pastor Wishart, is religion's question. Wishart is writing, of course, from a Christian perspective, but Christianity is hardly alone in considering that the reasons we do the things we do matter as much as the things we do. In proposing that motive should matter for everybody, not just for Christians, Wishart is proposing to universalize the values of his faith; he is trying, he believes, to improve the nation through improving its people. If people would only operate from the proper motives, he contends, many of the problems of industrial organization could be resolved.

But is any of this the business of religion? Wishart obviously believes that the answer is yes. In this he follows the teaching of the Social Gospel movement since its inception in the middle years of the nineteenth century: Wherever human beings are, there the Gospel must go. Every human activity, the preachers of the Social Gospel believed, would benefit from application of Christian morality. When Reinhold Niebuhr called for the "Christianization" of American industry, that is what he had in mind: not that Christians must run everything or that the workers must meet for Bible study, but that industry itself should be remade according to a vision of love and caring that was quite foreign to the laissez-faire society of his time (and is, probably, quite foreign to the laissez-faire society of our time, too).

Or consider, once more, the role of religion in the civil rights movement. The prophetic voices of Martin Luther King Jr., Fannie Lou Hamer, and other leaders called people of all colors to nonviolent battle. Many white clergy who had never before involved themselves in a public way with issues of social change found themselves caught up in the opportunity to work for the betterment of God's creation.[10] The clergy joined the resistance. The cultural response is best illustrated, once more, by the confrontation between and Hubert Humphrey and Fannie Lou Hamer at the 1964 Democratic convention. If religion at its best is subversive, politics at its best proposes that the nation *stands* for something. Humphrey was arguing, in effect, that the nation should stand against racial exclusion, and that politics—working for the election of the Democratic ticket—was the best way to achieve that stance. Support us, Humphrey said, and the meaning the state will then provide through its politics is that racial segregation is wrong. Surely a pleasant prospect.

Hamer, however, did not see matters precisely Humphrey's way. Moved by her faith, she sought a somewhat different goal. At the risk of engaging in hyperbole, it is probably fair to say that she wanted more than an end to racial segregation: By calling for the establishment of the Kingdom, she was proposing a radical restructuring of American society, and a radical reordering of its priorities. She rejected the emphasis on "equality" propounded by most civil rights leaders, insisting on something more: "What would I look like fighting for equality with the white man? I don't want to go down that low. I want the true democracy that'll raise me and that white man up . . . raise America up."[11]

The reason Humphrey could not give Hamer what she wanted was not, really, because her vision was religious; it was that her religious vision was too radical to be considered in politics. Which is not the same as saying her vision was wrong.

And there lies the point. A thing may be right and yet impolitic. Or it may be popular and yet impolitic. Politics is the art of the possible; bargaining and compromise are its life's blood. Of election campaigns this is particularly true. No candidate ever comes before the voters clothed entirely in authenticity. Candidates who want to win are constantly shifting, shading, spinning, softening, omitting, emphasizing, sometimes even reversing field. This does not make politicians hypocritical. It makes them practical. To demand of a political candidate that he never change his public view of an issue is to demand of him defeat.[12] (I am reminded in this connection of a story, possibly apocryphal, about the economist John Maynard Keynes, during his service in the

House of Lords. Keynes rose to make an argument for some proposition. A member of the other party rose to ask whether Keynes had not argued the other side of the issue during the previous session. Keynes is said to have replied with something like this: "Yes, that's true. When I get additional information on a subject, I now and then change my mind. What do you do?")

This brings us back to the story of Humphrey's failed negotiation with Fannie Lou Hamer, whose solidly Christian faith, as Professor Marsh meticulously details, was the wellspring of her public activism. What happened next is quite instructive. Rebuffed by Hamer, who believed she was answering a divine call and was thus unwilling to compromise, the Democratic Party turned to other leaders of the Mississippi Freedom Democratic Party, people who were better educated than Hamer and who, in President Johnson's eyes, were easier to handle. They knew how the game was played in a way that Hamer did not; more important, they wanted to play it. A compromise was worked out behind her back, the lily-white delegation was seated, and the brief challenge to the segregationist Democrats was turned back by a president who despised them but also needed them.

It is fascinating to think that most Americans who have heard of her consider Fannie Lou Hamer a hero. In the linguistics of contemporary liberalism, Mrs. Hamer should surely be cast as a villain in her effort to use openly religious language in a nefarious scheme to impose a frankly religious order on the nation; and Humphrey and Johnson must be viewed as heroes for going behind her back, sabotaging her religious vision in order to negotiate with more practical MFDP members to destroy their leader, and their movement.

And let us make no mistake: The mass protest wing of the civil rights movement, the part that was moved by religious inspiration and in turn inspired a nation, did not truly achieve its goal. America was reformed but not remade. The state did not come to revolve, as Hamer hoped and Martin Luther King Jr. preached, around a Gospel of Love; rather, it retained its capitalist core and widened somewhat the set of beneficiaries. The state came to see its job, not as permanently changing the nation in a fundamental way in the search for a greater vision of love (for Hamer, Christian love), but rather as permanently establishing vast civil rights bureaucracies to monitor those aspects of equality that are measurable.[13] The existing order was not subverted; it was reformed in minor ways that siphoned off enough support from the more radical aspects of Hamer's vision (and King's) so as to avoid grappling with the more fundamental challenges that the civil rights movement posed.[14] The state, in short, refused to allow itself to be subverted by the religious resistance of the civil rights movement. It was a lot cheaper to invent affirmative action and buy people off.

The co-opting of the civil rights movement is a particular tragedy for America, even if matters could not have been otherwise. In the middle years of the twentieth century, no social movement was more plainly religious, in both its inspiration and its message. It is easy to forget (and some history texts seem to make a virtue of forgetting) that Martin Luther King Jr. was a preacher before he was an activist, and that he always credited his Christianity for both motivating him to lead and strengthening him to persevere. King never tried to hide the religiosity of his message, even from secular audiences. "[B]oth God's will and the heritage of our nation speak through our echoing demands," he told the National Press Club in 1962.[15] In a 1961 commencement address, he said, in effect, that rights need not be argued for: "To discover where they come from it is necessary to move back behind the dim mist of eternity, for they are God-given."[16] In his famous speech at the conclusion of the march from Selma to Montgomery in 1965, he borrowed from Micah: "Let us march on ballot boxes, until we send to our city councils, state legislatures, and the United States Congress men who will not fear to do justice, love mercy, and walk humbly with their God."[17]

The civil rights movement, in Mrs. Hamer's day, the middle years of the 1960s, was still characterized by a remarkably radical energy, a vision of a nation fired by love and commitment rather than profit and self-seeking, a nation in which the very meaning of life was defined by the Gospel commandment to love one's neighbor. That vision was explicitly Christian, and it was doomed from the start—doomed in the sense that it could not possibly be realized through politics. The flaw lies in politics, not in religion, which is no knock on politics; but religion, at its best, is a higher path to some of the truths that politics dimly perceives.

IV

Black Americans are, by many measures, the most religious people in the Western world.[18] The religion of the community is overwhelmingly Christian and evangelical.[19] The voting of that community is overwhelmingly liberal and Democratic. There is no necessary inconsistency here: The fact that white evangelicals tend to vote Republican should not lead to the generalization that all evangelicals do.[20] On the other hand, these African American evangelical Christians hold positions on most social issues far closer to the positions of, say, the Christian Coalition than the New Deal Coalition. For example, black Americans are strong supporters of school vouchers and classroom prayer and (in most surveys) hold serious reservations about abortion rights.[21] But the black community votes consistently for a political party that would never take seriously its views on these issues.

The most commonly suggested reason for this seeming anomaly is that the Republican Party's record on racial justice has been so terrible that few African Americans can stomach a yank on the GOP lever, no matter what areas of agreement there might be. There is some truth to this suggestion, but it is surely incomplete. After all (to take one example), a higher proportion of Republican than Democratic senators supported the Civil Rights Act of 1964 and the Voting Rights Act of 1965. But that counter example is also misleading. At the time of those votes, the Republican Party had not yet fallen fully into the hands of the conservative movement. The prominence of white evangelicals in the party also gives many black evangelicals pause: The memory of the segregationist Christian academies of the 1960s still burns. The Southern Baptist Convention's apology for that era (and for earlier support of segregation—the SBC was founded over the issue of slavery) is a helpful step toward eradicating long-standing black skepticism, but only a step.

Yet the explanation that rests on the history of segregation is only a small component of a larger truth. The larger truth is that the black clergy themselves have largely chosen to become the reliable allies of the Democratic Party. The larger truth is that after the pivotal moments of 1964 and 1965, the encounter between religion and electoral politics sapped the radical religious energy from the civil rights movement, leaving the black church as a reliable and important block in the Democratic coalition and—for just that reason—unable to witness publicly to that which is most radical (radical in American terms) in the Christian tradition. The black church dares not articulate the messages that most challenge the dominant culture, for fear of losing its place; and those messages it does press, at least in public, tend to resemble press releases from the liberal wing of the party.

The theologian Cornel West has lamented the state of black leadership, especially among the clergy, arguing that there is too much self-seeking, too much patronage, even too much race consciousness—and not enough transcendence. He longs for the days when the black clergy were able to press the cause in a way that resonated with some deep wellspring of justice in the national soul.[22] If Professor West is right, the reason may well be that the fortunes of the black clergy's leadership (and of black people generally) have become so bound up with the fortunes of the Democratic Party that it is no longer possible for the leaders to press ideas that their religious understanding of the world might demand. The redistributive justice of the civil rights era thus becomes affirmative action; the Reverend Jesse Jackson, having been, for most of his career, passionately pro-life, suddenly is forced to become pro-choice when he wants the party to take him seriously. As for Mrs. Hamer's vision of the establishment of the Kingdom, or at least the preparation of the way . . . well, that is a favor that politics cannot bestow.

The short of the matter is that the idea that is most right—or most righteous—may not be one that politics is able to accommodate. True, American politics has been remarkably successful at accommodating seemingly radical ideas without yielding its core. Our political system does not exactly screen radicalism out; very often, it invites radicalism in, in order to tame it, to take energy that might have been devoted to the restructuring of the culture or the economic system, and twist that energy instead into the gaining of minor triumphs in the political system. Social movements are domesticated, softened, absorbed. Radical challenges to the status quo morph into demands for a moderately larger piece of the pie, and the basic social structure remains unchanged. The women's movement has almost nothing left but the needs of professional women, women who work in the upper reaches of capitalism: preserving abortion, preventing sexual harassment, breaking the glass ceiling. The labor movement has left behind its anti-capitalist roots and now fights for profit sharing and seats on the board of directors. The civil rights movement is reduced to building a rickety wall around affirmative action programs, which themselves have been reduced to getting the right number of places in colleges and thus in the professions for minority students, and, now and then, offering such bizarre arguments as the claim that a "zero tolerance" policy on violence in the public schools discriminates against black students.

This technique of co-opting radical energy is only possible, however, when radicals are willing to be co-opted. Religious radicals are, or should be, harder to co-opt, because although politics deals with compromise and negotiation, religion, at least in the Western experience, tends to deal in absolutes. Dietrich Bonhoeffer wrote in his never-completed *Ethics* that compromise is the enemy of the Word.[23] He was writing in the context of the struggle by many German churches to resist the orthodoxy being imposed upon them by the Nazi regime, which wanted to control the content of the Christian message. But his point may be generalized. Religion that is not pure in its fidelity to its vision of truth—religion that is unfaithful—begins to lose its distinctively religious character and becomes much like everything else. When a religion enters politics, it at once finds itself bombarded with demands for compromise. The message must be softened, or hardened, or omitted altogether. As we shall see in the next chapter, the risk is especially great when a religion enters electoral politics. Candidates, as we have seen, will do what they must in order to win. They will likely welcome religious supporters as they would welcome anybody who might be able to raise money, ring doorbells, or generate votes. But that support, as we shall see, always leads to infidelity—infidelity of religion to its own best self.

It is no accident that Mrs. Hamer is one of the heroes of Professor West's critique, for he complains that the tattered remnants of the civil rights movement long ago passed from the hands of those of genuinely radical religious vision, those truly willing to resist the culture, and into the hands of professionals, insiders, more interested in making sure the slice of the pie is the right size.[24] But West's critiques, although well taken, are also a little bit unfair to the leadership; or, if the criticism is apt, he has perhaps picked the wrong cause. The self-seeking that so alarms him is not a problem in itself but a symptom of a larger problem. The activists among the black clergy made the decision in the 1960s to become a part of the Democratic coalition. With minor exceptions, they and their inheritors have stuck with that decision ever since.

Why does this matter? Because injustice comes in many varieties, and some of its forms flow from the system. The theologian James Cone has written about the risks of a black theology too wrapped up in Martin Luther King—not because Cone has no respect for King, whom he calls the most important theologian in American history, but because emphasizing King to the exclusion of the more radical thinkers "makes it easy for whites to ask for reconciliation without justice and for middle-class blacks to grant it, as long as they are treated specially"[25]—a reference, presumably, to affirmative action. Cone, like West, wants black leadership, especially the church leadership, to focus on justice understood more broadly than ensuring that the proper number of black students are admitted to the best colleges.

As a matter of politics, the choice is perfectly understandable. The situation of black folk in America has been so desperate that the turn to electoral politics was perhaps inevitable. And what a turn it has been. The Democratic Party consistently receives nearly 90 percent of the black vote (at least in national elections), even though a recent survey by the Joint Center for Political and Economic Studies showed that the median African American is more conservative on social issues than the median white voter.[26] An important reason for this consistency is the perception that the conservative movement (nowadays associated with the Republican Party) has opposed just about every important civil rights initiative of the past half century. The Republicans are seen as the party of big business, which few black Americans see as their ally. I am not here concerned with whether these reasons are sufficient. One might answer, for example, that the De-mocratic Party is dead-set against voucher programs that might help poor black children escape the horrific schools of many an inner city, programs that African Americans overwhelmingly support.[27]

But assessing the *political* merits of the black clergy's decision to go with the Democrats is beside the point. What matters is that, in *religious* terms, the decision has been disastrous. Once the decision to become electorally active was made, the power of prophetic ministry was lost.[28] If you are in the business of endorsing candidates and pushing for their election, you can hardly pretend to stand outside the corridors of power to call the na-tion to righteousness. You are far more likely to soften the message, rein-terpret the Gospels, and do what is necessary to retain the status of the insider. Cone complained, correctly, back in 1976 that too many black churches "adopt their value system from the American capitalistic society and not from Jesus Christ."[29] But the villain may not be capitalism alone. The villain may be politics itself.

The black clergy, like the black community, are overwhelmingly Chris-tian, and, within Christianity, overwhelmingly evangelical.[30] As evangeli-cals, they must believe, truly believe, in a divinely inspired Bible. They must recognize, therefore, that their reward lies in the next world, not in this one. This is not to say that there is anything wrong with calling on the world to renew itself for the benefit of those who suffer—only that the church must not confuse that prophetic obligation with the very different vocation of influencing the election returns.[31] Neither Christ nor any of the apostles involved themselves in governance. They were too busy bringing the Word—too busy witnessing—even when it meant they were reviled as outsiders. Perhaps they understood that one cannot be an insider and an outsider simultaneously. One is a prophet, calling the world to account, or one is helping to run the world, and therefore resisting the call of the prophets.[32]

3

Politics, Not Elections

LET US NOW JUMP FORWARD TWO DECADES to the middle of the 1980s, a moment when the Reverend Jerry Falwell's umbrella organization, Moral Majority, Inc., seemed to stride the political world like some conservative colossus, crowning and defrocking candidates for electoral office at will. That, at least, was the image of the group in the panicky imagination of liberal activists and commentators. Perhaps it is difficult, looking back from today's perspective, to recall the level of the rhetoric. Senator George McGovern, one of several prominent Democrats who lost their Senate seats in the 1980 conservative sweep, derided what he called Moral Majority's "militaristic approach," adding that "their narrow, arrogant attitude is destructive to the political process."[1] Another critic proclaimed the group "a dangerous threat to the lives and liberty of the real majority: women, lesbians, gay men, black, Latino, Asian, native, undocumented, youth, elderly, the disabled, poor people, and working people as a whole"[2]—a weird, catchall list sufficiently long to leave Moral Majority not only without a majority but without more than a handful of members.

But—surprise, surprise! Before the decade was out, Falwell, unable to raise enough money to keep the group running, folded it up. And, despite the histrionic warnings of Moral Majority's critics, scholars who have studied the group have been unable to find much political influence. It turned out Moral Majority could not end political careers by "targeting" senators whose views it did not like. It turned out Moral Majority could not deter Hollywood from creating films it did not like. (The group's much-ballyhooed effort in the mid-1980s to scare ABC out of running the made-for-television movie *The Day After*, a polemic against nuclear weapons, served only to increase interest in the program.) It turned out that Moral Majority's membership was a tiny fraction of Falwell's public claims, or the media's public fears.[3] And, as far as history is able to record, Moral Majority never persuaded a single legislature to take away a single fundamental right from a single person.

By the standards of politics, Moral Majority failed. It is the nature of that failure that suggests some commonalities with the experience of Fannie Lou Hamer, who was, if sincere, at least as fundamentalist, at least as radical, at least as much a religious fanatic, as Jerry Falwell. Indeed, despite the differences of some of their ideas, Fannie Lou Hamer and Jerry Falwell had in common not only their shared evangelical Christianity but their insistence on engaging politics on overtly religious terms. Neither of them was doing anything remotely un-American by trying to persuade politicians to do what (in the radical vision each presented) the Lord required. But their common failure, their shared inability to win in politics what they were sure God wanted, helps to illustrate the problem with religious activism in public life. The religious voice, as I have argued, should always be welcome, its words taken seriously, respected, and honored, even if, in the end, the society chooses to go another way—but, at the moment the prophet begins to relish that welcome, the power of prophecy begins to drain away.

II

In 1941, the British writer C. S. Lewis published a short essay entitled "Meditation on the Third Commandment"—an essay, it is worthwhile noting, that nowhere either mentioned or quoted the Third Commandment. His goal was to forestall the creation of a "Christian Party" in England.[4] The United States would shortly be going through a similar antidisestablishmentarian spasm: Just about a decade after Lewis's essay was published, the "Christian Nation" amendment to the Constitution was introduced in the Congress, which stated explicitly that all the laws of the United States were to be subject to the Word of God and his son Jesus Christ.[5]

The Christian Nation Amendment disappeared into the Congress without a trace. In later years, it would reappear with depressing regularity, only to vanish again. John Anderson, later a liberal hero, was elected to Congress in the 1960s on a platform supporting the amendment, a platform he subsequently and sensibly repudiated, although not, evidently, until he decided to run for President.[6] But the desire to create a kind of

Christian party of the sort Lewis feared has stayed with us—and, despite the ahistorical lamentations of some of today's media and academic critics, the temptation has hardly been limited to Christians on the right. It is, however, Christians who fall on the conservative side of the political divide who have lately been yielding, and who, when they yield, stimulate the agonizing and often shrill cadence of "Keep religion out of politics!" So it is with those pesky conservatives that we should begin.

Unfortunately, few scholars have tried to understand the concerns and aspirations that gave birth to the upsurge of conservative Christian activism in the late 1970s and early 1980s, preferring to explain the movement away as an aberration or as somehow un-American. Alan Brinkley, one of the few serious historians to take the movement seriously, has pointed out that the rise of the loose coalition of organizations often called (disdainfully) the Religious Right actually had strong roots in a mounting discontent about the direction society was taking, which helps account for the early successes that so stunned its critics.[7] Indeed, as a signal of the existence of a large and unhappy group of citizens, the movement was in the grand tradition of American democratic pluralism; the politicians who were accused of pandering to the groups were simply responding to normal imperatives of representative government. Unfortunately, many liberal critics have refused to take the groups at face value, insisting that they must be, somehow, the products of irrational impulses, perhaps of shameful manipulation as well. Dismissals of this kind probably helped account for the astonishingly rapid growth of the organizations, for nothing creates political energy quite so well as insult, and nothing makes organizations harder to slow than the ignorance of their critics. When a 1993 article in the *Washington Post* derided conservative evangelicals as "largely poor, uneducated, and easy to command," a few biased readers might have cheered, but contributions to the politically organized groups very likely increased.[8]

Voter surveys indicate that it is still quite unusual in America for clergy to suggest to congregants how they should vote.[9] Yet the conservative religious activists, even if they usually stop short of endorsing candidates, plainly form an important part of the Republican electoral coalition. Many scholars see the Supreme Court's 1973 abortion decision[10] as the transformative moment in the development of conservative Christian organizations.[11] I have made that claim myself.[12] And, no doubt, issues (as we call them in our politics) have been important—not only the widespread availability of abortion, but the abolition of organized classroom prayer, the sexual revolution, and the growing pressure on the traditional family. Abortion can perhaps be set aside, because of its status, for many Christians, as, literally, a matter of life or death: Activism in the pro-life cause is inevitable. If one truly believes in the humanity of the unborn child, it is difficult to be satisfied with the weirdly complacent slogan, IF YOU DON'T BELIEVE IN ABORTION, DON'T HAVE ONE. The other issues, however, make an interesting set. Together they represent a culture that many Americans see as threatening, not to themselves, but to their children—and, in particular, to the ability of families to raise their children with the religious values they consider vital. Perhaps it is not the proper role of the state, and perhaps not even of the culture, to assist. Many Christians fear, however, that the state and the culture are getting in the way. In a basically democratic nation, it should not even occasion surprise that they turn to politics to try to alter the direction of both.

But the groups grew swiftly for other reasons as well: particularly their resonance, even in a basically liberal age, with the deep aspirations of significant numbers of Americans. Whether or not the United States really is, as some conservative observers insist, mired in a culture war,[13] it is certainly fair to say that the dominant liberal ethos of our public life is only that—the dominant ethos of our *public* life—and is often in conflict with the hopes or plans or most cherished beliefs of many Americans. In particular, Americans with traditional views on matters of sex and family life, as well as on the very nature of authority (is morality a set of God-given absolutes or a constantly evolving set of cultural constructs?), often feel themselves screened out of the mosaic of contemporary America.

The problem of authority is, for many traditionalists—especially evangelicals—far more troubling than many of the "social issues" that, because they seem amenable to political solutions, capture the attention of law-centered journalists. But authority is about culture, not law. It is, at bottom, a question of whether there are any binding moral rules. Traditionalists tend to believe in morality as a set of God-given absolutes, rules of behavior that humans are not free to vary. The contemporary culture, especially in education, is wary of absolutes, preferring to view morality as a constantly evolving human construct. A family raising its children to believe in God's rules can hardly be happy with a dominant ethos that is not so much morally relativistic as morally skeptical—for the answer to every moral argument seems to be, "Well, that's just your opinion." Few, if any, religions actually teach a morality as vapid as the morality American culture tends to preach.

Once we understand that for millions of Americans, moral rules are God-given, we can perhaps track down the source of some of the discontent that so often seems to bemuse, or just befuddle, the media. For example, if you situate yourself within the context of traditional Judeo-Christian sexual ethics, it is easy to understand the opposition among some religionists to allowing men and women to serve side by side in combat positions, not as a matter of sexism but as a matter of trying to structure all of life in a way that avoids temptation.[14] If you take a moment to try to understand the origin and the continuing appeal of the belief of many evangelicals in the literally inerrant Bible, it is easy to see why they would oppose the teaching of the theory that Homo sapiens evolved from other animals, a theory they believe to be false.[15] If you take a moment to contemplate the traditional Christian teaching that God and only God is the source of goodness, it is easy to see why many fundamentalists would oppose courses in the public schools suggesting to their children that morality rests on anything else. To say, as liberals too often say, that it is fine for these disgruntled citizens to have their views as long as they keep them private is, ironically, to concede the basic point of the conservative critics, to wit, that we are after all mired in a war for the culture; the rule that unhappy-conservative-Christians-should-shut-up-and-go-away-and-let-liberalism-win sounds, to those who think they are in the trenches, like the thunder of heavy artillery.

Evangelical churches grew explosively in the closing decades of the twentieth century. I think it is wrong to conclude, as the conservative commentator David Frum has suggested, that this remarkable growth was somehow a product of a shift in American Christianity "from an ethic of rectitude to an ethic of forgiveness."[16] Although many mainline Protestant denominations began in the 1960s to abandon the idea of serious rules of conduct, many evangelical churches began preaching them all the harder. I also think it is wrong to conclude, as have some observers, that much of the growth can be accounted for by evangelicals' early and skillful use of communications technology, especially television. The simpler explanation—and one that is largely borne out by the data—is that the evangelical churches grew because they offered a message of hope, values, and discipline that appealed, and continues to appeal, to those they aim to convert.[17]

Which leads us to the great liberal bugaboo of the age, the Christian Coalition. Almost from the day of its founding in 1989, the Christian Coalition has been a force in the Republican Party. With its member churches, its ability to drum up letter-writing campaigns as well as votes, and its stated goal of training 10 political activists in every electoral district, of any size, in the United States—a projected total of 1.75 million activists—it has been, for many conservative candidates, a welcome source of energy and on-the-ground troops . . . and a group nobody wants to have for its enemy. The Christian Coalition has generated, if anything, even more histrionics than Moral Majority ever did.[18]

One must of course be wary of lumping together groups that are often quite distinct. To take a famous example from the literature, Jerry Falwell's Moral Majority was designed to appeal to fundamentalist Christians. The Christian Coalition was not. Observers unwilling to study the carefully nuanced distinctions among evangelicals might miss this point and would then lack the tools to explain why, in his 1988 presidential campaign, the Reverend Pat Robertson (who is not viewed by evangelicals as a fundamentalist) ran less well among white voters attending fundamentalist churches than among whites as a whole.[19] The monolithic Religious Right is, in short, a media invention.

Indeed, much of what we think we know about religion and actual voting seems to have been cobbled together from guesses, errors, and misunderstandings. To take an example that may seem trivial—but leads, if uncorrected, to further errors—mainline Protestants are significantly more likely to vote than are evangelicals.[20] Moreover, the group sometimes referred to as "low-status whites," which is heavily evangelical, might have the lowest rate of political participation of any segment of the population.[21]

If one does not take the time to understand the distinctions among American Christians, even among evangelicals, one cannot make sense of much that happens in politics. Take the 1980 presidential election. The conventional wisdom has it that the Southern Baptists who turned out to elect Jimmy Carter in 1976 turned against him and voted for Ronald Reagan in 1980. In fact, even many conservative activists seem to believe this. Writes Ralph Reed, longtime executive director of the Christian Coalition: "[T]he burgeoning religious conservative movement went to work, delivering a huge vote for the first divorced man ever to sit in the White House and helping him defeat two of the most devout Christians in the history of recent politics, Jimmy Carter and John Anderson."[22]

But the data do not quite bear out the generalization. Reed quotes a national poll, issued immediately after the election, stating that Reagan defeated Carter among white Baptists by a remarkable 56 percent to 34 percent.[23] But the somber calculations by scholars of voting do not bear this out. Carter's margin among Southern Baptists (by far the largest white Baptist group) shrank considerably from 1976 to 1980, but he retained a majority. The source most relied upon by scholars of presidential elections is the data collected in the National Election Statistics of the Center for Political Studies at the University of Michigan. According to the NES figures, in 1976, Carter received 59.1 percent of Southern Baptist votes versus 37.6 percent for Gerald Ford. In 1980, Southern Baptists split slightly in favor of Carter. The NES puts the numbers at 50 percent for Carter, 46.6 percent for Reagan.[24] Why then did Reagan win so handily? Because he trounced Carter among most mainline Protestant groups, gaining, for instance, 66.7 percent of the Presbyterian vote, 56.7 percent of the Lutheran vote, 68.8 percent of the Episcopalian vote, and 53.2 percent of the Methodist vote. (Certainly many of these mainline Protestant voters are also evangelicals; but none of them are "white Baptists.")[25] In addition, Reagan received 49.5 percent of the crucial Roman Catholic vote. Among identifiable religious groups other than Southern Baptists, Carter received a clear majority only of the Jewish vote.

Interestingly, all the same religious groups that split against Carter in 1980 also split against him in 1976—with one exception, which turned out to be the key to the election. In 1976, Carter won the Roman Catholic vote by a landslide, 56.2 percent to 40.6 percent for Ford. Thus, contrary to the popular story, it was Catholics, not evangelical Protestants, who elected insurgent Carter in 1976, and it was their massive defection to the Republican nominee that defeated incumbent Carter in 1980.

But Protestants elected George Bush in 1988. The Roman Catholic vote returned to the Democratic Party, with Michael Dukakis picking up about 52 percent, but Bush won every other religious group handily, with the exception of the Jewish vote (72.7 percent for Dukakis) and the Baptist vote (a statistical dead heat among Southern Baptists, and a 55.2 percent majority for Dukakis among other Baptists, including the black Baptist churches).

And how did Bill Clinton fare in 1992? He held onto the Catholic vote and won every measurable Protestant group, with the exception of nondenominational Protestants (61 percent voted for Bush, 26.8 percent for Clinton, 9.8 percent for Ross Perot); those who indicated no denomination other than Protestant (43.6 percent Bush, 35.9 percent Clinton, 20.5 percent Perot); the "independent" Baptist churches (45.4 percent Bush, 36.4 percent Clinton, 18.2 percent Perot), and those who answered "just Christian" as their affiliation (44 percent Bush, 32 percent Clinton, 24 percent Perot). What have all these groups in common? All of them, as nonaffiliated Protestants, tend to lead lives a little bit separated from the culture, and tend to be conservative in their outlook. Democrats never expect to get their votes, and Clinton did remarkably well among them. In fact, in 1996,

Clinton actually won the group describing itself as "just Christian" by a margin of 2 to 1 over Bob Dole. Dole wrested away a few of the mainline Protestant groups, piling up strong majorities among Episcopalians and Presbyterians, but was unable to make inroads among Roman Catholics.

Contrary to another popular story, however, Roman Catholics are not the largest religious bloc in the country—assuming that it is even fair to think of religious voters as blocs. As far back as 1960 (the earliest figures evidently available on the NES web site),[26] Roman Catholics have been the third largest bloc, behind mainline Protestants and evangelical Protestants. The Catholic share of the electorate has risen substantially, from 20 percent in 1960 to 26 percent in 1996, but there has been a larger change in the makeup of the Protestant community, accounted for principally by the long-standing decline of the mainline churches. Mainline Protestants were a staggering 45 percent of the electorate in 1960, with evangelicals constituting another 29 percent. By 1996, evangelicals accounted for 33 percent of the electorate, mainline Protestants only 22. The main beneficiaries of the decline have been, not evangelicals, but Catholics and the ubiquitous "none," which soared from 1 percent in 1960 to 13 percent in 1996.

III

But even if the organizations of conservative Christianity have a little less electoral clout than commentators often seem to think, their influence is far from insubstantial. Arizona senator John McCain discovered this during the Republican presidential primaries in 2000, when he went to Virginia Beach, a stronghold of several of the organizations, to denounce the Reverend Jerry Falwell and the Reverend Pat Robertson as "agents of intolerance" who were more interested in building their influence in the Republican Party than in winning elections. He also called Falwell and Robertson "evil," which, he announced days later, was meant as a joke. The tone of the speech was angry. A week before the speech, one of Robertson's organizations had made telephone calls (featuring the taped voice of Robertson himself) to potential Republican voters in the Michigan primary, assailing McCain's record and supporting his opponent, Texas governor George W. Bush. McCain was trying to turn the tables, implying, perhaps, that whatever Robertson and Falwell stood for, voters should believe that Bush stood for the same thing.

The move predictably backfired. Although McCain took pains in his speech to distinguish between the leadership of Christian conservative organizations and the members, nobody paid close attention to that nuance. Politics is not about nuance. As one scholar pointed out, the speech "surely energized Christian conservatives by giving them an enemy in the race."[27] Voters affiliated with the Christian Coalition and other groups turned out to vote . . . and, in the Virginia primary, at least, they went for Bush, by a margin of 8 to 1. It seems that rumors of the death of the Christian Right in Republican politics have been greatly exaggerated.

The Christian Coalition hardly holds the stage alone. Over the last two decades of the twentieth century, organizations of conservative religious activists blossomed everywhere—not just everywhere in America, but everywhere in the world.[28] In the United States, the groups come in remarkable variety: the Traditional Values Coalition, the Christian Action Network, Excellence in Education, the Eagle Forum, and many others. James Dobson's Focus on the Family movement has millions of followers, and his daily radio program, some observers believe, generates far more political activity than the more organized groups.[29] Indeed, there is among traditionalist Christians what is sometimes called the "electronic church," self-described Christian radio stations that carry much of the same syndicated programming, a good deal of it political (if not specifically electoral) in nature, so that even Protestants who are unchurched, or who attend services at a mainline denomination, may, if they so choose, listen to the message all day long. Some estimates place the daily listenership in the tens of millions.

Here I have some personal experience, for my family and I would have to be described as regular participants in the electronic church. We attend an Episcopal church, but we listen frequently to a local Christian radio station, especially when driving. As believing Christians, we find it both more enjoyable and more informative than more traditional stations. It is also much cleaner: We do not have to worry about our children being exposed to repulsive lyrics or lurid details of violent crime. To be sure, the political content is substantial, and we do not always agree with it, but religion, as I have emphasized from the start, can hardly escape being political.

Yet, even as the electronic church booms, few of the political organizations of the Christian Right seem to have maintained the vitality they possessed in the 1980s.* The political scientist Robert Booth Fowler, in a thoughtful analy-

---

*Some skeptical scholars have argued that even if the influence of the groups seems to be waning at the national level, they still maintain significant influence on local politics.

sis, attributes the decline to a number of factors, including an inability to pen-
etrate elite Washington culture, the hostility of the mainline Protestant denominations, the indifference of most Americans to the battles the groups
want to fight, and the failure to enact any serious part of the agenda.[30] Further, as Fowler and several other analysts have pointed out, it is not easy to
measure the influence of the organizations even in the 1980s: Most of the voters the groups claim to target seem to be voters who would have gone Republican in any case.[31] Moreover, as the journalist E. J. Dionne has noted, not
all skepticism about Christian conservatives amounts to mere liberal bias:
Anti-Semitism and anti-Catholicism are facts of evangelical history, not media
inventions designed to undermine the Republican Party.[32] On the other hand,
the commentator John Judis has suggested that the groups have become, in
effect, victims of their own success. Having gained a measure of power in
Washington, Judis contends, they have lost their traditional focus on grass-
roots organizing and have substituted instead all the tricks of political con-
sultants: telephone calls, direct mail, and surveys.[33]

One might cut through all these other explanations—and some commentators do—with the suggestion that Christian conservatives have
harmed themselves in the court of public opinion because of their purported extremism on a number of social issues. But this is not a plausible
story. The Christian Coalition, for all that it is vilified in the mainstream
media, probably holds positions closer to the median voter on a greater
number of issues than do more durable liberal groups such as the National
Organization for Women or the American Civil Liberties Union. For example, the group's support of classroom prayer in the public schools, anath-
ema to liberalism, has, throughout the coalition's history, been the position
of a significant majority of American adults.[34] And although only a minority of Americans ever supported the Christian Coalition's early call for a
ban on nearly all abortions, fairly strong majorities agree with the group's
more recent and more nuanced position that most late-term abortions
should be illegal.[35] The Christian Coalition, in other words, can often
make a stronger claim than many liberal groups to have its finger on the
pulse of the public. But NOW and the ACLU know something that the
Christian Coalition, as a self-proclaimed religious group, should know but
seems to have forgotten: Partisan politics is dangerous.

What is so dangerous about politics? From the Christian point of view,
the first and greatest danger is theological: the loss of prophetic power when
one chooses the path of coercion. It is more than a little ironic, as the conservative commentator Cal Thomas points out in a recent book, that many of

the same preachers who insist that God is on their side nevertheless seem to think that their side cannot prevail except through coercion.[36] Could it be, he wonders, that the faith of some politically active Christians is not as strong as it should be? If Christians lead the lives God intends, Thomas argues, the culture will eventually come along—but because of the example of Christian living, not because Christians have their hands on the levers of coercive power.

Thomas's fears that the political activism of evangelicals might signal a lack of confidence in God echo the recent arguments of other evangelicals. Dean Merrill, a former vice president of Focus on the Family, makes a similar point through a series of rhetorical questions: "Are we convinced that our Lord is fundamentally stronger than the devil and his followers? If so, then why all the dismay? Should not a great, almighty God be able to handle the local five-member school curriculum committee, for example, or a panel of nine black-robed judges?"[37] These contemporary arguments have their roots in the Baptist separationist tradition, stretching back into the nineteenth century and on into the early years of the Republic. As late as the 1960s, Jerry Falwell continued to preach the traditional Baptist message of separation, urging his congregants to place their faith in God rather than in government.

This theological concern has a practical side. Politics is antithetical to religion for another important reason: Politics generates the desire to win. And the desire to win, in turn, generates the willingness to do what is necessary to win. And, for the group that begins with a radical religious impulse, the what-is-necessary often winds up being a compromise. So (the reader may demand) what is wrong with compromise? Nothing, if one is a politician. But, potentially, everything, if one is a religionist.

We return to Dietrich Bonhoeffer, whose stance on compromise I mentioned in the previous chapter. Compromise, to quote his *Ethics* more precisely, "hates the word."[38] (By which he means the Word.) "Compromise," he wrote, "always springs from hatred of the ultimate."[39] For Bonhoeffer, "the ultimate" meant God—or, more precisely, the *idea* of God. The desire for compromise arises, according to Bonhoeffer, from the desire, even among the religious, to flee from God's word: "Even the raising of the question of the ultimate, even the endeavour to give effect to God's word in its authority for life in the world, is now accounted radicalism and apathy or antipathy towards the established orders of the world and towards the men who are subject to these orders."[40] The religious desire to compromise the Word, he argued, is the desire to avoid the label of radicalism.[41]

Perhaps the Christian Coalition has flown from the Word. When the group was young, its brash and uncompromising rhetoric probably accounted for much of its appeal. As Justin Watson points out in his book on the group, its basic stance, from the middle of the 1980s through the middle of the 1990s, was restorationist. What the Christian Coalition promised was a better future modeled on a more virtuous past. The path to this future would be politics. Watson quotes a 1990 speech in which Pat Robertson, the group's founder, called for a return to what he described as the nation's founding principles: "Back to the Bible, back to the Constitution, back to the greatness it knew through faith in God, through individual self-reliance, through moral restraint."[42] The power of this frankly religious vision gained millions of converts, and, to the extent that the vision was radically at odds with the dominant culture, it was subversive in the sense that I used the term in Chapter 2–it focused believers on the transcendent, thus equipping them for prophecy, and perhaps for more. In short, the Christian Coalition, like the Southern Christian Leadership Conference, was in the great American tradition of radical public activism by religious groups moved to act by their radically different understanding of the meaning of the world.*

IV

Yet the Christian Coalition, like Moral Majority, has faltered. What has gone wrong?

Let me propose an answer somewhat different from the mainstream analyses. I suspect that the group is suffering because the radical energy that once fired it has gone out of it. And the reason the radical energy has gone out of the Christian Coalition is that the organization has become, with time, less and less prophetic and more and more political. In so doing, it has been forced to make the very trade-off that Dietrich Bonhoeffer would have predicted and Fannie Lou Hamer disdained: compromise versus the Word. For the coalition is now a basic building block of the Republican electoral coalition; it has, in effect, suffered the same fate as the black preachers who have cast their lot entirely with the Democratic Party.

---

*Again, I emphasize that I am drawing an analogy, not an identity. One should be able to appreciate the radical diversity of religious activism without endorsing all the ends that the various radicals might seek. Indeed, as a believer in genuine diversity I particularly want to carve out spaces for the nurture of sources of meaning radically different from whatever happens to be dominant in the culture of the moment. My desire to create these spaces is independent of whether I happen to agree with the meaning thus generated. I return to this point in chapter 5 and again in chapter 12.

To see why such trade-offs matter, let us return to the C. S. Lewis essay I discussed earlier in the chapter. Lewis argued, with devastating brevity, that the problem with the establishment of a Christian party was that it either would not be a true party or would not be truly Christian. If purely Christian, he proposed, the party would not succeed in electoral politics, for it would be too small to make a difference and would, probably, include parts of Christ's message that nobody quite wanted to hear. If successful in politics, the party would cease to be distinctively Christian, because it would compromise the purity of doctrine for the sake of transient political advantage.

The second point is the more salient. In order to win elections, Lewis warned, a Christian party might be "tempted to accept help from unbelievers who profess themselves quite openly to be the enemies of God." Moreover, because not all Christians agree on all issues, the party would very likely represent only a minority of voters, even in a country overwhelmingly Christian. Thus, wrote Lewis, the party would have little choice but to form an alliance with "the un-Christian party nearest to it in beliefs."[43]

Why does this matter? Let us extend Lewis's argument a bit. The alliance he describes would be political, not religious; its purpose would be the attainment of secular goals on which the groups agreed. The "un-Christian party" to which the Christian party was allied would have its own reasons, presumably "un-Christian ones," for fighting for the same political program. It might seem, at first blush, that such a choice is pragmatic, the way to get things done. But note the trade that the Christian organization makes. It steps into politics, into the realm of negotiation and compromise—away from the Word. Its price of admission is to surrender the very language, the very understanding of the world, that first generated its reason to be . . . and its power of resistance. Suddenly, the secular political party will speak the language of faith—and the supposedly religious organization will speak the language of politics. And, although neither one will quite be speaking its natural language, each will quickly find itself passably fluent, if still outside its native tongue.

The Christian Coalition, as it maneuvered toward this trade-off, faced two signal moments. The first was the 1992 Republican Convention. The second was the release of the coalition's official platform, the *Contract with the American Family*, in 1995.

The 1992 Republican Convention, many observers believe, helped Democrat Bill Clinton to an upset victory over President George Bush. Although it is not fair to suggest, as have some commentators, that the convention was in effect run by the Christian Coalition, there is little doubt that religious conservatives were a strong and influential presence. How strong? So strong that when Vice President Dan Quayle, addressing a roomful of delegates meeting at a nearby hotel, called out, "Who do we trust?"—expecting to hear cries of "George Bush!"—he was startled when the assembly yelled back, "Jesus!"[44] How influential? So influential that Pat Buchanan was given the opportunity to deliver a fiery speech in prime time, where, some political experts have argued, he doomed Bush's reelection chances when, describing the effort needed to turn the culture around, he uttered the words "religious warfare" in describing the effort needed to turn the culture around. The *positions* espoused at the convention were not particularly radical, but much of the rhetoric was sufficiently fiery—*religiously* fiery—that many voters were scared, especially when the news media played and replayed the most worrisome moments.

Supporters of the Christian Coalition have long complained that the group's influence over the 1992 convention was exaggerated by reporters.[45] Even the windy rhetoric, they insist, was blown out of proportion. (Buchanan, for example, is not affiliated with the Christian Coalition, or with any other organization of the Religious Right, but some news reports blurred this distinction.) Those concerns, however, even if legitimate, are beside the point. Politics is politics. If one does not want to be misquoted, one must not provide anything to misquote. Which leads to the second signal moment.

The second moment was the release, in 1995, of the *Contract with the American Family,* the official public platform of the Christian Coalition. What is immediately striking about the *Contract* is its entire lack of the restorationist tone of the coalition's early pronouncements. In fact, there is little in the *Contract* that could not have been produced by any conservative think tank. The *Contract* supports lower taxes, a balanced budget, and school vouchers, for example—but none in explicitly biblical terms. Peculiar though it may appear, the *Contract with the American Family* contains not a single quotation from the Bible. Even when discussing so controversial an idea as the Religious Equality Amendment to the Constitution, the *Contract* defends it in secular terms, as a matter of correcting judicial misunderstandings of the First Amendment. When Ralph Reed, longtime executive director of the Christian Coalition, presented the *Contract with the American Family* to the public and the media, he explained that it contained only "the ten suggestions, not the Ten Commandments."[46]

Despite Reed's gentle tone, the *Contract with the American Family* provoked blistering attacks for its purported extremism. But they were unwarranted and, indeed, missed the point. Justin Watson, in his study of the Christian

Coalition, notes the criticisms of the *Contract,* then adds: "[A] closer study of this document reveals, especially in comparison with earlier manifestos of the Christian Right, a striking avoidance of radical positions."[47] Some critics dismissed the document as a smokescreen. In fact, the document was powerful evidence that the radical religious energy that had given birth to the coalition was in the process of being domesticated—the very fate, as we saw in the previous chapter, that befell the civil rights movement.

Ralph Reed defended the evident secularism of the *Contract* by pointing out, correctly, that the religious conservatives to whom the Christian Coalition tries to give voice care about and are affected by such matters as tax rates and budget deficits.[48] But, once we take account of C. S. Lewis's dire warnings, we can quickly see that the problem with the *Contract with the American Family* is not that no religious people care about the issues it raises—obviously, tens of millions do. The problem is that the *Contract,* even though produced by the *Christian* Coalition, is not even a religious document, to say nothing of a Christian one. It is a secular political document, setting forth a secular political program, justified with secular political argument. Why is this a problem? Because the *Contract* entirely lacks the hard, radical energy of the coalition's early days. The document does not defend its program on the ground that God wants it, or even that morality demands it; the document defends its program by offering what amounts to a series of op-ed articles, suitable for the most secular of newspapers.

From the point of view of liberalism, this remarkable transformation should be counted a good thing. Some liberal critics of the coalition cynically derided the *Contract* as a smoke screen, written in secular language in order to mask a perhaps different religious program.[49] But contemporary liberal philosophers insist that religiously inspired arguments, before being presented in our public debates, should be translated into a common secular language.[50] I have set forth elsewhere, at some length, my reasons for disagreeing with the translation requirement, which seems to me both undemocratic and unrealistic.[51] But if liberalism indeed requires that religious language undergo a translation before being presented in public debate, then liberals should be pleased rather than suspicious to find the Christian Coalition engaging in it.

C. S. Lewis, however, would have been appalled. So would Fannie Lou Hamer. And Dietrich Bonhoeffer. And so were many of today's conservative activists. As the coalition became more and more a building block of the Republican Party, former allies—especially on the abortion issue—began to attack the group with such words as "treachery," "unprincipled," "betrayal," and "deceit."[52] Criticisms of this kind are precisely what the Electoral Objection predicts: Once a religious organization wants a role in determining the outcome of election contests, it will do what is needed to enhance and preserve that role. If purity of doctrine would weaken its influence, then doctrine is impurified in order to be influential.

Lewis would have been appalled in part because watering down the message in order to gain acceptance would be at war with one of his larger projects: to place the question of religious truth beyond secular moral judgment. Lewis believed that Christians should never defend their faith to others by arguing that it was useful (for example, that one would lead a healthier, happier life upon conversion to Christianity) or by arguing that it led to morally good results (that a good Christian would, by virtue of the faith, adhere to an admirable secular moral standard). Lewis was quite vehement in support of the proposition that the *only* reason for anyone to accept Christianity was that it was true. In other words, those who should be Christians were those, and only those, who took Christian revelation to be an actual set of facts about God's relationship with the world; and, for those who believed the facts, nothing else was as significant.[53] Consequently, for Lewis, a political party that appealed to voters on the ground of some secular policy proposal would already cease to be Christian. It would not be Christian because it would be asserting not the truth of Christianity, but only its utility.[54]

Viewed in this light, the *Contract with the American Family* is, to say the very least, a bit unsettling—not for its conclusions but for its arguments. The decision to offer a secular argument for the social agenda of a religious organization is a decision for compromise, for alliance, for political victory, rather than for doctrinal purity. It is a choice to stand inside rather than outside, to be kingmaker rather than prophet. It exemplifies the Integrity Objection. No doubt compromise is the pragmatic choice, and religionists who refuse to engage in it will lose more political battles than they will win. But this justification does not really answer Lewis's point. Religious organizations making pragmatic compromises for victory should ask themselves two simple questions: *If we win, what are we winning? And at what cost?*

To be sure, any organization that survives will fall, sooner or later, into the hands of pragmatists, much as the Mississippi Freedom Democratic Party did. But members originally attracted by a group's radical vision are unlikely to remain members once the nature of the vision itself seems to change. After all, if the public program of the Christian Coalition turns out to be indistinguishable from—say—the public program of the Heritage Foundation, then what special niche is the coalition filling? The special religious niche, as Mrs.

Hamer knew, is the niche of the prophet, the niche that calls the world to account without attempting to become a broker of political power. In his book *Active Faith,* Ralph Reed tells the story of how Pat Robertson once quit the Religious Roundtable, an umbrella group of religious conservatives, because of the roundtable's support of Ronald Reagan. Robertson, says Reed, "felt strongly that evangelicals should not tie the gospel to any single political party or leader."[55] The coalition has in some ways forgotten that wisdom, thus running afoul of the Electoral Objection, for the *Contract with the American Family* reads eerily like the output of a group that has tired of being accused of costing the Republican Party votes. It reads like the product of compromise.

Compromise is what politics demands. In a multireligious democracy, the need for political compromise is so extreme that the putatively religious organization that decides to be actively political will, inevitably, be transformed into a political organization that was once religious—in the same way, for instance, that Yale, where I teach, is a secular university that was once religious.[56] This, I believe, is what is happening, or perhaps has already happened, to the Christian Coalition. That is why liberal theorists who oppose religious language in politics should be pleased that the Christian Coalition has gained so much power in the Republican Party, and why religious conservatives should be uneasy: The process of domestication of politically active white conservative evangelicals is well under way, and may be irreversible.[57]

Ralph Reed suggests that the problem faced by Christian conservatives is, in part, the lack of a national leader around whom they can coalesce: "In my view, when the helicopter carrying Ronald Reagan left the Capitol grounds in 1989 following the inauguration of George Bush, we witnessed the departure of the first and last individual who could unite all religious conservatives from the national political stage."[58] But, in so writing, Reed is still imagining his movement in political terms rather than in the terms of the prophetic voice of religious transcendence. And if conservative Christians insist on electoral politics as the path for gaining their ends, they will risk falling victim to all the various diseases of which C. S. Lewis warned. Cal Thomas puts the point simply: "If people who claim to follow Jesus and his kingdom get too cozy with government, it won't be the government that gets injured. It will be the church that is compromised."[59]

Among conservative Christians, Thomas's position seems to be gathering support. *Time* magazine reported in February 2000: "In the late 1990s, the hyperpolitical Christian Coalition went into steep decline, while

Promise Keepers, an organization that believes many of the same things but shuns political action as the route to achieve them, has grown."[60] Promise Keepers focuses on what (in its view) God requires of individuals and families, not what God requires of the Congress or the Supreme Court or the voting public.

Moreover, the faith-killing compromise that electorally active religions are tempted to commit involves more than the loss of focus on the problem of living as God commands. The compromise is also, for lack of a better term, attitudinal. When a religion learns to run the secular state, it risks the loss of humility. Humility is an indispensable virtue of the godly life according to all the Jerusalem religions—Christianity, Judaism, and Islam—and in many other traditions as well. Alas, American churches, both those identified as conservative and those identified as liberal, too often seem awash in complacency, with far too many believers unalterably persuaded that they already know all the answers.[61] And, in their complacency, too many of America's religious leaders are certain that their God-given task is to use the law to impose those answers on everybody else.

The prophet, facing a resisting world, must struggle with uncertainty and rejection. Through those struggles, the prophet learns humility—and perhaps reaches a richer version of truth. The one who wields the sword, however, struggles less, for he possesses the authority to force others to yield to his vision. Thus does the power of prophecy disappear.

4

The Religious Views
of the Candidate

THE DELICATE AND MESSY TRADE-OFF for religious activism in politics is that it often etches in sharp relief the religiosity of candidates for public office, and of their supporters. When George W. Bush spoke at Bob Jones University in South Carolina during the Republican presidential primary season in 2000 and failed to say a word about the racist and virulently anti-Catholic theology of its leaders, both of his rivals for the nomination criticized him for his silence. Bush's supporters (and Bush himself) shot back that his critics were injecting religion into the campaign—but were they? It is not as though Bob Jones University is not a religious school; and it is not as though it does not stand publicly for anything objectionable, having fought, and lost, all the way to the Supreme Court in the early 1980s in an effort to retain its tax-exempt status notwithstanding its racially discriminatory policies.[1] Whatever else there is to say, one must award the school points for integrity: When it lost the case, the university gave up its preferred tax status rather than yield on its beliefs.

But those are just about all the points the university gets. Bob Jones is a controversial stronghold of a particular brand of Christian conservatism, boldly proclaiming a forceful anti-Catholicism (one of its leaders had, in the past, referred to Roman Catholicism as "a satanic cult") and forbidding interracial dating, which it viewed as unbiblical—a stance the school suddenly abandoned after the controversy over the Bush visit.[2] Other Republican presidential candidates (including Ronald Reagan and Bob Dole) had spoken at the university during their campaigns, but Bush's appearance sparked a firestorm that the earlier ones had not. Perhaps what made the episode so fascinating to the media was the fact that Bush, asked during a debate a few months earlier to name the philosopher who had most influenced him, answered "Jesus." This, too, was derided as the injection of religion into the campaign, although, if the answer is true, it is difficult to imagine what the critics would have had him say instead. Perhaps they preferred a prospective President willing to tell a crowd-pleasing lie. More likely, their objection to the expression of Bush's view was really an objection to the view expressed: that is, that he was foolish, or perhaps undemocratic, to be influenced more by Jesus than by anyone else.

Here we stumble up against the problem. Most presidential aspirants—most candidates for elective office—would at least claim to hold some religious belief, and we can grant, for the sake of argument, that the great majority of them are sincere. If we take religion seriously as a component of human personality, we can hardly say with a straight face that a candidate's religion is irrelevant to the decision we make in the voting booth. Suppose the case of a candidate who happens to be a member of the Christian Identity movement, a white supremacist "religious" organization loosely affiliated with the Aryan Nations. It is difficult to see why a black voter would be wrong—morally or rationally—to take that fact into account. The candidate's evident acceptance of racist religious teaching would provide important information about how, if elected, he would likely govern.

If religion is real, it affects who an individual is. If it affects who an individual is, it must be relevant to how he or she would govern. If we insist on the solemn pretense that a candidate's religion is irrelevant, we are trivializing faith itself, proposing that it makes no actual difference in the life of the believer. Yet, what does this mean in practice? Suppose a pro-choice voter finds herself hesitating to cast a ballot for an avowed Roman Catholic. Suppose a pro-family voter is uneasy about supporting a proud member of a Protestant denomination that celebrates same-sex unions. Are these examples of rational self-interest, reflective policy analysis, or religious prejudice?

One answer might be to proclaim that religion is personal. But what might this mean? It cannot mean that the individual believer is unaffected by it. So "personal" must carry a more subtle message. Perhaps the message is this: "Yes, I understand that your religion affects who you are, and therefore will influence how you wield power. In that sense your religion is most certainly *relevant* to my decision on whether to vote for you or not. Nevertheless, I shall deny myself the use of this relevant information because of the greater threat of religious prejudice that might arise if every voter started wondering about every candidate's religion." This approach is not at all unusual. In a liberal democracy, we often deny ourselves access to useful information in order to preserve important values.[3]

Sometimes the candidate himself raises the issue, and everybody feels more comfortable inquiring about religion. For example, John Anderson, during his independent 1980 campaign for the presidency, was the darling of many liberals. But he was also the understandable object of suspicion by many Jewish voters, because he was a lay preacher who had first run for Congress on a ticket supporting the "Christian Nation" amendment to the Constitution. In fact, the 1980 election represented a particular political moment when all three presidential candidates raised the religion question. For the Baptist incumbent Jimmy Carter, the religion issue had been alive since his 1976 campaign, in which he taught many Americans who were unfamiliar with the term what "born again" meant. For the Presbyterian challenger Ronald Reagan, religion grew increasingly relevant as he marched across the country accepting implicit endorsements from prominent Christian conservatives. If, as Teddy Roosevelt said, the President has a responsibility to go to church, we would violate no solemn principle by asking him which one. And it surely would be appropriate to question William Jennings Bryan on how his professed faith would affect his presidency.

Candidates who raise the issue themselves should have their answers ready.

II

The Bob Jones situation also illustrates a problem with the casual way that the media and even many scholars talk about American religion. It simply is not true that most Americans are Christians—or rather, it is not relevant. For that shared label suggests commonalities that do not exist. Bob Jones University got itself in trouble in part because of the nasty way its leaders spoke of Roman Catholics, and the criticism was mostly justified. But there is a more complicated issue at the heart of the controversy: Christians have sharp disagreements.

For example, Protestants do not believe that the Pope is the successor of Peter and do not believe that the Bishop of Rome or any institutional church speaks with any special theological authority (*sola scriptura*, remember, was the rallying cry of early Protestants). Most important, Protestants generally believe that justification—loosely, salvation—comes from grace (God's unearned gift) and faith (loving belief) in Jesus Christ. Catholics believe that justification comes from grace, faith, and good works. This is not the place to persuade readers unaware of these controversies why any of this matters. Suffice to say that it does—indeed, in the Christian community, there is no question more pressing than the question of justification. The nub of the matter is that Christians disagree, and very sharply, on these issues. A Protestant has little choice but to say that a Catholic is just plain wrong in what he believes—and the Catholic has little choice but to reciprocate.

In the same way, of course, Jews believe that Christians are wrong in thinking Jesus to be the Messiah and Christians and Jews both believe that Muslims are wrong in thinking Muhammad the messenger of God. We are, for the most part, too polite to discuss these matters, especially around election time . . . but, in truth, many, many American religionists are certain, quite deeply certain, that many, many others are mistaken or even deluded.

The Bob Jones University episode, however, presented to the Bush campaign a challenge of a different magnitude. The anti-Catholic preaching of the school's leaders is an extreme version of a general evangelical theme. Here one must define *anti-* with some care. Unless we believe religion to be so trivial that none of it is true and thus none of it matters, it cannot be the case that we do something wicked when we describe someone else's belief as false. To be sure, we must tread carefully in such conversations, not only because of the risk of hubris—we, too, could be mistaken—but also because history, even in America, teaches us that my conclusion today that your religion is false might lead me, tomorrow, to try to use the power of the state to force you to join mine. Yet that risk is no reason to pretend that all religions can simultaneously be true, or that nobody can criticize anybody else's. Form matters: There is criticism, and then there is attack. And so does substance: There is exegesis, and then there is bigotry. Bob Jones's leaders, in talking about Catholics, failed both the form and the substance tests; but they were hardly the only believers of any faith to do so, and they certainly will not be the last. They deserve the criticism they received, but not for believing that other people's faiths are false, or even for saying so.

In America, where cultural norms prohibit making anybody feel bad about anything, it is not easy to talk publicly about theological differences. Still, if talking publicly about these disputes was all Bob Jones's leaders had done, the media would probably have treated them as curious and backward (who really cares about salvation?) rather than as intolerant bigots. But the leadership of Bob Jones has, over the years, said quite a bit more.

And here, I think, we come upon the crucial point. After visiting Bob Jones, candidate Bush was immediately attacked—first by Alan Keyes, one of his rivals, and later by just about everybody else—for failing to criticize the university's policies and teachings from the lectern when he spoke there. In political terms the attack made sense. But it was, really, a proxy for a harder public conversation. What people really wanted to know was whether Bush agreed with what the leaders of Bob Jones said. He told us, of course, that he did not. But what did this mean in Christian terms? Presumably, since Bush had announced just two months earlier that the philosopher who has most influenced him is Jesus, he meant that the leadership at Bob Jones had misunderstood the Gospel. What a lovely world this would be if he felt comfortable saying *that* in public. Not easy throwaway lines like "I condemn all bigotry and intolerance" or "I disagree with some of their teachings" but "They misunderstand Jesus Christ. They distort the Gospel. Christ's message was one of love, not of hate. It is because I follow Jesus that I am obliged to tell the world that the leadership of Bob Jones is simply wrong."

But that is not how candidates for office generally speak. We tend to want our public officials, especially our President, to espouse some religion, but we seem to want it the way that children want their parents to tell them that a trip to the dentist will not hurt a bit: It is not the truth of the claim but the claim itself that we find comforting. So although it might seem unlikely that many Americans would vote for an avowed atheist as President, few voters seem to want a president whose belief in God actually matters, who behaves differently because of his faith than he would behave otherwise. Indeed, were deep and serious and sustained religious devotion an important test for public office, we would surely have amended the Constitution by acclamation to allow Jimmy Carter to serve four or five terms.[4]

III

Article VI of the Constitution prohibits the imposition of any religious test for public office. We tend, nowadays, to lift the provision from its historical context. The authors of the document simply wanted to forbid the *federal government* from requiring that its officials swear to a given creed. Many of the states had religious tests for some or all of their officials, and a few of those requirements remained on the books until well into the twentieth century. In other words, anybody who claims that there is an American tradition prohibiting the imposition of religious tests . . . is simply wrong.[5]

During the debates over the Constitution, the clause aroused controversy. For example, Henry Abbott, a delegate to the North Carolina ratification convention, reported that many in the state harbored fears that "pagans, deists, or Mahometans" could become President. James Iredell, one of the drafters of the Constitution, answered by assuring Abbott that "it is never to be supposed that the people of America will trust their dearest rights to persons who have no religion at all, or a religion materially different from their own."[6] Even though, as the historian Jon Butler has shown, America's self-conception as a *Christian* nation did not begin until the middle of the nineteenth century,[7] there is little question that its self-conception as a *religious* nation stretches back to the framing.

Recognizing that we are a religious nation is not the same as creating an official religion. The use of religious tests for public office has been, throughout the world, a device for trying to ensure the fealty of government officials to a particular faith. In the Christian tradition, what came to be known as the "test-oath" had special force. The idea of the oath was to pick a proposition to which a believer in the wrong branch of Christianity could not swear: asking a follower of the Eastern Orthodox Church to swear that the Holy Spirit proceeds from the Father and the Son, for example, which is what Western Christians believe, whereas Eastern Christians believe that the Spirit proceeds from the Father alone.

Even if one believes that test-oaths for public office are a good thing, they are doomed to failure, a point made by Oliver Ellsworth, a delegate to the Constitutional Convention, whose words were later quoted by Justice Hugo Black of the Supreme Court: "In short, test-laws are utterly ineffectual; they are no security at all; because men of loose principles will, by an external compliance, evade them. If they exclude any persons, it will be honest men, men of principle, who will rather suffer an injury, than act contrary to the dictates of their consciences."[8]

Black quoted these words in *Torcaso v. Watkins,* a 1961 decision in which the Justices ruled unanimously that the state of Maryland could not refuse to commission a man as a notary public based on his refusal to take an oath affirming the existence of God.

Of course, an oath that God exists is not the kind of oath that scared the Framers. They were worried about using the test-oath to separate Christians from Christians, not to separate Christians from non-Christians. I am not suggesting that their values should be our values; I am suggesting the serious limits of a rhetoric that puts into the mouths of the Framers values that we have developed for ourselves. If we think—and I hope we do—that it is wrong to discriminate, in the voting booth, say, between Christians and non-Christians, the reason is not that the Framers were worried about it. They were not. The reason is that history has taught *us* to be wary of it. If we are irritated at, or frightened by, groups who, today, seem willing to reimpose test-oaths, let the reason for anger be stated clearly: not that the Constitution is against it, but that history is.

The record of the American people has not, goodness knows, been perfect. In the middle of the nineteenth century, voters in several states turned to the unabashedly anti-Catholic Know-Nothing Party, which controlled both houses of the Massachusetts legislature and elected some seventy-five members to the House of Representatives. Those who joined the party had to swear never to vote for anyone not born in the United States or anyone who was a Catholic.[9] This was quite a horrific moment in our history, and not as large an aberration as we might like to pretend. There has long been a vigorous anti-Catholic strain in American public life, as Al Smith discovered during his 1928 presidential campaign and, a few decades later, John Kennedy nearly did. It is not dead yet.

Still, we should be absolutely clear: The constitutional ban on religious tests can, at best, refer to official religious tests. It cannot, and should not, affect the conscience of the individual voter, and any suggestion to the contrary is ridiculous. The notion that I, as a voter, should never take into account the religious affiliation of a candidate means that I would be acting in an illiberal fashion were I to oppose a nominee who belonged to the Christian Identity movement or the World Church of the Creator, both adamantly racist groups that consider themselves religious. If the religious beliefs of the candidate give me serious and relevant information, I, as a voter, will surely take that information into account.

There is, of course, a danger of misuse. Prejudices against Jews or Catholics—or, for that matter, against Protestant fundamentalists or Pentecostals—might creep into the voter's calculus. The security against such dangers, however, will not be found in any broad principle. There is no litigation or press conference or op-ed piece or school curriculum that will put an end to the evil of prejudice. The security will be found, like so much in a true democracy, only in the common sense and goodwill of the voters themselves. If we genuinely do not believe that the majority of the American electorate is capable of or interested in rising above such biases, we should be on the barricades after all, for we have a revolution to fight.

5

The Single-Sided Wall

Y ET THE BOUNDARY IS NOT ONE that the state should police. Few threats to religious freedom could be greater than an effort
by the government to decide which speech by religious institutions should be
rewarded and which speech punished. Imagine for a moment a state so in-
secure and, at the same time, so totalitarian, so determined to invest every
corner of society with a single, state-imposed vision of right and wrong, that
it actually doles out benefits to those churches that preach the right messages
and denies those benefits to churches that preach the wrong ones. So great a
horror, one might think, is the stuff of the old communist empire or one of
the few remaining dictatorships in the Third World, precisely what the Western-style tradition of constitutional rights is designed to oppose.

One would be wrong.

The nation I describe is the United States of America, and the grim
threat to religious freedom is already in place, with the tragic complicity of
civil libertarians, the courts, and, worst of all, even many religious leaders,
who seem to think it a good thing for the state to penalize those religions
that speak words of which the government does not approve.

The instrument of this oppression is the tax code, and it is wielded reck-
lessly by a coalition of agencies and interest groups determined to stifle the
ability of religious groups to speak out on a subject that the members of the
coalition believe beyond the religious purview. That subject is electoral politics, and, in the interest of truth, it must be admitted that most Americans
probably agree that religious groups should keep their noses out of it. By
now the reader is aware that, I, too, think we are all better off—and religions

in particular are better off–if those who claim to speak for God avoid the endorsement of candidates or parties. But I do not confuse my own views on this question with God's, and my respect for religious liberty is sufficient that I also think that those religions that disagree with me (or with the majority) should not be penalized for their advocacy. Sadly, many Americans seem to believe that only those religions they like should be permitted to prosper, and that those they don't should be penalized.

II

The story should be familiar, even to the most casual consumer of the news. An interest group with a religious-sounding name, or an actual church, caught endorsing political candidates, whether directly or indirectly, is threatened with the loss of its tax-exempt status ... and, very often, the threat is carried out. The legal argument is that the group in question, by endorsing candidates, has behaved in a way that is inconsistent with its special tax status. Certainly that argument correctly states the law, for Section 501(c)(3) of the Internal Revenue Code could hardly be more explicit in prohibiting electoral activity by all entities, churches included, that are tax-exempt under its provisions. So the Reverend Jerry Falwell's Liberty Lobby, the Christian Coalition, and a variety of other religious or quasi-religious groups have lost their special tax status for violating the code. The troubling question for the advocate of religious liberty is whether the law thus stated is a good idea.

Consider the lengthy, and ultimately inconclusive, litigation against the Catholic Church, seeking to end the church's tax-exempt status on the ground that its advocacy against abortion–especially at election time–represents a violation of the code. The lawsuit, filed in 1980 by supporters of abortion rights, claimed that the church was opposing specific candidates, charges that were backed with a copy of a letter from an archbishop urging parishioners to vote against candidates who favored abortion rights.[1] The lawsuit made headlines in 1982, when the federal judge hearing the case ordered the church to turn over internal documents on subjects ranging from how the bishops arrived at their position on abortion to what connections existed between the church and right-to-life organizations. The bishops understandably refused to comply, and the court levied a fine of $50,000 a day for contempt–a fine that the Supreme Court held in abeyance until the church could appeal the judge's decision that the plaintiffs had standing to bring the lawsuit. It was on that ground–a lack of standing–that the suit was eventually dismissed.[2]

What concerns me is less the question of standing than the question of religious liberty: It should at least occasion a bit of comment that the federal government decides which benefits to grant or deny to religions depending on the content of their teaching. I seem to recall that the First Amendment contains a distant, whispery hint that there might exist a constitutional right to freedom of religion, and that America used to pride itself–or do I remember wrongly?–on not being the sort of place where preachers have to watch what they say. Perhaps this is a matter to which our rich national community of civil libertarians will soon turn its attention–although, given their long-standing silence on the problem, that is not the way it pays to bet.

In 1993, for example, when the Internal Revenue Service lifted the tax exemption of Falwell's Old-Time Gospel Hour and fined it $50,000, an approving newspaper editorial warned that tax exemptions must be "reserved for groups that devote themselves to spiritual causes alone,"[3] ceding to the state both the remarkable power of deciding which causes are spiritual and the authority to punish religious groups that happen to disagree. The late Arthur Kropp, head of People for the American Way, called the decision "an encouraging sign that the IRS is taking a hard look and taking action."[4] It is not clear, however, who is supposed to be encouraged, and action that punishes religious groups for speaking the words they believe the Lord requires of them has only recently become the American way.

Even assuming the truth of the charges in the lawsuit, the Catholic bishops were only doing what communities of faith around the world have always done: advocating and working for the world they believe God prefers. The Catholic Church teaches that abortion is wrong, that it is a grave sin, in part (there are other reasons too) because, from the moment of conception, the fetus is a human life. Abortion then becomes, in the words of Pope John Paul II, *"the deliberate and direct killing, by whatever means it is carried out, of a human being in the initial phase of his or her existence, extending from conception to birth."*[5] Some secular critics of Catholic theology, and even some religious ones, shrug off such arguments, suggesting that the answer for those who are against abortions is not to have them. But this argument simply fails to take religion seriously. If the Catholic Church sincerely believes abortion to be the snuffing out of innocent life, it can hardly be blamed for declining to take the view that the only unborn children worthy of protection are the unborn children of Roman Catholics. (This would be a little like the Protestant preachers of the Social Gospel movement in the early years of the twentieth century taking the view that only Protestant workers should have higher wages.) If the bishops believe abortion to be so great an evil, they have no choice but to work for its abolition.

Now, to be sure, nobody threatened to lift the tax exemption of the Catholic bishops back when they were trying to sway politicians away from support for school segregation or to find a way to rid the world of nuclear weapons. Indeed, before we go any further, we should take the time to note the embarrassing—or perhaps the correct word is outrageous—political bias in the enforcement of the provisions that bar political involvement by 501(c)(3) organizations. It is a matter of simple fact that the rules are almost always invoked against churches and other groups that fall toward the right end of our rather narrow political spectrum; the left is all but immune. One of the principal players in this little drama is a self-proclaimed watchdog known as Americans United for Separation of Church and State. Americans United does some important work in the cause of religious liberty, such as arguing that public-school students possess the right to express their religious views freely. But the group also has a terrible blind spot when it looks at regulation of churches involved in politics, for it is unable to see the threat to religious freedom. Americans United arguably makes things worse, for, while styling itself as protecting churches from their worst selves, the organization is probably the principal filer of complaints with the Treasury Department about religious groups overstepping the bounds of the tax code.

As we shall see, this campaign suggests that Americans United has the wrong name, for the effort to use law to rein in the speech of clergy runs contrary to the origin and core meaning of the separation of church and state.[6] But, given that our culture understands the separation so badly, the flaw is forgivable. What is more troubling is the identity of the subjects of Americans United's many complaints. As of this writing (autumn 1999), the group has filed more than twice as many complaints about churches supporting Republican candidates than about churches supporting Democrats. One easy answer to this evident imbalance is that churches that lean to the right are twice as likely as churches that lean to the left to engage in activities that are inconsistent with their tax status. There are no data on this point, nor is it easy to see how they might be assembled. Intuition might suggest that electoral activism is a phenomenon of churches that support Republican candidates, and, indeed, American history since the development of modern political parties offers no antecedent for the highly organized conservative Christian groups that exercise so much influence in the GOP. Yet the notion that white evangelical churches are the only places where electioneering occurs ignores the experience, as so many of our generalizations on religion tend to do, of the black churches.

Among the evils of which liberals complain are implicit or even explicit endorsements of candidates from the pulpit, distribution of "voter guides" to tell the faithful how to cast their ballots, and raising of campaign funds during services. In the churches of the African-American tradition, these practices are commonplace. During the aforementioned litigation over the tax-exempt status of the Catholic Church, many black clergy were terrified.[7] The former pastor of one of the largest African-American congregations in Connecticut described to me the panic the lawsuit set off among the black clergy, leading to a meeting of powerful pastors at which they tried—and failed—to lay out contingency plans.

One might argue (and some do) that the political organizing activity by black churches is different from similar activity by white churches because, in the inner cities—where most black churches are found—no other forums for organizing exist. Impoverished communities tend to lack basic social structures. Much has been written in recent years about the decline of the institutions of civil society, the places apart from either government or work where people congregate, exchange views, form opinions, inspire fellow citizens, and plan action. In many inner cities, the institutions of civil society are not merely declining—they are absent.[8] That is, they are absent except for the churches. (Among black Christians, church involvement seems to correlate with political involvement even more strongly than among white Christians—that is, those who do not attend church tend to be politically inactive.)[9] Consequently, if residents of the inner cities cannot organize politically in the churches, it may be that they cannot organize anywhere.

III

Of course, African Americans are not alone in the belief that the ideal place for political activity is the church. There are tens of millions of Americans of other colors for whom the church is at the center of their lives. Many of them cannot conceive of a politics divorced from church. Such conservative groups as the Christian Coalition and the Traditional Values Coalition have tried to sign up churches rather than individuals as members in part because of a sense that, among people for whom church is truly central, if you get the church, you tend to get the members. I have questions about whether churches *should* sign up as members or partners with groups possessing overtly political agendas, but it is quite easy to understand why the churches *do* sign up as members: They see a culture that is not only spinning out of control but evolving in ways that many of them consider actually hostile to their religious vision. The hostility matters because that culture—especially through its media and public schools—tends to send messages at odds with what many faithful parents want to teach their children. Could it be that we tend to ask the question backward? Suppose that the culture and its creature, the state, are making it more difficult to practice a particular vision of God's will or to raise children to practice it. If so, then arguably it is the state that presses, not the religion that resists, that is violating the separation of church and state.[10]

I do not mean to suggest that there is no room for constitutional controversy on the tax code and the role of religion. But I am not sure there is room for very much.[11] Our jurisprudence of church and state has become almost silly, a satire on itself, struggling to enforce an ahistorical fantasy—that it was the power of religion, not the power of the state, that the Founders so feared that they wrote a clause about religion into the First Amendment. The modern way is to treat the metaphorical separation of church and state as a protection for a secular public space against religion's incursions, even though the idea of a secular public space is a late-twentieth-century invention, and the notion that there exists some sphere of life into which religion ought not incur would have astonished the authors of the Constitution.

Thus "Religion's Sphere," the title of this first part of the book, is meant to be ironic. Why? We saw in the preceding two chapters that it is the habit of religion to resist. One of the things religion resists is our contemporary understanding of the separation of church and state. I do not mean that no religion teaches that a degree of separation of the two is important; in the American experience, most religions do. I mean that every serious religionist understands that complete separation is impossible. I mean that Justice Stanley Reed was absolutely right to suggest in the middle of the twentieth century that "a rule of law should not be drawn from a figure of speech."[12] He was right because rules of law, especially constitutional law, should be practical principles of government operation. The separation of church and state, as understood in the modern era, is not.

As any serious student of religion knows, religion has no sphere. It possesses no natural bounds. It is not amenable to being pent up. It sneaks through cracks, creeps through half-open doors . . . and it flows over walls. The concept of *religion* is itself an idea that is necessary only if one plans to divide the world into multiple spheres, one of which is somehow related to the life led according to a narrative about God, and the other of which is somehow related to . . . well, to something else. Serious religions, however, do not conceive of the world in this way. In particular, the principal Western religious traditions, Judaism, Christianity, and Islam, all reject it. I do not mean that none of them preaches separation; I mean that none of them conceives of the world as divided into that which God created and therefore rules and that which God did not and does not.

To be sure, not every religion makes universalistic claims, if by universalistic we mean the ability to explain the destiny of all human beings, not just adherents of the faith. But the proper sphere of a religion can only be defined by that religion, not by some instrumental definition of the term. Religion itself—as an idea, as an entity—has no inherent bound. If my Christianity teaches me that murder is wrong, I am not next required to conclude that the only murders that should be prevented are those done by Christians. I am not equipped to look at the world and decide that part of it belongs to God and part of it does not.

As understood in ordinary conversation, the separation of church and state supposes, wrongly, that it is possible to pick a sphere of life and confine all religion to it . . . simply by virtue of its having been identified as a religion. So we say that religion is private. We say that it is to be kept apart from politics. As though religion does not shape believers. As though the people who believe that God wills proposition **P** are not different from those who disagree.

Yet what sort of sense does this argument make? I am a citizen of the United States and owe it my allegiance. But my first allegiance is to the God who created me. My faith in the God of the Christian Bible makes me a different person than I would be did I lack that faith. My faith does not call me to be a different person only in some hidden persona. My God requires of me that I live a changed life. If my life is changed, then my interactions with others are changed too. Whether in the marketplace or in the workplace or in politics or in my family, in whatever sphere of life I might enter, it is my faith that is to lead me.

An old ditty from the labor movement went something like this:

> *Mr. Businessman, he went to church, he never missed a Sunday. Mr. Businessman, he went to hell, for what he did on Monday.*

Putting aside theological difficulties–Protestants in particular teach that salvation is by faith and by grace, not by works–the rhyme nevertheless captures as well as anything the ideal of all three of the Biblical religions, Judaism, Christianity, and Islam, that the rules the Lord sets down are rules for all of life, not merely for particular spheres of life. The business executive cannot, consistently with a serious religion, insist on being free of God's laws when he enters his workplace. God teaches the religious what life means. The state might prefer to impose its own meaning on the sphere of politics and try to confine the meanings discovered by religion to some smaller, less significant space. But it is all folly. Rushing past boundaries is what religion does.

That is why conversion plays such an important role in the Christian narrative. The idea of conversion supposes resistance, that the individual who converts at some point prefers not to.* He tries to wall off the call of God. But the boundary does not hold. God makes a way. Because religion will not be confined.

A religion can of course confine itself, or try to. Some religions believe that their adherents should not work for change in the world; others, that working for change is fine, but working for coercive change (changes in the law, for example) is not; still others that the answer depends on the nature of the society in which the religion is currently existing. A religion cannot, however, be confined by a legal fiction. God cannot be held back by constitutional law.

I am a great believer in the separation of church and state, but it is important to explain what it means, for the metaphor, properly understood, is instructive. The federal courts have been harshly criticized for overreliance on the separation metaphor, which the Supreme Court first mentioned in its 1947 decision in *Everson v. Board of Education*.[13] There the justices quoted from Thomas Jefferson's famous 1802 letter to the Baptists of Danbury–stating that the wall existed–and added that the wall "must be kept high and impregnable."[14] The Court went on to explain that the motivation for the religion clauses of the First Amendment was a fear of the

---

*I should clarify this point for non-Christians. All Christians believe that human beings are saved by God's grace and our faith. As sinful, fallen creatures, we cannot "earn" salvation; we cannot make God our debtor, putting him in a position in which he has no choice but to save us. God works within us to prepare us for salvation. A principal split among Protestants is on the following question: Is God's grace "prevenient"–that is, irresistible among the Elect, those he has chosen to save, the position of John Calvin and the Reformed tradition? Or have human beings the ability to say No to God's offer, even when God is working within them, a position described as Arminian after Jacobus Arminius, an early exponent whom some regard as a heretic? In either case, the human might try to resist God's saving work; the split among Protestants is over whether resistance is futile. (The Roman Catholic position on salvation includes, in addition to faith and grace, the necessity of good works, done by God's grace.)

kind of bitter religious warfare that once swept across the European continent. Certainly the Founders were aware of and troubled by the European
experience of sectarian conflict. They were troubled by many things, and,
as the historian William Lee Miller has pointed out, locating the precise single concern that led to the adoption of the religion clause is impossible.[15]
We can, however, say something about the origin of the American ideal of
separating church and state. And the fascinating truth is that neither Jefferson nor that sad, violent history is the source of the separationist ideal.

The true origin of the metaphor, as Mark DeWolfe Howe pointed out in
the 1960s and most legal scholars have accepted since, does not lie with
Thomas Jefferson's coinage, which occurred over a decade after the First
Amendment was adopted. Rather, its origin is in Protestant theology. Indeed,
instinct in the Reformation was the idea that God had created not one but
two forms of authority, the spiritual and the temporal, each with its own
sphere of legitimate power. The Reformers believed that God was sovereign
over both and that both were required to exercise power in accordance with
God's law; nevertheless, their purposes were quite different, the one to prepare men's souls for salvation, the other to maintain order in the material
world. To be sure, the early record of both the Lutheran and Reform traditions was one of considerable overlap between church and state, and it was
left to the dissenters—the Anabaptists in the Old World, the Baptists in the
New—to show why a degree of genuine separation was theologically desirable. Indeed, the Anabaptists believed in a separation not only of church and
state but of Christians from the state. They believed that the ability to exercise the coercive power of the state would inevitably be a corrupting force
among Christians. The consequence was that they opposed service by Christians as magistrates, legislatures, even soldiers. Their American descendants,
including the Mennonites and the Amish, hold similar views.

Howe back in the 1960s, as well as legal scholar Timothy L. Hall in a
more recent book,[16] have shown how the separationist ideal was brought
into the American dialogue on the proper roles of religion and the state by
Roger Williams's evocative seventeenth-century metaphor of the garden
and the wilderness. For Williams, a Baptist, the garden was the domain of
the church, the gentle, fragile region where the people of God would congregate and try to build lives around the Divine Word. The wilderness was
the world lying beyond the garden wall, uncivilized and potentially quite
threatening to the garden. The wall separated the two, and the reason for
the wall was not that the wilderness needed protection from the garden—
the wall was there to protect the garden from the wilderness. In particular,

the garden needed protection from the wilderness so that the people who joined in community within it would be free to come to their understanding of God's will safe from the coercions of a society that might disagree.

And yet, wrote Williams, if the wall was ever breached, it was the responsibility of the people of the garden to go out into the wilderness and try to civilize it—that is, to make all the world a garden. Thus, not only did the wall not protect the wilderness; the metaphor, as originally understood, envisioned that the garden would ultimately overwhelm the wilderness. Wrote Howe:

> When the imagination of Roger Williams built the wall of separation, it was not because he was fearful that without such a barrier the arm of the church would extend its reach. It was, rather, the dread of the worldly corruptions which might consume the churches if sturdy fences against the wilderness were not maintained. . . . The principle of separation epitomized in Williams' metaphor was predominantly theological.[17]

Williams was not worried that the people of the garden might have too much influence over the wilderness. His worry was the other way around: "[T]he commonweal cannot without a spiritual rape force the consciences of all to one worship."[18] Religious freedom, for Williams, as for the later Protestant tradition, meant protecting the garden. True, the people of the garden might be required to work for the betterment of the wilderness (Protestants have long argued over just how much), but the wilderness was never as important as the garden. The wall was needed to keep the garden pristine. For the Baptist Williams, it was the responsibility of the wilderness to stay out of the garden—not the other way around.

This does not mean that Williams gave no thought to the state, and Hall has corrected Howe's misreading of Williams on this point. In keeping with the Reformation vision, says Hall, Williams believed that the state, like the church, had a sphere set out for it by God. He did not believe the spheres would overlap, because the state would be "occupied with fundamentally different concerns from religion."[19] Each power should, he believed, remain on its proper side of the boundary. But if the state ever crossed the line, the believer must choose to follow the commandments of God and ignore those of the state.[20]

The concern that led Williams to explore the metaphor of the garden wall was religious persecution, which he and his followers experienced firsthand in the Massachusetts Bay Colony. The power that he feared was the power of the secular world, not the power of the religious. In the present day, the people of the wilderness often complain about incursions by the people of the garden—for example, about religious activism in politics, the subject that has partly inspired the present book. Yet there is far more historical and constitutional merit, as well as far more theological merit, when the people of the garden complain about incursions by the people of the wilderness. The wilderness does more to threaten the garden than the other way around; there is no serious comparison between the temporal power of the two. (I am reminded of a scene in the film *A Bronx Tale* in which a priest tries to persuade a little boy who has witnessed a murder to confess to what he has seen. The boy is reluctant because he is afraid of the gangster who did it. The priest tells the boy that God will protect him. The boy answers, "Your guy has more power up there. But my guy has more power down here.")

The religion clause of the First Amendment is designed to limit what the state can do, not what the church can do.[21] Strict separationists of the current era like to cite Thomas Jefferson's vision of church and state as forever separate, but Jefferson, in confining state and religion to their distinct spheres, never suggested, in any of his work, that it was the task of the state to police the boundary between the two. Besides, it boggles the imagination to suppose that the Framers adopted the First Amendment in order to incorporate a Jeffersonian interpretation that would not occur for another twenty years. More likely, they knew how fragile a thing is faith, and they understood how its nurture requires the construction of a wall, not to keep the faithful in, but to keep the world out.

There are many reasons why it is desirable to protect the garden from the encroachments of the wilderness. I want to focus on a single one: the importance of protecting the ability of the religious to resist the dominant understanding of life and the world that the state will try to impose. The school has always been a key site for that resistance. As the late Robert Cover put it, "There must, in sum, be limits to the state's prerogative to provide interpretive meaning when it exercises its educative function." Otherwise, "[t]he state might become committed to its own meaning and destroy the personal and educative bond that is the germ of meanings alternative to those of the power wielders."[22] The fact that the power wielders do not like the alternative meanings is not, by itself, reason enough to justify their destruction.

I like the phrase of theologian David Tracy, who has written that "the religions live by resisting."[23] If religion lives by resisting, then it dies by conforming. Christians in particular are under a strict injunction not to try to fit in, although, in America, it is easily forgotten: "Do not conform any longer to the pattern of the world, but be transformed by the renewing of your mind" (Rom. 12:2). The wilderness, unbounded by the wall of separation, will do all that it can to reshape religion into its image, that is, to domesticate the faith, eliminating its radical possibilities in favor of whatever set of meanings the dominant culture considers best. The survival of a religion rests on its ability to avoid being overwhelmed by the secularity of the wilderness. As long as a religion is able to teach the faithful the alternative meanings that its vision of God provides, it will help create people who form the core of dissent and thus of change. It is no accident that in the most important social battles in the nation's history—abolitionism and the civil rights movement—the forces of justice have been led by religious dissenters. And the religious dissenters were able to exist at all because the wall of separation protected the garden, enabling them to create meanings of their own. That resistance to the wilderness may not be the only truth and the only value of the separation of church and state, but it is, from the point of view of both religion and democracy, surely the most important.

The separation of church and state, in its contemporary rendition, represents little more than an effort to subdue the power of religion, to twist it to the ends preferred by the state. The separation of church and state is, in its way, an establishment of religion, for it allows paid state functionaries—we happen to call them judges—to define what religion is and assign it to the sphere in which it is permitted to function. If religion will not remain in the sphere assigned to it, those same functionaries are paid to hold it back, and the police and armed forces of the state are paid to help them do it.

What religion worthy of the name would allow itself to be pent up by the state? Liberty of conscience itself may have begun in the effort of religion to differentiate itself from the state, to propose that there is a higher authority by which the actions of the state can be judged, an effort that began with prophets of the Old Testament.[24] Before the prophets of Israel, the cultures of which we are aware almost always believed in the divinity, or the near divinity, of their rulers. And although the Aristotelian idea that God, to be God, must be perfect, came somewhat later, cultures that believed in divine rulers probably lacked the rhetorical tools to criticize the rulers' edicts. In short, the notion of separation probably began with the stripping of the mantle of divinity from leaders, which enabled the leaders to be criticized—*on the ground that they were not doing the will of God*. The separationist idea, in other words, began precisely to enable the religious to point to the flaws, in religious terms, of their leaders. In so doing, they tried to tap the conscience of leaders and subjects alike, and also warned of divine retribution to come, should the rulers or the people ignore their words.

It would be contrary to this great purpose, the purpose of fueling conscience, for the religions now to say to that very state, *Tell us the limits you prefer and we will keep to them!* King David surely did not much like being criticized by Nathan, but that does not mean that Nathan was wrong to do it, or that David should have tried to stop him. And the fact that David repented in the end (after he and Bathsheba lost their first-born child as a punishment) suggests that Nathan was on the side of right.

Nothing is different when a religion tries to influence policymakers today. I do not think the state should create official religions or try to persuade people to choose one sect rather than another. I do not think that anything in the Constitution prevents the state from listening to its religious constituents on the great issues that come before us. Yet we are, all of us, subjected to a steady drumbeat, from journalists and commentators, from lawyers and activists, and sometimes even from judges, to the effect that religion has a sphere and the state has a sphere, and the purpose of the wall of separation is to keep the two apart; and thus (so it is said) it is not only wrong but potentially unconstitutional for the state to pay attention to arguments couched in religious terms.

What nonsense! To use the separation metaphor as a device for disabling religious groups from participating in public dialogue has nothing to do with valuing religion and much to do with devaluing the people who believe in it. Roger Williams, understanding both the risks of state oppression and the risks of religious oppression, located his metaphor in the domain of the probable. He knew what faith was. He knew its place in the hearts and minds and lives of human beings, and he knew its place in the larger world. And its place can be described simply: Everyplace.

Religion, in short, has no sphere.

Which brings us to the following problem: The law today too often behaves as though it does.

IV

It turns out, then, that it is the state, acting through its judges, that decides when religion has crossed the wall of separation: a wall that Christianity built and, for many years, patrolled almost alone. And who decides when the state has crossed the wall? Why, the very same judges decide—that is, the state. Unsurprisingly, then, religion is often found to have breached the wall, whereas the state almost never is. When one of the two parties to a compact takes it upon itself to determine the bounds of the compact and to decide whether each side is in compliance, it is entirely predictable that the side holding the power will make all (or nearly all) the decisions its own way. As the state does today.

One might remark that the state of affairs I describe does not make religion any worse off than any other entity in America: Everybody and everything is subject to state power. But one would be pardonably mistaken. The difference is that groups with other motivations, when they believe that the state has overstepped its bounds, may organize to force political change; and, if they convince enough of their fellow citizens, may gain sufficient leverage over the state to lift its yoke from their necks. But the state has decided (as the patroller of the wall) that religions, and religions alone, may not do the same. If Smith the environmental leader says to vote against Jones on the ground that Jones is an enemy of the environment, millions cheer. If Smith the preacher says to vote against Jones on the ground that Jones is an enemy of the faith, millions say that Smith does not understand the proper place of religion in a democratic system.*

We have turned poor Roger Williams inside out. The wall of separation is no longer for the protection of the people of the garden; it is for the protection of the people of the wilderness. And what is the evil against which the people of the wilderness need protection? Why, it is *the ideas, the words, the persuasions of the people of the garden*—the very things the wall itself was originally designed to nurture. The metaphor that was meant to explain how the religious come to evangelize has been inverted. There is still evangelizing, only now it is the state that is the evangelist, pouring through the soft spots in the wall, using its coercive authority to alter the very structure of the ideas and words that were once spoken freely. And speaking the right words—or avoiding the wrong ones—now turns out to be the only way the church is able to preserve such tatters of protection for religious liberty as the state now offers.

So the wall of separation turns out to be not a garden wall but prison wall, surrounding the church to keep the people of the garden inside, with barbed-wire escarpments, angled inward, lest the religious try to clamber

---

*To be sure, a 501(c)(3) environmental organization is subject to the same rules regarding political activity as a 501(c)(3) religious group. My point here, however, is not about the tax code. My point is that the separationist metaphor should not be used to distinguish among possible grounds for casting a vote.

over. This tortured modern vision of separationism is reminiscent of the fourth-century Emperor Constantine's arrogant justification for keeping the early Christian Church under his thumb, even while heaping praise upon himself for forcing the world to tolerate it: "You have been appointed bishops by God for the internal affairs of the Church. I on the other hand have been designated bishop for external affairs."[25] Constantine styled himself the protector of the Christians, who had been persecuted, in and out of the empire, for hundreds of years. In return for not killing them, he expected Christians to refrain from criticizing the way he ran his government. Much of the freedom struggle of the early Christian Church was to escape the grasp of emperors and tribunes who used "toleration" as a device of control. The church tolerated, after all, is the church that survives by virtue of the forbearance—the toleration—of its protector.

A wall conceived as imprisoning the garden leaves the church without any tools of self-protection. In a democracy, perhaps the most obvious of those tools is politics. Every other group of citizens, if dissatisfied with the way it is treated by the state, has resorted to advocacy and even the electoral process to improve its situation. For that matter, every other group of citizens, if dissatisfied with the way somebody else is treated by the state, has resort to advocacy and the electoral process to improve the situation of those others. To suggest that the First Amendment's protections for religious liberty were designed to limit the ability of the religious to change the rules under which they are required to live is to invite us into Wonderland, where everything is a mirror image of what seems obviously true: Chess pieces can talk, clocks have eyes, and every pleasant country lane twists and turns as you try to walk it, depositing you at last at the same spot where you began your journey.[26] In Wonderland, it might make sense that a constitutional clause drafted to protect religion from the interference of government actually does the opposite; and only in Wonderland would anybody seriously imagine that we protect religious freedom when we punish churches that speak the wrong words.

6

The Separation of
Church and Slavery

B UT WAS THERE AN EARLIER CONSENSUS? Was there
a moment in the nation's history when separation of church and
state was differently (not to say properly) understood? Perhaps the most
useful focus for our investigation would be the first great era of religious
activism in American history: the nineteenth-century campaign to abolish
slavery.

I

The historian Don Fehrenbacher once wrote that the reason slavery was
able to persist for so many decades was that those supporting it were
moved by interest whereas those opposing it were moved by sentiment. In
other words, the slaveholders would actually be affected in their daily lives
by the discontinuance of the institution, whereas the abolitionists, by and
large, did not suffer any personal consequences if slavery continued.[1] It is
an uneasy truth of history that materialism tends to trump idealism, even
though subsequent events often prove that the idealists were right all along.
Much human misery could have been avoided had enough others, at key
moments in the past, spun political interest out of idealistic sentiment.

One force that can weave sentiment into interest is religion, for religion,
at least in its Western model, tends to point the believer away from the material and toward the transcendent. The Western religions teach their adherents to put God first, to take a moral understanding and make of it a
rule by which to live; in Fehrenbacher's terms, to take that which is mere
sentiment and, for God's sake, elevate it into interest.

The era of the public campaign for abolitionism in America spanned roughly the last three decades of the eighteenth century and the first six decades of the nineteenth. The leaders of the campaign, almost all of them clergy, always cited religious reasons—the Christian Gospel, basically—for their activism. The Quakers were probably the earliest Christian opponents of slavery in the New World, forming America's first anti-slavery society in Philadelphia in 1775.[2] There were eighteenth-century southern evangelical abolitionists as well, but their efforts were uncoordinated and their movement faded.

In the north, Charles G. Finney, considered by some the greatest abolitionist preacher of them all, was an unapologetic Christian evangelist who mixed the passion of his antislavery convictions with the fervor of the tent meeting. (In his later years, he moved on to a struggling little college called Oberlin in Ohio, where he taught students why the message of Christ forbade humans to hold other humans as chattel.)

One of Finney's most famous sermons on the subject of slavery included this call to his audience: "We see how we are to treat those who are oppressed and in slavery. We are to put ourselves in their position and inquire what we should ask them to do for us, in their circumstances." And what would this empathy produce? Finney reminded his listeners that the 1860 elections (in which Lincoln faced Stephen Douglas) were right around the corner, then told them, in so many words, how to cast their ballots: "I should be very prone to think that no one ought to cast his vote against [a slave's] liberty for the mere sake of money or office. Even politicians can see how shameful and how outrageously wrong it is to hold any person as a slave."[3]

And why was holding slaves wrong? For Charles Finney, as for most of the abolitionists, the reason was simple: The Bible commands Christians to love their neighbors as themselves. To the antislavery preachers, the contradiction was so obvious as to need little argument. What the South was doing, the Bible forbade; and the responsibility of the Christians in the North—so the abolitionists insisted—was to end what the Reverend Theodore Parker, another prominent antislavery preacher, called "this plague-spot of slavery—the curse to our industry, our education, our politics, and our religion."[4]

Parker, Finney, and others preached against slavery during the first half of the nineteenth century, the years leading up to the Civil War. This was an era in which, we might say, the question of the proper role of public religious argument in the nation's affairs was very much in play. In one of those peculiarly American historical paradoxes, fears that the country's religious affairs might come to be dominated by institutional religions were leading, not to a high wall of separation between church and state, but to a burgeoning "Christian nation" sentiment. One reason might have been that the fear about the influence of religion, as many historians have shown, was really a fear about the growing influence of the Roman Catholic Church. Protestants after all understood the idea of "church" somewhat differently than Catholics did, and could easily envision a nation wholly Christian with its institutional religions wholly disestablished.

Thus the abolitionist fervor probably assisted the young nation in working out its views on what weight should be given to claims by religious leaders about what direction God wanted the country to take. Here, after all, were clergy–lots and lots of clergy–contending that the nation was obliged, both morally and spiritually, to free the slaves, for no other reason than that slaveholding was inconsistent with Divine Law. What the nation had to decide was not, at first, whether the antislavery preachers were right; but whether to listen at all.

To be sure, there was a degree of religious fervor against "the peculiar institution" even at the time of the framing of the Constitution. Abigail Adams, for example, opposed slavery for overtly religious reasons. "Of this I am certain," she wrote in an anonymous letter published in 1776, "that it is not founded upon that generous and Christian principle of doing to others as we would that others should do unto us."[5] Back in the seventeenth century, this proposition seemed to attain widespread acceptance in the thirteen colonies–as long as the "others" were fellow Christians. As the historian Edmund S. Morgan has shown, prior to the 1660s, it was common for slaves in Virginia to convert to Christianity in order to take advantage of laws prohibiting (or at least making difficult) the holding of Christians as slaves rather than as indentured servants; and they were often set free as a result of the conversion.[6] (By the end of the century, Morgan tells us, slaveholding was more profitable, slaveowners held more power, and the relevant laws were changed; conversion was allowed but no longer led automatically to emancipation.)

Slavery was certainly debated at the Constitutional Convention and in the debates over the ratification of the new document, and, of course, Jefferson's draft language blaming slavery on the king and condemning the practice was removed from the Declaration of Independence before it was presented for signature, but it must be admitted that although antislavery feeling might have run high during the eighteenth century, antislavery activism was rare. When the great evangelist William Wilberforce, writing in his diary in 1787, referred to the abolition of slavery as one of the "great objects" God had set before him, he did so as part of a lament: He was expressing sorrow that his Christian brethren seemed to have cared so little about the issue in the century then tumbling toward its close.[7]

The historian William Lee Miller has argued that one must distinguish two distinct revivalist eras in American Protestant thought to understand why abolitionists might fail in the eighteenth century to force a ban on slavery into the Constitution, yet succeed eighty years later in moving the nation to war over the question. The First Awakening, Miller points out, was sufficiently grounded in the Reformed tradition "to insist that it was God's grace and not human effort that did all the converting and the history-changing."[8] Thus it was sufficient for such famous preachers as Jonathan Edwards to urge their listeners to improve themselves in preparation for the return of Jesus Christ.[9] The Second Great Awakening, by contrast, influenced by new ideas about democracy and the growing popularity of Enlightenment ideology, emphasized the believer's confrontation with the world, and the obligation to improve it.[10] As the historian Nathan Hatch has shown, few Christian denominations that arrived from Europe into the new nation were able to preserve the sturdy, cautious distance from the material world that so many preached back home.[11] True, the debate over the Christian role—to prepare for personal salvation alone or to work as well for the betterment of God's creation—is as old as Christianity, but it is that second impulse, the impulse to change the world to conform with one's vision of Divine Will, that has been victorious in America and has characterized most mainstream religion to the present day.

A review of abolitionist sermons of the era—as well as the responses by preachers who believed slavery to be consistent with, or even required by, God's will—indicates little doubt on the part of the preachers about the propriety of altering the world to fit the Word. Their only disagreement was on the appropriate tactics.

The fiery abolitionist preacher Theodore Parker, in an 1854 address to the New York City Anti-Slavery Society, came to the brink of calling for open warfare. He decried the reluctance of the wealthy North to fight against slavery and then predicted that some invader—Spain, perhaps—would do it in order to win territory:

> In case of foreign war, the North will not be the battle field. An invading army would attack the South. . . . Let an army set foot on Southern soil, with a few *black Regiments;* let the commander offer *freedom to all the Slaves and*

put arms in their hands; let him ask them to *burn houses and butcher men;* and there would be a state of things not quite so pleasant for gentlemen of the South to look at.[12]

But Parker finally backed off from his warlike imagery, reverting to a political solution, albeit one that under today's silly rules would cost a church its tax exemption: "Now is the time to push and be active, call meetings, bring out men of all parties, all forms of religion, agitate, agitate, agitate."[13] He even listed, by name, political officials whose careers should end as a result of their support for slavery.

Many other abolitionists were quite open in their call for violence if necessary to overturn the slaveocracy in the South. The black abolitionist David Walker's 1830 pamphlet calling on the slaves to rebel is one signpost. So is the publication, in 1831, of the first issue of William Lloyd Garrison's militantly antislavery newspaper, the *Liberator.*[14] Nat Turner's rebellion also took place in 1831—an important year for the cause, in which supporters of slavery could begin tarring all abolitionists, who were previously derided as fanatics, with the brush of violence.

Other abolitionists managed, rather cleverly, to hide a call for violent warfare inside a call for peace. One, the Reverend Charles E. Hodges, in a tract entitled *Disunion Our Wisdom and Our Duty,* conceded the claim of the pro-slavery forces that the Constitution itself protected the institution. Therefore, Hodges explained, Christians were required to view the Constitution as immoral and, because "it is wrong to sustain sin," to work for the end of the Union—a result, as everybody knew but Hodges failed to mention, that could hardly be brought about peacefully. "[C]an you do otherwise," he demanded, "than commit yourself to this cause . . . ?"[15] It is unlikely that Hodges had to point out to his readers that a commitment to the cause of abolishing slavery by abolishing the Constitution was, in the politics of the time, little different from a call for civil war.

Understandably, most of the abolitionist preachers were careful to avoid any talk of violence, and some of them spoke against it directly. For example, the Boston antislavery preacher Ezra S. Gannett, in an 1854 sermon, issued a sharp warning: "Violence in the support of truths dear to us, or disorderly resistance to offensive legislation, is as unwise as it is improper, and as unchristian as it is injurious."[16] The New York abolitionist preacher Seth Williston—who, like many nineteenth-century American Protestants, saw the United States as the New Jerusalem—called for an end of slavery, but not at the cost of warfare: "If it has war, it should be from invasion, not from her own citizens. We are required to pray for the peace of Jerusalem, accompanied with an assurance that they shall prosper who love her."[17]

Others took a more nuanced view, especially once the war arrived. The abolitionist Henry Darling suggested that the war was God's way of purifying a nation that had sinned mightily, and in many different ways. But, once the war began, Darling argued, there was no choice but to fight it to a conclusion. In response to efforts to negotiate an end to the war that would allow slavery to continue, he offered withering contempt:

> Are other demons to be exorcised from our body politic, and this one to remain? Is God bringing us through this terrible baptism of blood, to cleanse the white robe of our national purity from a few of its minor impurities, but yet to permit this deepest, darkest stain to remain? That would be a strange teleology, indeed, that would lead any to such a conclusion.[18]

Even as most abolitionist preachers eschewed the violence of Turner and others, however, they embraced activism in the cause of making God's will a political reality. They forcefully rejected charges that they were, through their advocacy of the abolitionist cause, breaching a barrier that should remain pristine. An 1859 sermon by Nathaniel Hall was explicit:

> I undertake to say that there was never a more senseless assumption put forth in all Christiandom—one more to be resisted, if need were, to the very death—than that the pulpit, standing as the visible exponent of God's truth and law, should have nothing to say in reference to the fact that millions of human beings, in the nation in which it stands, are forcefully deprived of their natural rights, and crushed beneath the heel of lawless oppression.[19]

Like Parker, Hall came close to calling for violent warfare: "[W]ith the North should be the unalterable decision, We will no longer be partners in the upholding and cherishing of this accursed barbarism. We will no longer be tied up to a complicity in this intolerable outrage and affront to Christianity and the age."[20]

And, lest his audience think he was simply speaking of breaking up the Union, Hall ended his sermon with a telling biblical quote: "'Wherefore, put on the whole armor of God, that ye may be able to stand in the evil day, and, having done all, to stand.'"[21] This followed Hall's sermon of the previous week, occasioned by the execution of John Brown, in which he lauded Brown, despite his violence, for standing firmly against a violent institution. Hall implied, although he did not actually say, that "aggressive force," as he called it, was appropriate in ending oppression, and he pointed out that Americans of his day (like those of our own) tended to applaud the use of force in causes with which they agreed—at least when the violence succeeded.[22]

The abolitionist preachers did not think it possible to confine their vision of justice to a narrow, walled-off region called "church"; they considered action in the world not only justified but imperative. Ezra Gannett explained that the survival of the institution of slavery "is not purely a political question." Why not? Because "it has its moral side, and religion and Christianity are entitled to examine it as entering within their domain."[23] That which touches morality, in other words, is precisely that which religion is "entitled" to examine; no argument about separation of church and state can prevent the church from protecting its own side of the wall. One might reasonably ask, of course, what falls on the church's side of the wall—what aspects of life religion is entitled to "examine"—but Gannett, like other abolitionists, seemed quite sure that the question of the size of religion's sphere was one for religion, not the state, to decide. And, having made its decision, said Gannett, religion had to act in the world. Those who oppose slavery on religious grounds, he argued, "may take all constitutional and lawful methods for securing an abrogation of those enactments, and of those provisions of the fundamental law [he meant the Constitution], which offend our moral convictions."[24]

This is, indeed, the very point of the change in the American Protestant understanding of the believer's obligation during the early nineteenth century. The Christian, many and perhaps most pastors were by this time preaching, was to work for the betterment of God's creation—especially in a nation that was, in the minds of many Protestants, specially favored by God to lead the world to truth and justice. That special land, the preachers believed, had to be made fit to live in.

Many abolitionists believed that the land would be more fit when it was more Christian. They supported abolition largely as a tool for evangelizing. It was imperative to convert the slaves to Christianity, as it was imperative under the Great Commission to convert everybody, but the effort to evangelize the slaves was that much harder, wrote one abolitionist preacher, because of "the heathenism of oppression" created by enslavement.[25]

Of course, not every preacher was persuaded of the unfitness of the New Jerusalem in the first place. Public preaching on the question of slavery was by no means limited to those who opposed it. On the contrary: There is no reason to suppose, especially during the first half of the nineteenth century, that anywhere near a majority of the American public opposed slavery. Even among those who did not happen to like it, few were, so early, willing to see young men fight and die in order to end it. And then there were many people, including many clergy, who believed that slavery—in particular, African slavery—was simply the will of God.

The historian Jon Butler has shown how an entire theology of authority and obedience was worked out in the colonies (especially in Anglican Virginia) in order to justify and reinforce the dominance of master over slave.[26] Although many Southerners, as Don Fehrenbacher puts it, went through the motions of complaining about the unfortunate necessity of slavery, the truth was that it was defended, from an early moment, with all the available arguments, secular and religious, that the slaveowners and their tame clergy could muster.[27] During the eighteenth century, as American slavery grew progressively more violent, and thus less like slavery in most of the rest of the world, slave revolts (often led by Christian slaves) grew more frequent.[28] In response, the defense of the practice on Christian grounds grew ever more didactic: Accepting the Gospel truth might make men free, but that freedom, argued the pro-slavery clergy, was only spiritual, not political.[29]

Some defenders were vulgar, or at least over-simple, in announcing that there were slaves in the Bible and that was the end of the matter.[30] (One pointed out that it was not enough for the abolitionists to say that the biblical examples were not of *American* slavery: biblical marriage, he teased, was not American marriage either—should Americans therefore not marry?[31] Another, having offered a similar analogy between biblical images of both slavery and the family, concluded: "[O]ur heart and our home relations shall never be more Christian than they are now."[32]) But there were more sophisticated criticisms of the antislavery preachers, including a very thoughtful pamphlet by Nathan Lord, the president of Dartmouth College, who argued that all human institutions, including slavery, serve in some mysterious way "the all-wise purposes of God." He warned against "Utopian" thought and the zeal to found the New Jerusalem before its time.[33]

This style of reasoning was not unusual. It was a holdover from the vision of many eighteenth-century Protestants that the believer's task, whatever his station in life, was to prepare for salvation. Remaking the world stood a far distant second to remaking the self. The historian Forrest McDonald, writing about the moment of framing of the Constitution, summarized the mindset of many Christians this way:

Slavery was not necessarily condemned . . . for in an ultimate sense moral accountability was to God: blacks and whites were equal in His eyes, and that should be enough for any man. In a society in which almost everyone believed in a future state of eternal rewards and punishments (and in which reminders of one's own mortality were almost continuous), that was no trivial abstraction.[34]

Lord's gently pro-slavery pamphlet is less important for his argument than for his style of argument. Once having argued, in a reflective and scholarly way, that slavery was consistent with the will of God, he concluded firmly, "That all contrary suppositions, theories, and interpretations must be false, wherever the fallacy lies."[35] The source of the fallacy was, for Lord, "specious humanitarian philosophy," which "substitutes the natural sentiments, sympathies, tastes, volitions, purposes, and resolves of the human mind for supernatural grace; or puts the latter in subserviency to the former."[36]

Here Lord was making a rhetorical move that truly believing religionists, sooner or later, have no choice but to make. If God wills a proposition **P**, God cannot also will **Not P**; so those who believe that God's will is actually **Not P** are in error. Lord took the view, in other words, that God could not simultaneously be for slavery and against it; that is, God could not hold to **P** and **Not P** at the same time. The reason is that God, being perfect, cannot be the author of any contradiction. This is a very old proposition in theology, going back to Thomas Aquinas and, before him, to Aristotle. Thus the pro-slavery preachers and the antislavery preachers agreed on at least one premise: A perfect God could not be on both sides of the issue simultaneously.

The preachers of the Second Great Awakening believed in doing God's work in the world. If God's will was **P** rather than **Not P**, then **P** rather than **Not P** was what the world should reflect. And if the world instead continued to reflect **Not P**, it was the duty of God's people to change it, until **P** was both God's Word and living truth. If God's immutable Word, **P**, condemned slavery as a sin, then God's creation had to be made free of the practice. Nowadays, as we have seen, a significant body of thought holds that activism of this kind is a bad idea, perhaps prohibited by the Constitution. It will be instructive, therefore, to consider how Americans caught up in the debate over slavery in the first half of the nineteenth century conceptualized what might now be described as a conflict between church and state.

II

Few of the pro-slavery preachers disputed the right—indeed, the responsibility—of members of the clergy to speak out on issues of morality. The Southern apologist Henry J. Van Dyke, in a sermon preached in 1860 just after the election of Abraham Lincoln, conceded the point. After first explaining that Abolitionists, in order to be Abolitionists, had to believe that slaveholding was sin, he went on to say that, given their beliefs, it was not surprising that they militated for legal change: "And you will perceive it is just here that Abolitionism presents a proper subject for discussion in the pulpit; for it is one great purpose of the Bible, and therefore one great duty of God's ministers in its exposition, to show what is sin and what is not."[37]

Van Dyke went on to explain, in blistering language, why the Abolitionists were wrong in their understanding of God's will. He further argued, in language reminiscent of some of today's fervor against religious activism in public life, that "the influence of the Christian ministry is hindered . . . by the constant agitations of Abolitionism in our national councils"[38]—in short, that another reason for Abolitionists to cease their efforts was that they were hurting the image of the church itself.

One fiery pro-slavery preacher, the Reverend Iveson L. Brooks of South Carolina, attacked Abolitionism as "a fanaticism near the borders of lunacy," but only because the antislavery clergy misunderstood the Bible.[39] The African slaves, he argued along with many other Christians, were the children of Ham, condemned in Genesis 9 to serve. He added, once more in keeping with slavery's other defenders, that the Africans were actually better off as slaves than they would have been in their native land, for in the United States they received the benefits of Christian civilization.

Some of the clergy worried about Abolitionist efforts to influence voters, but for reasons of wisdom rather than separationism. One pro-slavery preacher complained about single-issue politics in the 1860 election, aided by clergy who presumed to state God's will: "Men who, in the better days of the republic, could not have obtained the smallest office, were elected to Congress upon this single issue; and ministers of the gospel descended from the pulpit to mingle religious animosity with the boiling caldron of political strife."[40]

Yet I do not mean to suggest that nobody who opposed the abolitionist cause worried about the separation of church and state. The worry was unquestionably present; what is useful as we look back on the era is to consider how it was raised. Slavery, its supporters insisted, was one of the institutions on which society rested. Its abolition, therefore, was not a moral question but a practical one: Would its ending be helpful or harmful to the social order?[41] (Since the social order was a slaveocracy, the question of course answered itself.)

For example, George D. Armstrong, pro-slavery pastor of a Presbyterian church in Norfolk, Virginia, explained that Christians, whatever their views on slavery itself, should oppose abolition because economic and political arrangements are not the proper business of the Church of God. The church, according to Pastor Armstrong, is not "intended to do all the good which needs to be done in the world, and wage war against every form of human ill."[42] He added: "God has assigned to the Church and the State each its separate province, and neither has ever intruded into the province of the other without suffering therefor."[43] The only Christian responsibility to the slaves, Armstrong insisted, was to preach the Gospel to them.[44] A South Carolina newspaper editorialized along similar lines: "It is vain to present the matter [of abolition] in a religious dress; its bearing under any garb will be political, for it strikes at the foundation of our domestic institutions."[45] Thus, in the Southern view, the abolition question was about the political and economic arrangement of society, and therefore was one on which the Church should not presume to speak. The separation of church and state, then, meant that the church must not upset the existing institutional order but must work within it in order to accomplish its proper goal of saving souls. (As in the present day, the critics presumed to know the proper role of the church.)

Moreover, as the historian Mitchell Snay has shown, the theological struggle on behalf of slavery was bolstered by a general anticlericalism in the South, a spillover of the region's anti-Catholicism.[46] The fact that so many abolitionist leaders were ordained ministers was, for many Southern preachers, a larger objection than the fact that their arguments were religious in nature. Consider, for example, what happened in 1854, when a coalition of 3,000 New England clergy presented a petition that opposed, on religious grounds, the expansion of slavery into the Nebraska territory. Pro-slavery members of the Senate were aghast. Religion, they contended, should remain in its proper place. Argued Senator Stephen Douglas:

> [H]ere we find that a large body of preachers, perhaps three thousand, following the lead of a circular, which was issued by the Abolition confederates in this body, calculated to deceive and mislead the public, have here come forward, with an atrocious falsehood and an atrocious calumny against this Sen-

ate, desecrated the pulpit, and prostituted the sacred desk to the miserable and corrupting influence of party politics.[47]

Douglas went on to say that these "political preachers" (as the pro-slavery side liked to call the Abolitionist clergy) "ought to be rebuked, and required to confine themselves to their vocation."[48]

In the same debate, Senator Mason sounded a pure separationist note. The substance of the petition, Mason argued, was beside the point. What mattered was the identity of the signatories*—for not everyone enjoyed equally the right to petition the government for redress of grievances:

> But I understand this petition to come from a class who have put aside their character of citizens. It comes from a class who style themselves in the petition, ministers of the Gospel, and not citizens. . . . Sir, ministers of the Gospel are unknown to this Government, and God forbid the day should ever come when they shall be known to it. The great effort of the American people has been, by every form of defensive measures, to keep that class away from the Government; to deny to them any access to it as a class, or any interference in its proceedings.[49]

And the next speaker, Senator Butler, complained that the signatories "have dared to quit the pulpit and step into the political arena, and speak as the organs of Almighty God."[50] He added: "When the clergy quit the province which is assigned to them, in which they can dispense the Gospel . . . when they would convert the lamb into the lion, going about in the form of agitators, seeking whom they may devour, instead of the meek and lowly representatives of Christ, they divest themselves of all respect which I can give them."[51]

Senator Houston, responding to the attacks on the petitioners, offered a middle course between the wall of separation and the domination of politics by clergy:

> I do not think there is anything very derogatory to our institutions in the ministers of the Gospel expressing their opinions. They have a right to do it. No man can be a minister without first being a man. He has political rights; he has also the rights of a missionary of the Saviour, and he is not

---

*The identity of the signatories mattered in more ways than one. Twenty years earlier, in 1836, the House of Representatives had voted overwhelmingly that slaves were not among those who were able to exercise the First Amendment right to petition for redress of their grievances.

disfranchised by his vocation. Certain political restrictions may be laid upon him; he may be disqualified from serving in the legislatures of the States, but that does not discharge him from political and civil obligations to his country. He has a right to contribute, as far as he thinks necessary, to the sustentation of its institutions. He has a right to interpose his voice as one of its citizens against the adoption of any measure which he believes will injure the nation. These individuals have done no more.[52]

In short, Houston argued, the status of being a member of the clergy, although it might disqualify a person from government service, had no effect on the other rights of the citizen.

What should be striking about the nature of the Senate debate over receipt of the 1854 petition is that the members who worried about separation of church and state did not complain about religious argument, or biblical citation, or the invocation by the Abolitionists of the name of God. They worried only about the identity of the signatories—the fact that the petitioners were all clergy. It was that class that was, in Senator Mason's terminology, denied all access to the proceedings of government. The prohibition, in other words, even as understood by those who cited it, was not on petitions by religious people but on petitions by religious *leaders*. This history is consistent with a proposition vigorously argued by the legal scholar Steven Smith—that the original understanding, if there was one, on the separation of church and state was only to separate the *institutions* we call church and state. It was, says Smith, the church, not the people of the church, that was banned from holding power over governance. And it was arguments by the institutional church, not religious arguments by ordinary citizens, that the founding generation puzzled over how to control.[53]

This understanding makes perfect sense when we recall that the American tradition of religious liberty owes at least as much to the dissenting Protestant preachers of the seventeenth and eighteenth century as it does to the Enlightment thought that so influenced Thomas Jefferson and James Madison. The dissenters were interested less in building a secular America than in creating one in which Christians would be free of the control of the institutional churches—Rome, in particular, but the Anglican tradition as well.[54] For dissenting colonial Baptists like Isaac Backus, as well as prominent names from the Founding Generation (including John Jay), "free" religion meant religion free of the corrupt and worldly churches of Europe: in a word, Catholicism.[55] Few of the dissenters did not want a government free of religious influence, and, indeed, could scarcely have imagined such a state; they wanted a government (as well as a private sector) free of control by an ecclesiastic hierarchy. (That is the reason, for example, that the Puritans required magistrates rather than clergy to officiate at weddings.) This fear of clergy domination often expressed itself in rabid anti-Catholic animus; but the fear unquestionably formed a central motive for many supporters of religious liberty.

So when Mason and other slavery advocates pointed to the fact that so many Abolitionist leaders were clergy, they were attempting to link their cause to the popular fear of churchmen ordering the government about. One need not concede that they properly understood the doctrine they were citing to understand why they would cite it.[56]

III

All through the twentieth century, historians searched for ways to explain the Civil War in particular, and the abolitionist struggle in general, without the need for resort to religion. So, for example, we have all been told that the war really represented the struggle of the cheap-labor North against the free-labor South, or that it was really all about immigration, or railroads, or even what Lincoln kept insisting, an ideological struggle to keep the Union whole. Yet it was slavery, and nothing but slavery, that caused the Southern states to secede; it was slavery, and nothing but slavery, that the war's most ardent Northern supporters addressed.

The historian Sydney E. Ahlstrom put the matter this way: "Had there been no slavery, there would have been no war. Had there been no moral condemnation of slavery, there would have been no war." The Civil War, says Ahlstrom, was a "moral" war, but not "because one side was good and the other evil, nor because purity of motive was more pronounced on one side than on the other." In other words, it does not matter if some supporters of the Union were racists or cared not a fig about slavery. It does not matter if Lincoln himself was moved by more motives than one. What matters is that the underlying dispute was a moral dispute: "It was a moral war because it sprang from a moral impasse on issues which Americans in the mid-nineteenth century could no longer avoid or escape."[57] The impasse could not be escaped because sentiment, in Fehrenbacher's term, finally became interest: People cared, passionately, about the answer to the moral question.

All one needs to make sense of the war over slavery is to accept religion as a force that actually can shape people's outlook, and thus their lives and their behavior. There are and have always been tens of millions of Americans for whom God is a living truth, whose ordinances we are bound to obey. Our understanding of God's Will will ever be imperfect, and our sinful imperfection will always keep us from perfect obedience; but for those who believe, that Will is as palpable, as relevant, often as irresistible, as any secular argument of law or morality. Religion at its best works in its adherents genuine transformation; did it not, there would be no reason to fight for either religious liberty or religious disestablishment.

There is good reason to think that without the steady drumbeat of Christian condemnation from the abolitionist preachers, there would never have been sufficient antislavery sentiment—to say nothing of antislavery interest—to enable the nation finally to go to war over the issue. Equally important, there might never have been sufficient antislavery preaching if not for the tireless evangelizing of such abolitionists as Charles Finney and his protégé Theodore Weld, who successfully targeted, among their many audiences, young college students who would, they knew, be the nation's future leaders. From town to town they went, crisscrossing the North, the West (as it was then known; nowadays we would say the Midwest), and the border states, at every stop bringing their message that slavery was contrary to the Gospels. Until, finally, people came to believe it.[58]

In the beginning was the Deed, wrote Goethe, but his ironic play on the famous Gospel text was simply wrong. In the beginning of the campaign against slavery was the Word; in the end was the War. Had our national discourse been snarled then, as it is now, in the spider's web of our misunderstanding of separation of church and state, the Word would have been harder to spread . . . and the Deed would have been harder to do.

It is a commonplace of public dialogue in our current era—at least among elites—to treat religionists working for change as presumptively fanatical, not amenable to reason. In the first half of the nineteenth century, the abolitionists, too, were described as fanatics and, as Miller notes, often met the fanatic's end:

> Mobs North and South could give vent to their appraisal of these fanatics, these bloodhounds, with *action*: by tarring and feathering, by blacking the offending fanatics' faces and putting them on the next train, by breaking up abolitionist meetings and running the speakers out of town, by looting Lewis Tappan's home in New York and burning furniture in the square.[59]

Most antislavery preachers were not murdered, or tarred and feathered, or run out of town on a rail. But all of them, arguing in religious terms, for religious reasons, for a fundamental change in American society, were considered dangerous.

In an important sense, the charge was true. The Abolitionists *were* fanatical. They *were* dangerous. They believed themselves the custodians of God's Word, and, for the more radical among them, the William Lloyd Garrisons, the Nat Turners, the Frederick Douglasses, no force on God's Earth was going to prevent them from building the New Jerusalem. The end of slavery is the legacy of their fanaticism, but so is the bloody war that preceded it. Yet the question in political terms is not whether they were wrong to invoke God's Will, but whether the gain was worth the candle. I believe that it was; and this belief disables me from saying to others who invoke God's Name in their causes that they are acting undemocratically. I only pray that they take the time and the caution to be as certain as they can be that they are right.

Not long before I completed this manuscript, the voters of Alabama, one of the nation's poorest states, unexpectedly and resoundingly defeated a referendum that would have created a state lottery. Lotteries have grown enormously popular in our modern era, when selfish voters demand more services from government but insist on lower taxes, and politicians, more worried about reelection than either morality or common sense, scramble to please them. Lotteries, like taxes, do indeed enable states to raise revenue—but in a most regressive manner. The poor spend a significantly higher proportion of their income on lottery tickets than the rich do. On the other hand, the expected return to the bettor (the jackpot in dollars multiplied by the chance of winning it with a dollar bet) is much lower than in the illegal numbers games that lotto-happy politicians pretend to abhor but, obviously, secretly envy. In short, there are many excellent reasons to oppose lotteries. In the view of many critics, however, the voters of Alabama chose a bad reason: religious conviction.

Week after week, preachers thundered against the lottery from the pulpit. Lotto backers did not take this religious opposition seriously, evidently certain that enough voters had been seduced—that antilottery sentiment would never mature into interest. Polls, after all, showed the public voting for the lottery by a margin of 60 to 40. Then, when the religious voice triumphed, supporters retreated into sour grapes: There were the religionists again, imposing their fanatical opinions on everybody else.[60] Of course, this argument cuts both ways. Another view might be that the fanatical lottery backers were trying to impose their opinions on everybody else. It is not enough for supporters to answer that nobody is forced to play. Available choices are not simply available choices. A culture defines itself in large part by what it chooses to make available. It is not at all fanciful for religious parents (or, for that matter, nonreligious parents) to suppose that it will be harder to raise good (disciplined, unselfish, thoughtful) children in a state that encourages its citizens to gamble (and to make very bad bets at that) than in one that abstains from such an assault on the will. Religionists who fought the lottery, like religionists who fought against slavery, were working to make God's creation better—or to prevent others from making it worse. Maybe they were right. Maybe they were wrong. Either way, one cannot help but hear echoes of the old pro-slavery separationism in the shrill insistence of lottery supporters that their opponents, because they were moved by religion, should not have forced an entire state to live according to their morality.

7

The Separation of
Church and Wealth

RELIGIOUS FAITH, IN ALL ITS DELIGHTFUL and dangerous variety, has always been a part of the nation's public life. No era has been untouched by political advocacy of the religiously devout, and no era before our own has seen an organized effort to screen religion out—unless, of course, one counts the battle to preserve chattel slavery, and there, fortunately, the attempt to mute the religious voice was defeated.

The Second Great Awakening produced more than the abolition of slavery. All across America, Christians looked for opportunities to engage with the culture, using tools of witness, tools of politics, and tools of law for the betterment of God's creation. The historian Nathan O. Hatch has suggested that the upsurge of religious activism in the early nineteenth century was related to the splintering of American Protestantism, because, suddenly, there was a religious outlet for every cause: "[O]ne could worship on Saturday, practice foot washing, ordain women, advocate pacifism, prohibit alcohol, or toy with spiritualism, phrenology, or health reform."[1] The examples Hatch chooses are telling. As the historian Sydney E. Ahlstrom points out, one cannot understand the nineteenth century reform movements that swept the nation without understanding their roots in the Christian Gospels. Writes Ahlstrom: "If the collective conscience of evangelical America is left out, the movement as a whole is incomprehensible."[2] What movements does Ahlstrom have in mind? He lists, among others, the push for public education, the battle for women's rights, the improvement of prisons and hospitals, and the crusade for peace—in short, just about every important struggle for social change that occurred in the century.[3]

These early examples of what came to be called the Social Gospel movement serve as stark reminders of a more sensible period in American history,
when the voices of the religious were welcomed into politics, and Americans
of many different denominations spent, literally, hours upon hours debating
the proper Christian role in an increasingly complex (today we would say
multicultural) society.[4] Hardly anybody doubted that public expression of religious voices was a good thing, and their expression was regular and ca-
cophonous. Americans of that era asked the same question we should ask
today: not *Who should be allowed to speak?* but *What is the right thing to do?* And
nowhere was this debate more heated—and the religious voice more active
and welcomed—than in the decades-long argument over how to deal with the
massive social dislocations wrought by industrialization.

Imagine for a moment the America of the late nineteenth and early
twentieth centuries, the swift transition, over a period of perhaps thirty
years, from a nation in which nearly everybody worked the land in one
way or another to a nation in which the defining form of labor was working for a wage in the factory. Small communities that had preserved their
values for centuries were shattered as the young began to wander to find
work. The great industrial cities were built around the great factories, and
suddenly, for the first time in American history, great masses of strangers
lived crowded together in tenements. Many were immigrants from the
farms, many more were immigrants from abroad. Women and children
worked as well, often for pennies a day. In the tenements, there was neither
decent sanitation nor running water. In the factories, there was dangerous
work under oppressive conditions, but whenever the workers tried to organize unions, the police, private detectives, even the armed forces were
called out to put a stop to it.

The churches could hardly have stayed silent. And, although many
preachers spoke on behalf of the status quo, the situation of the workers inspired many others to challenge, publicly, both the policies of business and
the policies of government. And they were not alone. The nineteenth century flowed into the twentieth on the cusp of what has come to be known
as the Progressive Era, during which—at least according to popular history—the states and, later, the federal government adopted a number of
statutes and regulations aimed at curbing what were viewed as the abuses
of an unfettered laissez-faire economy.[5] Whatever the softness of the popular history, nobody denies that the motives of the reformers were pure, and
the reformers in the pulpit were prominent and provocative players in the
political drama of the age.

Consider the contemporary complaint that the late years of the twentieth century saw the government abandon most efforts to rein in business excesses, as long as prosperity reigned for most Americans. The complaint turns out to be as old as preaching–the great biblical prophets regularly issued injunctions against the rich who despised the poor–and it is certainly as old as America. Thus, the rector of a Philadelphia church lamented on All Saints Day in November 1914: "Our leading business men value tariff laws more highly than the Sermon on the Mount."[6] American business, he argued, preferred to make the Gospel "just the kind suitable for American business conditions." He added: "Wall Street has always kept tight hold of the Church, so the Church would not let Christ do any damage among stocks and bonds. Christianity, if allowed full swing anywhere, will, at times, close the stock exchange."[7]

Here is another example that sounds remarkably contemporary. Charles D. Williams, bishop of Michigan, lamented the moral state of the nation of 1917 in words much like those we sometimes hear today: "The one test of an administration is its effect on the stock-market and of a Congress its effect on business."[8] Then, after complaining that Americans had forgotten the connection between their rights and responsibilities, thinking of themselves now as individuals who could do as they liked rather than members of a greater whole, Williams charged religions with cooperating with this moral decline: "The same individualistic and atomic conception of society has permeated our popular religions. . . . Protestantism, the religion of the Reformation, has been almost purely individualistic and atomic."[9]

People, in other words, were simply out for themselves, which was hardly what the Gospel message envisioned. Bishop Williams announced, as a solution, the evolution of a "new social conscience" that would question "not only the acquisition of wealth but also the use and spending of wealth."[10] The development of this new conscience, and the altering of the course of law to enable it, was a Christian obligation, he argued, as part of the Great Commission to evangelize the world (Matt. 28:16–20). Poverty and inequality of wealth, according to Williams, were the enemies of the Gospel:

> There are everywhere in our modern world economic, industrial and social conditions which make the Christian life practically impossible. Is it not the business of religion to deal directly with those conditions and try to make the environment at least more favourable to the regenerate life? Our concern is with the soil as well as with the seed in our sowing of the Word.[11]

In other words, if the conditions of the workers were not improved, there would be no rich soil in which the Word could take root.

A similar argument was pressed by Pope Leo XIII in *Rerum Novarum,* his 1891 encyclical letter attacking both socialism and unbridled capitalism. Although criticizing preachers who believed that the Gospel message demanded a more equitable sharing of wealth, Leo nevertheless insisted that workers must not be oppressed by "greedy" employers but must be paid wages adequate to support their families, lest they be tempted into sin.[12] Those with the responsibility for running the country and the factories also had the responsibility to refrain from creating conditions in which it would be harder for workers to lead Christian lives.

The more radical of the preachers, not content merely to worry about the salvation of the workers' souls, challenged industrial capitalism itself. One vehemently anticapitalist preacher, David C. Reid of the Congregational Church in Stockbridge, Massachusetts, published a book in 1910 entitled *Effective Industrial Reform.* Living and working in the Berkshires, he saw around him the hovels of the working class and the grand villas of the wealthy. It was not only the patent inequalities that disturbed him, but the effect of the economic system on the family, and thus on the faith. (He observed, for example, that the wage-labor system forced women into the workforce and children into day care, where they could not receive proper moral instruction.[13]) Christians, Reid argued, were obliged to pursue "Christ's ultimate aim," which was "to transform human society itself." Jesus, Reid insisted, envisioned "not only regenerated men and woman, but also perfected institutions and laws."[14] He was prepared to fight for constitutional amendments, if necessary, to accomplish his plan.[15] And Reid, like Williams, saw socialism (although, he emphasized, not Marxism) as the only available system that would offer these "perfected institutions and laws."

Some put the point as a rhetorical question. "Is it right for people who call themselves Christians," demanded an executive of the Federal Council of Churches of Christ, "to live in comfort, accepting the dividends of industries where women toil for ten hours a day in the heat and noise of a factory for thirteen dollars a week? How many people who live on dividends even know what are the wages and conditions in the industries from which their money comes?"[16] But the call of the preachers was not merely, or mostly, for Christians to reassess their lifestyles; it was a call for government regulation of industry for the benefit of the workers. A few years later, Reinhold Niebuhr would propose the "Christianization" of American industry; but he was merely building on the work already done by the Social Gospel preachers of the Progressive Era.

The reformers well understood—indeed, often cited—the link between the preaching of the Abolitionist Era and that of the Progressive Era. The organization of labor unions was often explained as the logical outgrowth of the struggle against slavery. The abolitionist movement, argued a professor at the Yale Divinity School, rested on moral and religious foundations, plus one pragmatic idea: "the growing realization that to make the workman the natural and bitter enemy of his master was bad economics and bad business."[17]

Although many of the Social Gospel preachers refrained from suggesting that wealth was bad in and of itself, not all were so reticent. Bishop Charles Williams put it this way: "Particularly is wealth by its mere possession apt to distort spiritual vision, materialise all the standards of life and blind its possessor to the finer issues, the ideal values and ends of life."[18] The solution, for Williams, was socialism, or something much like it, for he believed the profit motive itself to be the enemy . . . and true Christianity to be impossible as long as the profit motive was present.

Yet the Social Gospel preachers were not, by and large, prepared to join the socialist movement on all issues. Indeed, many of the "evangelical liberals" at the heart of the Social Gospel movement—including Walter Rauschenbusch, perhaps the most famous of them all—considered themselves quite orthodox in their Christianity.[19] Their slogan was "Back to Christ," and they were, on most social issues, quite traditional in outlook.* Harvard's distinguished professor of Christian morals, Francis Greenwood Peabody, warned in 1924 against Christian alliances with forces seeking to overturn the family. Battling the excesses of industrial capitalism was one thing, Peabody argued; but to yield on the importance of marriage was impossible: "The family is to Jesus the elementary type of the kingdom of God, the microcosm which represents the divine plan for the world; and as the principles of the kingdom are, in his teaching, spirituality, personality, and will, so the family in its own interior sphere finds its stability in the same fundamental principles."[20] Far from seeking to transcend or eradicate the traditional family, according to Peabody, reformers should be trying to build a society based on its model.

Peabody believed that the more radical reformers had the wrong idea. They thought that God wanted a particular and very different form of in-

---

*To be sure, the evangelical liberals did not constitute all of the movement. There were also more modernist liberals, for whom orthodoxy was just another enemy to be fought.

dustrial organization, and their writings were aimed at bringing it about. But what God wanted, Peabody objected, was a particular and very different form of human being. After quoting from the Gospels, he summed up the attitude of Jesus Christ toward the idea of business:

> The fundamental sins of industrialism . . . are not those of the social order, but those of the unsocialized will. No rearrangement of production and distribution can of itself abolish the instincts of ambition and competition, or even the baser desires of theft, covetousness and deceit. Whatever the future of industry may be, the key to that better world is to be found, not in circumstances, but in character. That was what made it possible for Jesus, even while recognizing the perils of business life, to find in precisely that career a type of the kingdom of God.

Peabody pointed out that much of Christ's ministry, as described in the Gospels, seemed to be to "the industrialists of the world"–that is, of the world of biblical times:

> The sower in the field, the shepherd with his flock, the merchant buying pearls, the fisherman casting his net, the laborer waiting to be hired–these, and people like these, are, according to his teaching, concerned, not with demoralizing vocations from which they must free themselves if they would become disciples of Christ, but with a service worthy of the kingdom. They are instances of practical religion; their tasks may be illustrations of discipleship.[21]

A 1911 sermon by George H. Ferris of Philadelphia also addresses this point. Urging his listeners to remember that "Morality is spirituality at work," he warned that the Christian churches had to get involved, and quickly, in helping to resolve the social problems wrought by industrial capitalism. The church, Ferris declared, "must face the problems of her age, or go down."[22] In this he in effect joined forces with the Abolitionists, who, as we saw in Chapter 6, were persuaded by the Second Great Awakening of a Christian obligation not only to prepare the self for salvation but to work for the betterment of God's creation. And a part of that betterment, now that the slaves were free, was improving the conditions of those who labored. The Christian point was simple, and evangelical: Improving those conditions would improve the likelihood that more working men could be brought to Christ. Or, to turn the point around, improvements would reduce the likelihood that working men would turn to sin.

II

The anticapitalist preachers harbored no doubts about the proper role of religion in a democracy. Wrote one, with the fluid confidence that characterized so many: "[T]he place of the church and the ministry in the realization of democracy must be a place of directing power and influence; the minister must become the great mover and moulder of this great social order."[23]

Bishop Charles Williams, whose call for a greater attention by Christianity to social reform I reviewed earlier in this chapter, was also unimpressed by assertions that the church should stay away from certain spheres of life. He cautioned against "that most pernicious of heresies, the false distinction between the sacred and the secular."[24]

Social Gospel preachers who took the time to answer their opponents did not even bother to address the separation of church and state argument as it is now understood, because nobody seemed to raise it. Instead, they responded principally to religious critics who believed that the true work of the church was to save souls rather than to reform society.[25] One anticapitalist preacher, Charles Macfarland, scoffed at the critics' argument: "It is to be remembered that [Jesus] never once mentioned the Church. He always talked about the Kingdom."[26] Macfarland was wrong on one point: Christ may not have uttered the word "church" very often, but Matthew has him using it three times.[27] Still, Macfarland's theological point was an important one—the Kingdom was to be built outside the church—and his emphasis was one that the other Social Gospel preachers shared. The old Reform tradition, in which believers would look after their own souls and let the world look after itself, was not the canvas on which they wanted to paint. Like the abolitionists before them, they argued consistently for the church as a force in the world. Thus the missionary Sherwood Eddy would write in 1927 that the Christian responsibility was to replace the existing, oppressive order "by the constructive building of the new social order, the Kingdom of God on earth."[28]

If Eddy's words remind the reader of the argument between Fannie Lou Hamer and Hubert Humphrey at the 1964 Democratic National Convention (see Chapter 2), the reason is that there is a clear theological link between the two. Christians who believe that they are called to work in God's creation to prepare the way for the coming of the Kingdom will always engage the culture, often at the level of politics, in order to leave the world better than they found it. The desire to move the nation closer to what God wants it to be fired the abolitionists as well as the preachers of the Social Gospel—indeed, all through the nation's history, the same desire has led to the active involvement of Christians, speaking in their own religious voices, in our public debates over proper policy. Not until the closing decades of the twentieth century did anybody craft a serious argument that they were doing something contrary to America's constitutional inheritance or its political traditions.

There is, as we shall see in the second part of the book, a great need for the religious to engage with the culture, on issues ranging from how we value humans (by their test scores when they are young, by their wealth when they are older) to how we fight our wars (with as little sacrifice as possible) to how we decide who dies (inconvenience and expense turn out to be two reasons). The fact that not every religious voice will offer the same answers to these and other pressing dilemmas does not mean that religious voices have nothing to offer. All human beings possess, and most human beings acknowledge, an abiding hunger for transcendence, a yearning for answers—and even for questions—that press beyond the usual limits of our materialistic political thinking. We need conversation not merely about our rights but about what is right. Liberalism tends to resist this conversation by insisting on a plurality of visions of the good. But pluralism is not the same as relativism. The fact that we hold differing opinions does not mean that none of the opinions are correct. Whether our pressing dilemma is the distribution of wealth or the prevalence of abortions, when we try to shut the religious voice out of our debates, we close our eyes and ears to radical possibilities that might transform us, did we but listen.

To be sure, the possibility of our own transformation often scares us. Our human need to talk about the good—to use conversation and narrative to make moral sense of the world—is balanced by our fears of what outcome the conversation might reach. As the philosopher Charles Taylor has put the point: "[W]e can readily see why some people distrust articulation as a source of delusion or fear it as a profanation." By talking about the good, he reminds us, we may justify the bad. The very words we choose to discuss right and wrong have a power of their own, as do the sources, often sacred ones, from which we choose them. Thus our narrative of goodness, whatever its source, "can be rhetorically imitated, either to feed our self-conceit or for even more sinister purposes, such as the defence of a discreditable status quo."[29]

If we cut through some of the nonsense written about religion in public dialogue, it seems plain that the fears Taylor describes are at the core of the liberal effort to build a wall against it. The true concern is often not the form of religious argument, or whether it fits comfortably into the proper form of democratic dialogue, but rather the ends that liberals are afraid the religious voice might seek. The reason that religion was not derided as the enemy of liberalism until the 1970s is that the conservative religious populism of the early twentieth century had, by that time, been politically dead for fifty years, perhaps longer.[30] Public religion was triumphal in the middle years of the twentieth century, but liberals could march comfortably under its banner. King and the Niebuhrs were heroes in the liberal story.

But after the school prayer cases in the 1960s and the abortion decision in 1973, the banner of religious populism was raised once more.[31] The Bible that inspired Martin Luther King Jr. inspired Jerry Falwell and Pat Robertson. The difficulty for liberals was that the sources were leading, suddenly, in a direction liberalism found distasteful. It was one thing to quote the Gospel command to love thy neighbor in order to battle against racial segregation—but quite a different matter, in the liberal vision, to quote the same words to battle against abortion. The sources were the same. The cause was different.[32] So up the barriers went. The separation of church and state, which yesterday was no bar to religious activism in politics, today became the barbed-wire escarpment described in Chapter 4.[33]

So, for example, when the Roman Catholic archbishop of New Orleans threatened back in the 1950s to excommunicate Catholic legislators who voted in favor of a pending bill forcing racial segregation on private schools, no liberal voices were raised in protest. In the 1960s, when some Catholic segregationists in the South were actually excommunicated by their church, only a few white supremacists objected. Yet in the 1980s, when the Roman Catholic archbishop of New York said a few words that merely hinted at the excommunication of Catholic politicians who supported abortion rights, the firestorm of liberal indignation might have made it seem that nothing of this nature had ever happened in America before. Whereas in truth it was the cause, not the tactics, that drew liberal ire.

It is not right to call this move hypocrisy, as some conservative critics have done. It may be, as Charles Taylor acknowledges, simply fear. The power of argument resting on sacred sources was now being wielded by people whom liberals did not trust. Taylor says this fear is the fear of the activists' goals. I think the fear is the fear of losing the argument. Because the liberal answer to the rise of conservative Christian activism has been to try to construct rules for public dialogue that make it difficult, if not impossible, to express certain positions at all. These rules pretend to be merely epistemic—that is, rules about proper forms of argument and legitimate sources of authority—but they really are, as critics on the Left and the Right have pointed out, rules about substance. To take a simple example, if my religious motivation bars me from entering politics to fight against abortion, then I cannot carry on the fight at all. I call this a fear of losing the argument because we often discover, no matter how many theorists insist that free religious voices in public life will be an incoherent cacophony, that the religious voice is persuasive when other voices are not. Taylor's point is that liberals know this, and that it is that unspoken fear— the fear that resort to sacred sources might actually carry the day—that is the reason, and the only true reason, for the effort to keep the sacred sources out.

Taylor's argument suggests that, from the liberal point of view, the most important reason Moral Majority had to be destroyed was that it might otherwise turn out to represent a majority. The democratic risk is always that the other side might prevail; the current extremist version of separationism is designed to reduce that risk. But religious populism is like the Hydra: Cut off one head and two more shall take its place. Liberals imagine that the problem is the organizations of conservative Christianity, that if these groups would only go away, everything would be fine. In this, liberals are mistaken. The problem is the conditions in a materially prosperous but spiritually impoverished America that give rise to popular religious discontent. The lesson of the 1960s has been forgotten by liberals, perhaps because they are now the establishment, with a considerable stake in the status quo: If you do not change the underlying structure, you do not get rid of the problem. If one has fears of the steadily rolling tide of conservative religious activism, the answer is not, Canute-like, to decree that it must cease; the answer is to calm the storm. But calming the storm would require compromise; and compromise requires conversation; and if the religious voice is not welcome at the table, conversation is impossible.

So the storm continues to rage.

III

The argument against religious engagement, as we have already seen, is both dangerous and wrong, to say nothing of undemocratic. But the power of the argument in the contemporary culture should not be underestimated. Consider a single example. In 1997, the Pontifical Council for Social Communications, an arm of the Vatican, issued a short paper entitled *Ethics in Advertising*. This rather modest document suggested that consumer advertising be governed by an ethical code that would, among other things, resist the sexualization of human beings and the use of deceit or outright falsehood as selling tools. The response of Madison Avenue was depressingly common, but at least succinct. In the words of one advertising executive, "They should stick to religion, and we'll stick to advertising."[34]

Ah, how depressingly common the refrain—even when, as in this case, those speaking in the religious voice were careful to be prophetic rather than coercive. The Vatican paper did not call for a new state regulatory regime to force advertising agencies to do the right thing. It did not demand a boycott or threaten litigation. The report tried instead, in the manner of the great prophets, to persuade the executives themselves to do the right thing. But the cultural wall of separation between religion and morality is often higher than the constitutional wall of separation between church and state. Even the prophetic voice, it turns out, is often dishonored, treated as though it should be ignored simply because it is religious. Our culture is so awash in self-seeking and self-fulfillment and simple selfishness that the merest suggestion of voluntary self-restraint is viewed as an interference with individual freedom . . . the freedom, that is, to hear no contrary moral argument. Maybe advertising agencies, like abortion clinics, should be entitled to the physical protection of special zones designed to prevent those who believe they are speaking the Lord's words from getting too close to those who do not want to listen. To make sure that the religious stick to religion, which is, according to our dominant cultural ethos, unconnected with life.

I suppose a factory owner, his profits threatened by the Social Gospel movement, could have made the same argument a century earlier: "They should stick to religion, and we'll stick to manufacturing." As could the slaveholder responding to the abolitionist: "They should stick to religion, and we'll stick to running the plantation." But they would have been just as foolish, just as limited in their vision, as the advertising executives who want no religious criticism of their work—and just as wrong about the proper place of religion in a thriving democratic culture. For religion, as we saw in the opening chapters, has no sphere, and the river of serious belief cannot be dammed. The waters will flow where the waters will flow, because the Lord will go where the Lord will go.

8

Other Possibilities

I HAVE ARGUED SO FAR that the religious voice is needed in democratic politics and should be welcomed there; that religions nevertheless should be cautious about deciding when and how to involve themselves in public issues, for their religious integrity is at risk; and that when they do decide to take an active part in our public debates, they should, with rare exceptions, avoid the temptation to take sides in electoral contests. I have suggested that religious believers are at their best when they spend more time in the garden than in the wilderness, so that, if they are called to enter the public fray, they come to it purified, as prophetic voices calling the nation to account for its wrongs rather than as angry voices telling the nation what to do. Still, as I have emphasized throughout, these rules are but guidelines. Sometimes a moral wrong will seem so great that a lengthy and strenuous engagement in politics cannot be avoided. The abolitionists in the nineteenth century set themselves the goal of working to end slavery even if it could not be accomplished in their lifetimes. Many in today's pro-life and antipoverty movements would say they are doing the same. I do not propose to choose for other religious believers which issues are of such moment that they have no choice but to battle in the wilderness; I urge only that they take the time for prayer and discernment to be sure that they have chosen the right issues, the right tactics, and the right moment. The alternative is to rush headlong, the mistake that so many white clergy made in the 1980s and 1990s and many of the black clergy two or three decades earlier.

So, what are some other possibilities for the religious who want to maintain their own way of life, refuse to embrace the culture, and do not want to resort to politics? In this chapter, will briefly sketch three ideas.

PARALLEL INSTITUTIONS

In February 1999, Paul Weyrich, head of the Free Congress Foundation and one of the fathers of the contemporary conservative movement, fired off a letter that stunned his many supporters, a letter that seemed to sound retreat. Weyrich had long argued that conservative evangelicals should be more politically involved. He was instrumental in the founding of both Moral Majority and the Christian Coalition. But, in 1999, he wrote that although conservatives "got our people elected," electoral success "did not result in the adoption of our agenda." Why not? Because "politics itself has failed."[1]

Weyrich was writing, it must be noted, in the wake of the Clinton impeachment battle, which many conservative activists considered a kind of referendum on where the culture is now. Clinton's supporters, having won the fight, wanted to move on. According to the polls, so did most of the country. But movement conservatives by and large felt otherwise. If Clinton could remain in office despite being caught in an extramarital affair and then lying about it under oath—so the basic argument ran—the nation was in very bad shape.

Not every conservative activist agreed with the impeachment centeredness of the movement during 1999. Many religious conservatives argued against drawing broad conclusions about the national mood from analyzing the Senate's decision not to remove Clinton from office.[2] And the syndicated columnist George Will, never short of a one-liner, announced that the machinery of impeachment proved "too large to employ against someone as small as Bill Clinton."[3]

To Weyrich, however, the result was no joking matter: "If there were a moral majority out there, Bill Clinton would have been driven out of office months ago." Then how did Clinton manage to hang on? He survived, wrote Weyrich, because "we are caught up in a cultural collapse of historic proportions, a collapse so great that it simply overwhelms politics." The nation's entire culture was in the grip of "the ideology of Political Correctness," which meant that "the enemy" had taken over most cultural institutions—he named specifically the public schools, the federal government, the media, the courts, even many churches—and those institutions were now making war, he argued, on traditional values. He announced flatly: "I believe that we probably have lost the culture war."

His solution was separation, separation "from the institutions that have been captured by the ideology of Political Correctness, or by other enemies of our traditional culture." He urged evangelicals to consider ways to avoid the influence of the culture, particularly on children. He pointed to home schooling, to private courts,[4] to television-free households. "I'm not suggesting that we all become Amish or move to Idaho," he explained, but "I do think that we have to look at what we can do to separate ourselves from this hostile culture."

Well. For me, an evangelical Christian who is hardly a movement conservative, the Weyrich letter nevertheless carries a certain poignancy, even though he is discovering nothing new. John Calvin told us half a millennium ago that the world was a place of depravity, and Christian reformers all through history who have gone to politics to try to advance their agendas have run up against the same blank wall that Weyrich now finds so frustrating. But the Christian life should not be about getting the right candidates elected or advancing the right agenda. The Christian life should be about living in a way that Christ's light shines forth. In that sense, by calling for a separation from the culture, Weyrich is returning to what most evangelical preachers argued through most of the twentieth century.

There is, however, a deeper point to Weyrich's argument, a point missed by both liberal critics who have derided his analysis of the culture and conservative critics who have derided his solution to the problem.[5] The deeper point is that the devoutly religious need more time in the garden, less in the wilderness. The parallel institutions that Weyrich describes are exactly what people of faith should have built from the start—not so much to avoid the culture but to create a moral cocoon in which to raise children, strengthen families, and work in community with other believers to reach a deeper understanding of God's will. The state, of course, prefers to have all children (and, preferably, all adults) involved in institutions over which it exercises a degree of control. That is one reason that liberalism places so much emphasis on public schooling and so strongly resists placing many educational choices in the hands of parents.[6] But that is no more than the instinctive totalitarian impulse of every successful state, and should not be taken seriously by religionists.

Dissenting evangelical preachers insisted well into the twentieth century that Christians should separate from the culture and from the state in order to preserve their purity. Journalists report that this movement, which not long ago seemed to be dying, may once more be picking up steam.[7] Setting to one side Weyrich's political concerns, reasons are easy to identify. Indeed, with the traditional conception even of so religiously fundamental an institution as marriage nowadays up for grabs, there may be fewer and fewer reasons for traditional religionists to remain engaged with the culture. (Perhaps Weyrich should have listed in his letter, as an institution that should be privatized, marriage itself, for traditionalists could insist on religious marriages run by religious rules rather than secular marriages subject to state regulation.)[8] The state, as we have seen from the start, has one set of meanings it wants to pronounce. The religious faiths that are called to resistance should stand for a radically different set. Resisting faiths can only develop those different meanings, however, if they exist at some distance from the dominant culture. Otherwise, Weyrich is exactly right: Religion will simply be overwhelmed.

The appeal of Weyrich's argument should not rest on whether one happens to share his politics. It should appeal, to some degree, to anyone who believes in religion as a serious and transcendent enterprise, and anyone who thinks, as the Western religions all teach, that God has a knowable will and that human beings are obligated to discover it and to follow it. Indeed, I would argue (although many liberals would scoff) that the argument should appeal to anybody who believes in genuine diversity, for Weyrich contends that the culture should respect the spaces in which radical differences are nurtured. Of course believers should have avenues of escape from the culture. Of course believers should have space to make their own decisions, without state interference, about what moral understanding their children need, both to function in this world and to prepare for the next. Of course a society that truly values diversity and pluralism should support the development of communities that will reach radically different conclusions from those of the dominant culture.

Contemporary liberalism, unfortunately, is skeptical of what seems to many religious believers quite obvious. Liberalism is suspicious of parents: What if they teach their children something wicked?[9] Evangelicals are suspicious right back: What if the state does?[10] The answer is not, as much of the literature of liberalism suggests that all children learn certain critical skills. (Critical skills are fine but it is not possible to teach them without carrying along a large set of ideological assumptions.) The answer is to nurture many different centers of meaning, including many different understandings on how to find meaning, so that the state will have competition. To do otherwise is to yield to the totalitarian impulse, the impulse that says everybody must abide by *my* ideology.[11]

The other point of Weyrich's letter is that the Electoral Objection, as I have been calling it, turns out to be true. Politics, in the long run, cannot succeed in advancing the cause of religious truth, and overreliance on politics is damaging to religious integrity. I do not mean that there can be no successes. Abolitionism was a success. But it succeeded only through long and patient agitation and, in the end, a bloody civil war. Thus, as I have argued, politics—especially electoral politics—should be the rare choice. The better choice is witness, speaking to the culture in the prophetic voice. Witness is part of what can be taught and nurtured and supported in the separate institutions that Weyrich wants evangelicals to build. After all, as Roger Williams understood, the garden wall will eventually be breached: The culture will find a way in, no matter how far away the religionist might burrow. And, when the breach occurs, as Williams argued, the religionist must leave the garden and go out into the wilderness prepared once more to do battle.

THE GIFT OF TIME

If religious believers are to resist, they will have to spend more time in the garden, just as Paul Weyrich prescribes. No easier solution is available. Believers will have to invest time from their precious, irreplaceable store of hours and days. Time away from the wilderness, time with families, time spent walking in the garden (figuratively or literally) with other believers, time in community, time in prayer, time searching for the best version they can discover of transcendent purpose: These are the gifts that religious believers must give to one another if resistance and renewal are even to be attempted.

But American culture nowadays demands as much of our time as it can get.[12] And, by allowing us all less time, our culture is beginning to devalue the very act that makes us humans unique in the animal kingdom. I refer to thinking itself. We devalue thinking. Not thought—not intelligence—but *thinking.* And not the swift, intuitive thought of the *I-need-an-answer-right-now* society, but the pondering, reflective thought of one who knows that hard questions are called hard questions for a reason. Thinking as action, thinking as discipline, thinking as time-consuming ritual.

Hannah Arendt, in her wonderful book about thinking, pointed to something that most previous commentators on Plato's dialogues had missed, or at least thought not worthy of mention. Now and then, when confronted with a difficult question, Socrates, instead of tossing off a quick, breathtaking argument, would simply stop and think.[13] Often Plato would put it that way: "Here Socrates paused to think." The phrase, or one much like it, occurs in the *Crito.* It occurs in the *Republic,* in that marvelous passage where Socrates is gently mocking the idea of the state that maintains its members in luxury. It occurs in other places, too. Socrates, we are told time and again, stopped to think.

That is something that contemporary life does not encourage in us—that we stop and think. The idea of stopping to think—as opposed to the thinking fast that we tend to reward—proposes that there are advantages to reflection. To *stop* and think proposes that we cease to do what we were doing when the need to think came upon us. Sometimes, when we take a bit of our precious time and ponder a problem rather than leaping at its throat, we will come to a wiser solution. Perhaps a scientifically wiser solution; perhaps a morally wiser one. The short of it is that in a society that truly cares about either morality or science, there should be rewards for those whose intelligence is of a patient, reflective character, and not just those whose minds tend to work very fast. Unfortunately, we tend to omit patience when we measure worth.

Consider standardized tests for a moment. You have two hours, maybe three, to answer a set of questions. The premium is not really on knowledge, or on reasoning, and it certainly is not on reflective character. No, the premium is on speed. We value the student who can solve all the problems in three hours above the student who might need five or six. We label the faster student more intelligent, but what we really mean is just that he is faster. And in rewarding the quick answer, we penalize the reflective one; indeed, nothing in all our complex testing machinery seeks to figure out what our young people can do upon reflection . . . that is, in true Platonic fashion, after stopping to think. We train them not to stop and think but to think fast.

And that is the style of our culture. Television talk shows, quite famously, are arranged around a rapid and fluent patter of conversation. Television producers hate guests who stop and think about their answers: "Dead air," they call these silences, and the hosts are trained to avoid them. As though silence is the enemy. As though taking the time to think is un-American.

When we lose Socrates, we lose reflection, and when we lose reflection, we lose wisdom. And it is not only wisdom that we lose, although that is bad enough. When we lose Socrates, when we lose reflection, we lose a kind of closeness to reality, the ability to see the things that exist only in nuance, in hidden corners, in the uncommon details of life. And when we lose sight of detail, we lose sight of God, of our createdness, of our connection to, and obligation to, something larger than the fulfillment of immediate desire or need. Yet if we have no connection to anything larger than ourselves, if the daily grubbing for existence turns out to be all there is of existence—well, small wonder in such a world that we cannot talk about morality. We cannot talk about it because we do not at bottom believe in it.

This trend is one against which the religious should do battle. God rarely delivers quick and easy answers. The process of discernment is a reflective one. It costs us time.[14] And time seems to be in ever shorter supply. We Americans spend more hours at work than we used to. For professionals especially, the barrier between work life and home life has disintegrated. There is never a moment, it seems, when we simply shut our desk drawers and leave. We take our work with us. Bulging briefcases are out of fashion, but the technologies of information flow keep us always in touch with our work. Weekends are meaningless. Even vacations are becoming meaningless, for work comes along. Worst of all, for many otherwise deeply religious people, the Sabbath is meaningless: It has become, for millions, simply a day like any other day, a day for little rest and lots of work. We are told in Genesis that God rested on the seventh day, but our work is evidently much more important than his.

THE POWER OF THE PURSE

My next suggestion is that the religious spend more time contemplating what is, for most of us, one of the toughest sacrifices we can make: not buying things we want and can afford. I am not referring to a general norm of frugality, although that, too, used to be a staple component of many different traditions. I am referring, as the saying goes, to putting your money where your mouth is—or, more precisely, not putting it there. I am referring to boycotts.

Contemporary American culture is enthusiastically materialistic. Disposable income, personal possessions, and the value of investments seem more important than anything else in measuring the individual. Religions, by and large, teach otherwise, although some Christian preachers have built large followings for versions of what we might as well call the Gospel of wealth.

But the principal point is this: Whatever religions may value, the culture values money. So, if politics fails or looks too dangerous, and yet the religionist wants to influence and improve the culture, one way to do so is to look for opportunities to boycott, and urge others to boycott, products that seem culturally destructive. For boycott, too, can be a form of witness, and, if many join, can hardly be ignored. For example, religious groups were instrumental in 1992 in persuading a number of stores to remove from their shelves rapper Ice-T's *Cop Killer* album, although the opposition of police groups probably helped as well. Religious objections in 1989 seem to have led Pepsi-Cola to drop a series of commercials featuring pop singer Madonna, some of whose videos were perceived as mocking important religious symbols.

Now and then, I read of some Hollywood mogul complaining about people who express views on films they have not seen—as though the only reasonable plan is to pay money to see the movie and only then to decide whether to boycott it or not. Other critics argue that consumer boycotts amount to censorship, but that argument is surely sufficiently weak to need no answer. (Well, maybe a small answer: If I refuse, on principle, to pay to see films in which black actors behave in the idiotic fashion so common in Hollywood of the 1930s and 1940s, am I censoring the films or merely acting as a consumer in the marketplace and expressing my preferences? If I persuade others to join me—well, is that not how market solutions are supposed to function?)

To be sure, not all boycotts are successful. For example, 135,000 Americans in 1992 signed on to a new television and motion picture code, promising to boycott "all motion pictures except those that do not offend decency and Christian morality." (One Jewish organization also signed.) But it is not at all evident from the output of films and television programs that the boycott has had much effect on Hollywood. In the mid-1990s, the Southern Baptist Convention called on Christian families to boycott the Walt Disney Company, both because of what was seen as a turn away from family values in Disney's entertainment fare and because of the company's extension of health benefits to the domestic partners of its gay employees. Several other religious organizations, both Protestant and Catholic, eventually joined the protest. That boycott, too, was a failure, if the measure of success is a change in company policy. (According to media reports, not many Southern Baptists even stopped going to Disney World.)

One explanation for the different results is that most Christians, like most people, feel far more threatened by gun violence and a culture of indiscriminate sex than by the acknowledgment that gay people exist, form stable partnerships, and are not going to disappear. Another is that a target of a boycott that relies upon the substantial profits it earns in the Bible Belt—a chain store, for example—will be more susceptible to pressure than a more settled and (internationally) powerful entertainment conglomerate. A third is that the would-be boycotters are just as likely as anybody else to give in to the many temptations our seductive culture displays.

Whatever might be the explanation, it is perhaps unfair to say, as I did above, that any of the boycotts actually failed. That depends, once more, on how success and failure are assessed. As I noted, if by success we mean the accomplishment of change in the challenged practices, then many more boycotts surely fail than succeed. But that measure may not be the correct one. Paul Weyrich, in his 1999 letter calling for the establishment of separate institutions, pointed out that religionists who choose the path of boycott might or might not affect the culture, but they certainly affect themselves: "They separated themselves from some of the cultural rot, and to that extent . . . succeeded."[15] He was speaking not of political activism but of protection—protection of self, of family, and, especially, of children—from a culture that amounted, in his words, to "a sewer."

And this argument, it seems to me, is correct. Boycotts—that is, refusals to participate in the dangerous activities of a dangerous culture—are also a part of separating, of remaining in the garden. If others can be persuaded to move to the garden as well, the garden is better for it; and, in the long run, so is the wilderness. Religion, as we have seen from the start, resists. The space in which resistance is nurtured must be shielded from the ravages of a culture that would gleefully destroy it. A culture as powerful as ours has a teleology of its own. It sweeps aside opposition. It tries to draw everything to itself. It denies differences when they threaten its hegemony. And, just like the state, it tries either to domesticate religion or to destroy it. Which is why the religious must resist, even when the resistance consists of a simple refusal to participate . . . or to buy.

In the coming chapters, I will discuss some issues over which religions might choose to resist. As I hope the reader will quickly see, I am not attempting to establish a correct religious position, or even a correct Christian one, on the problems I analyze. But I do look for places where religions might find surprising commonalities as they struggle to preserve themselves and their powers of resistance.

PART II

Religion's Voice

9

Wars . . .
And Other Violences

IN THE EARLY SPRING OF 1999, a group of religious leaders publicly requested that NATO suspend its bombing of Serbia during the Easter weekend. After all, they pointed out, the White House had chosen to end its recent attack on Iraq prior to the start of Ramadan, with an eye to avoiding offense to Muslims. If it is inappropriate to attack a Muslim country during the holiest season in the Muslim calendar, the argument ran, might it not also be inappropriate to attack a Christian country during the holiest season in the Christian calendar?[1]

Evidently, the analogy fails. Nobody ever said why, but the leaders of NATO—including the President of the United States—did not so much reject the appeal as ignore it. The bombing continued, right into the Orthodox Easter weekend and, indeed, on the day on which Orthodox Christians observe Easter itself.

What is striking about this episode is not the fact that military and political leaders decided to pay no attention to religious concerns when they interfered with fighting—that has been the rule rather than the exception throughout our history, whether during the war in Vietnam or the Civil War. What is striking, rather, is the vast religious silence into which the Easter 1999 protest dropped. And not only the Easter protest—the entire war. The call for an Easter recess in the bombing was the product of conservative activists—one of the many odd twists in recent political and ideological history. But liberals sat this one out. There was no rush of religious leadership to demand a halt to the bombing; there was none of the popular religious antiwar fervor of the Vietnam era; there were, apparently, few sermons or prayers on the war, other than prayers for the swift success and safe return of "our" people.[2] The last great American war of the 1900s was in this sense like the last great American war of the 1800s, the Spanish-American War—the nation's religions, like the nation's people, just wanted to make sure that it finished quickly and the good guys won.

The change has been rapid and swift and unsettling. It seems only yesterday that John Updike, commenting on the American withdrawal from Vietnam, proclaimed that God had taken his blessing away from the United States. In the past (at least in our iconography), we always were the winners. Always. But not in Vietnam. Whether, as conservatives say, we did not try hard enough, or, as liberals say, we should not have been there in the first place, the fact is that America did not win. The withdrawal was hardly the fault of the war's religious opponents, but the national exhaustion after more than a decade of war without progress did seem to underscore one of their points: War is horrible and should be fought rarely, and only to avoid greater horrors. This solid, traditionally Christian position, is radical in American terms but could present an important voice in our public debates.

Except that the voice has vanished.

In Yugoslavia, NATO launched the largest bombing campaign in the history of warfare. The United States expended nearly every cruise missile in its arsenal. The cause, most people seemed to think, was a just one. But all the principled voices of opposition to wars past, voices reminding us of the Christian pacifist tradition, for example, or the Catholic "just war" tradition—voices arguing that all wars are wrong, or that most wars are wrong, or that rules of proportionality must apply—this rich chorus, already shaky by the time of the 1991 war against Iraq, seems to have disappeared from American political culture.

To be sure, the tradition of Christian pacifism is not rooted as deeply in American history as some might suppose. During the Revolutionary War and the War of 1812, one rarely heard religious voices objecting to the very idea of fighting violently for the ends of the state. As we saw in Chapter 7, the peace movement in the United States, an outgrowth of the Social Gospel movement, did not really take shape until the late years of the nineteenth century. There were religious objectors to World War I and even to World War II—although, aside from the fascists, they eventually quieted. And, certainly, there were religious objectors to the Korean War, including some religious dissenters who went to prison for their failure to register for the draft and stayed there until President George Bush pardoned them in 1992.

But nobody goes to prison over war anymore.

The religious voice that was so crucial in our debates over wars past has all but vanished from the politics of war. The omission is costing us.

Religious opposition to violence, including the violence of war, has become rare, or at least rarely covered in the press, perhaps because it seems boring and irrelevant in a country not the least bit reluctant about projecting its fantastic military power as long as no risk is involved . . . no risk, that is, to any Americans. We act nowadays in accordance with the weird new politico-military doctrine that we might call Unidirectional Isolationism: There are loads of causes around the world worth killing for but none worth dying for. As with everything else in society, the motto seems to be: No sacrifice. That sums up the method by which America evidently plans to fight in the new century. We will kill as many of the enemy as we can, so efficiently that journalists will not even bother to report the numbers, but we will not put a single soldier of ours in harm's way. The implicit message of Unidirectional Isolationism is that American lives are worth far more than the lives of anybody else in the world. This doctrine is perfect for the consumerist age, proposing as it does that there is no reason to feel guilty about sitting at home and watching the war on television. There is no reason to risk our lives, because there is nothing worth dying for. One might suppose that so profoundly antihuman a notion of warfare (if indeed there are any pro-human notions) would generate intense and relentless opposition from a religious community that is supposed to call us to be different and better than we are.

One would be wrong.

The nation's religions—particularly the mainstream Protestant denominations—are far too busy worrying about who can marry whom and which songs are too offensive to sing. Why spend precious resources fighting over fighting? It is not, after all, as though any of this warfare affects anybody who actually matters, like a congregant or a member of a favored minority group. There is no draft any longer, which means no American goes to war who has not chosen the military life, and we prefer not to risk the lives of even our volunteers. So although the churches might pray for the safety of "our" forces, and the wiser among them (wiser in the sense in which the word *wisdom* is used in the book of Proverbs) might pray for the people on the other side of the battle as well, there is little if any marching in the streets. No candlelight vigils, no denunciations of war profiteering, nobody chained to the gates of a military base. Or, at least, none is sufficiently interesting to gain more than a passing mention in the news columns. Either the press has gone to sleep or the religions have. It is the second of these two possibilities that worries me more. Our new warfighting doctrine is an immoral horror, and the political and media cultures that allow it and even encourage it ("The

Pentagon says there were no American casualties"—therefore we can switch the channel) are cultures that must be lifted from their depravity.

Once upon a time, that was what religious witness was for.

11

The Bible is full of wars. Not only wars, but slaughters, genocides, in which entire nations, entire peoples, are wiped from the face of the earth. Believers—other than those who conveniently limit the binding biblical texts to those with which they happen to agree—must find ways to make sense of the horrors of which they read.

One solution is to be harsh but firm. The evangelical scholar Gleason L. Archer, a prominent advocate of biblical literalism, has this to say in explaining Joshua's extermination (Josh. 6) of the entire population of the city of Jericho:

> [W]e need to recognize first of all that the biblical record indicates that Joshua was simply carrying out God's orders in the matter. . . . Therefore we must recognize that our criticism cannot be leveled at Joshua or the Israelites but at the God whose bidding they obeyed. (Otherwise we must demonstrate our own special competence to correct the biblical record on the basis of our own notions of probability as to what God might or might not decide to do.)

Professor Archer has already raised the stakes: If we want to criticize the massacre, he insists, we must criticize the God who commanded it, not the humans who performed it, unless we possess the confidence to insist that Joshua was wrong, that we know better than he did, and better than the author of the passage did, what God's commands were likely to be. Lest we miss the point, Archer continues to build for us the awesomeness of the critical task:

> If criticism there be, we should not stop there, for the destruction of Jericho was far smaller an affair than the annihilation of the populations of Sodom and Gomorrah and their allies in Genesis 19:24–25. And then again this volcanic catastrophe was far less significant in the loss of life than Noah's Flood, which, except for Noah's family, wiped out the entire human race.[3]

We will return to Archer's argument in a moment, but let us pause at this point. Already he is offering an important theological proposition—that those who follow God's instructions are above criticism because God is above criticism. (This is quite independent of whether one agrees with Archer's belief, which happens also to be mine, that the biblical text is above criticism.) Is it obvious that Professor Archer is correct? Rabbi Harold S. Kushner, for example, has written that he is forced to believe the Holocaust was the product of human sin rather than divine command because he could never love or follow a God who would command so horrible an event.[4] Kushner implies thereby that it *is* possible to criticize God; or, rather, that a God who is above criticism would also have to be a God who is above certain acts.[5]

This is a useful way of construing the problem. Believers aplenty, including leaders of the pro-life movement, routinely condemn terrorists who bomb abortion clinics or kill doctors. The usual argument, both within and without the movement, is that violence is not the proper way to show respect for life. Yet why is it not sufficient for the terrorists to answer that they have done what they have done because God has commanded it? The believer cannot reply, "You are not to follow God if he so commands"—although the nonbeliever naturally has no trouble enunciating this proposition. One is reminded here of the Jewish philosopher Martin Buber's ironic defense of the great reformers Martin Luther and John Calvin for persecuting their theological disputants. Once you "believe that the Word of God has so descended among men that it can be clearly known and must therefore be exclusively advocated," Buber wrote, you have little choice but to do whatever is necessary.[6] (The irony flows from the double meaning: Buber seems to be referring not simply to the belief in one's rightness, but to Jesus himself. The image in John's Gospel of the Word made flesh and descending among men (John 1) is a claim not merely about physicality but about knowability. Buber, therefore, is suggesting that believing in a God whose physical presence has been and can be experienced is part of what might lead to persecution, a proposition that Christians must not forget.)

Buber thus reminds us that the believer who criticizes the person who perpetrates horror in the Lord's name must offer *theological* criticism. Therefore the believer, by criticizing the attacks at all, is implicitly responding, "No, you are wrong. God did not so command." And how does the believer know this? One possibility is that God has made a special communication to the believer, telling him that the terrorist is wrong. Another is that the believer simply knows, based on his own religious tradition, that God (a knowable God, obviously) would never issue such an edict.* In either case, the substance of the objection is the same: The reason the believer knows that God *did not* command the terrorism is that the believer knows that God *would not* command such a thing.

One must be wary of carrying this argument too far. In Chapter 6, we encountered the abolitionist preachers and their biblical arguments against slavery. Some historians would deny the role of belief in God's will as an important force in abolitionism, contending instead that the preachers either played a minor part or were actually motivated by other, nonreligious factors. I do not see much reason, apart from antireligious ideology, to accept this theory. But if one does accept it—and it must, I suppose, have been true of at least some of the abolitionists—then one might decide that the antislavery clergy, despite their vehemence, were actually fitting God's will to a previously determined secular moral view. In other words, they were simply saying that they could not accept a God who would will chattel slavery, and, therefore, since they did accept God, chattel slavery must not be a part of his will.

This rather seductive syllogism ultimately turns true religion on its head. It creates a God (note the order of verb and object) who is incapable of decreeing that which the listener does not want God to decree. If God does seem to decree something with which the listener disagrees, the interpreter must be in error. This approach to understanding God, an approach that disables God from requiring anything unpleasing to his people, is all too common in the modern world; but to call it religion is a little like calling the act of fulfilling a child's every desire raising that child. In both cases, the description is literally accurate but functionally nonsense. The traditional response of both Christians and Jews to this apparent contradiction has been to refer to some larger text—generally, the Scriptures—to determine what God is likely or unlikely to will. If what happens is inconsistent with God's rules or promises, it must be happening against his will.

This may explain why even a committed literalist like Professor Archer accepts the necessity of sometimes explaining why God would will some of the troubling things he evidently does, rather than simply accepting it. Archer does not imply that God's will is to be obeyed only when it is understood; I suspect he believes that there are times when what God wills seems to be so horrific that we have to try to gain an understanding as an

---

*A third possibility is that the believer holds no actual belief about the content of God's will on this point and is merely searching for an argument that will persuade the terrorist to desist. This approach, however, reduces the objection to blasphemy, which must be ignored.

aid to our own ultimate task of obedience. And so, when he offers an
explanation for God's judgment on Jericho, as on Sodom and Gomorrah
and on the whole world at the time of the Flood, his words begin to
sound harsher still:

> The loss of innocent life in the demolition of Jericho was much to be re-
> gretted, but we must recognize that there are times when only radical sur-
> gery will save the life of a cancer-stricken body. The whole population of
> the antediluvian civilization had become hopelessly infected with the can-
> cer of moral depravity (Gen. 6:5). Had any of them been permitted to live
> while still in rebellion against God, they might have infected Noah's family
> as well. The same was true of the detestable inhabitants of Sodom. . . . So
> also it was with Jericho.[7]

Professor Archer goes on to explain that there were a number of peoples who had to be destroyed or nearly so before it was possible for the people of Israel to reside safely in the land of Israel. If God had been more
merciful, he suggests, the people of Israel might not have survived.

The scary metaphor of killing humans like cancerous cells is not, of
course, original; it is a commonplace, for example, of radical secular thinkers
of a variety of political stripes who need a rhetorical tool to justify the resort
to violence.[8] And its weakness in Archer's argument is the same as its weakness every place else it is used: Individual human beings do *not* relate to humanity as a whole in the same way that individual cells relate to the body.
The cell's very purpose—and its only purpose—is the good health and survival of the organism of which it is a part. The cell is possessed of no independent importance or value; whereas, in biblical terms, individual human
beings stand at the apex of God's creation, each made in God's own image,
and each possessed of that horrible and wonderful gift of free will.

Yet it does seem to me that one must take Rabbi Kushner's objection seriously. We have no choice, in considering the Holocaust, to say that God
allowed it to happen, as God, until quite late, did nothing to prevent it. But
what God allows to happen is not necessarily identical to what God wants
to happen. The Holocaust was accomplished by very bad people aided by
very indifferent people and very frightened people. Most great evil is accomplished in a similar fashion. Ideology and tribalism help. It is not only
the Bible that is full of great slaughters; so is the rest of recorded history,
from virtually every corner of the globe. As a Christian, I agree with those
Jewish scholars who insist that the Holocaust is ultimately unexplainable;

or, if it must be explained, I cast my lot with those Christian scholars who consider it "an eruption of demonism" into God's world.[9]

Demons erupt when we humans cease tending with care to the barriers that keep them at bay. Many strong religious believers contend that we stand today in a world in which the barriers have been weakened by cultural, economic, and technological forces. Perhaps we do. (See Chapter 10.) My larger concern here is the way that the ability of humans to do violence is also an invitation to the demons. Violence has a teleology of its own, or so it often seems: Our ability to do it supplies the compelling reason to do it. It is quite striking—and should, for the religionist, be quite troubling—that we Americans have come to accept an ideology of violence proposing that there are many causes worth killing for but few or any worth dying for. Even the sweeping violence of war has changed. Once it was a shared and horrible ritual of sacrifice in which we were forced by the suffering and death rained upon us to reexamine constantly the principles that moved us to fight.[10] Today it is a kind of televised video game in which public participation is limited to watching broadcasts from the nose cameras of cruise missiles, and the reporters who bring us the stories believe they have done their jobs as soon as they have assured us that there are no American casualties. Casualties among the enemy are the enemy's problem.

The new rule seems to be that we should have no concern about what our armed forces are asked to do as long as our soldiers do not die doing it. This basically nationalist message is one that serious religionists in general—Christians in particular—should find troubling. What kind of a nation are we, after all, when we judge our leaders' decisions to fight simply on whether we achieve an appropriate kill ratio? During the Vietnam War, thinking of this kind was criticized harshly by religious leaders. Nowadays, although some few clergy express concern about how we choose to kill, there is mostly a vast religious silence. One hesitates to suggest the obvious: that the Vietnam-era Christian message that we as a nation should not so freely kill tends to resonate with congregations only when young Americans are actually dying.

III

Which leads to the heart of the traditional Christian criticism of war. Wars are fought by countries, for causes in which the leaders believe. Critics of religious participation in politics are fond of arguing that religion has been the cause of many wars in the past. Partly true—but only partly. The religious wars, almost always, were fought by princes and their armies for some tangible benefit, such as territory or trade routes. Religion was often a convenient excuse, but it was rarely the underlying purpose. (Even during the Crusades, no effort was made to convert the Muslims.)[11] I am not suggesting that religions bear no blame for the evil they allow to be done in their name. Often the leaders of the medieval church were eager to enlist the aid of princes in their yearning to create what the historian Paul Johnson calls a "total" Christian society—and if force was needed for that act of creation, then force it would be. But there is plenty of blame to go around—and, in particular, the princes who commanded the armies that actually fought the wars surely believed the causes were just. Even before the advent of the modern nation-state, wars were usually fought in the national interest.

The Roman Catholic doctrine of just and unjust wars is usually traced to Augustine and was resurrected in the Middle Ages, partly in response to the sense that too many horrors were being committed in God's name—although, to be sure, the doctrine did not stop the horrors. The doctrine is a complex one, and this is not the place for more than a brief outline.[12] As developed by Augustine, the just war doctrine has two parts—*jus ad bellum* (justice for war) and *jus in bello* (justice in war). *Jus ad bellum* allows war only when it is a last resort; when it is declared by legitimate authority; and when it is morally justifiable. The moral justification requirement leads to still more complex arguments still. Augustine, for example, did not think self-defense a sufficient justification for killing another human being. Later just war theorists believed that self-defense is an adequate ground for war, as long as the absolute minimum necessary force is used. All just war theorists apparently agree that one state may intervene in the territories of another to reestablish order that has broken down or to prevent a great injustice that the second state is refusing to correct.

Once a war has been justified by consideration of the principle of *jus ad bellum,* the just war theorist is hardly at the end of the analysis. Now the strategy by which the war is fought must be justified, by the principle of *jus in bello.* This principle in turn has two components: a rule of proportionality and a rule of discrimination. Proportionality requires the use of only the minimal force necessary to prevail; but even that minimal force cannot be used if the consequences are likely to be too terrible. Discrimination means, at minimum, that a nation cannot intentionally target noncombatants, such as civilians. Some theorists would add that one cannot even target enemy combatants unless they are behaving aggressively.

I am less interested in the moral truth of just war doctrine than in the questions it would force us to confront, could it but be a voice frequently heard in our national councils. In the first place, just war doctrine requires the believer to consider the cause for which the war is being fought. The Christian subject to the discipline of the just war doctrine can never claim "following orders" as a defense to a charge of immoral conduct. It is not enough, in just war terms, that the cause be a just one—for killing is not justified in all just causes. Rather, the war is justified only if there is no other way to prevent the occurrence of an even greater horror. A nation's desire for territory or trade, or even for security or revenge, is not, generally, enough. A war to stop the Holocaust could plainly meet this test. A war to end the "ethnic cleansing" of the Balkans might have met the test, but would have met it better had the war started when the cleansing did. The invasion of Grenada, if truly necessary to save lives, would perhaps meet the test . . . barely. But the invasion of Panama, to take one example of a popular recent American war, probably would not: It is difficult to justify killing so many in order to capture one.

Just war doctrine, as we have seen, also requires a test of proportionality. This does not mean that a nation is justified in doing whatever its enemy has done. It means that a nation is justified in using enough force, but just enough force, to prevail. The just war doctrine does not allow killing more of the enemy than necessary. It does not allow killing at all when other tactics are available. And it is impossible, in just war terms, to justify the deliberate targeting of noncombatants.* For example, when President Ronald Reagan ordered the shelling of Lebanon in retaliation for the killing of 239 American marines in 1983, it is unlikely that just war doctrine could have provided an excuse, for it was perfectly predictable that noncombatants would die and very hard to ensure that the shells would find the killers. And terrorist attacks on civilian targets would never be justified. Neither would attacks on military targets in the absence of war declared by a competent authority.[13]

---

*The natural law doctrine of double effect is the traditional guideline. A nation fighting a war may not take any action intended to harm noncombatants. It may take actions that result in harm to noncombatants if that harm is not the intention of the action, if the action itself is otherwise justified by the just war doctrine and if the harm to noncombatants is relatively minor. For example, if the enemy is advancing on an undefended city and has announced its intention of killing the civilian population, it is appropriate, in just war terms, to attack and stop the advance even if a side effect of the counterattack is to kill some civilians.

The reason the just war doctrine requires all of this caution is that it rests on the Christian supposition that the enemy's soldiers are also part of God's creation and are as entitled as one's own soldiers to the love that every Christian owes to every neighbor. If the neighbor we love is doing a thing we think wrong, how much force is permissible in preventing it? That, basically, is the question that the just war doctrine poses. It is a question, however, that the United States, with the most powerful (and perhaps the most active) military in the world, never seems to ask.

Of course, as with all efforts to translate religious argument into public discourse, any conversation about just and unjust wars in the Christian sense must rest on an understanding of the reasons for the doctrine. Accordingly, the theologian Stanley Hauerwas has argued that it might be a mistake to import the Christian doctrines of just war and pacifism unmediated into political debate, as though anybody can read and apply them.[14] Hauerwas argues that the doctrines make sense only for those raised in the discipline of Christian community—not that nobody else can make sense of them, but that they state not just a theory of war or violence but a way of life.

Hauerwas wants America's Christians, at least, to rediscover the early traditions of the church, traditions of peace and sacrifice, not violence and triumph. Although Hauerwas identifies himself as a pacifist, I do not think he is really arguing that there is nothing worth fighting for; I think he is arguing that America's Christians are often insufficiently discriminating. But Christian inconsistency on the matter of war is, in America, no new thing. William Jennings Bryan, to take a famous example, spent his career as a committed Christian pacifist—that is, until the Spanish-American War broke out, when he became a colonel in the First Nebraska Volunteers.[15] Then, as now, arguing about war was something American Christians did poorly.*

Nevertheless, imagine how our public dialogue over the role of the armed forces would be altered by serious attention to serious religious voices raising these serious issues. By considering issues of proportionality

---

*Indeed, the Anabaptists believed in a separation not only of church and state but of Christians from the state. They believed that the ability to exercise the coercive power of the state would inevitably be a corrupting force among Christians. The consequence was that they opposed service by Christians as magistrates, legislatures, even soldiers. Their American descendents, including the Mennonites and the Amish, hold similar views. It is a mistake to assume, as we casually do today, that conservative religionists will always line up in favor of war and liberal religionists against it. In the debate over entry into World War I, for example, the Social Gospel theologians (especially Shailer Mathews of the Chicago Divinity School, viewed by some as the greatest of them all) led the fight for intervention, whereas more conservative theological thinkers opposed it.

and necessity, rather than the infinitely malleable concept of "national interest," we might actually make better decisions. Better in an old-fashioned
sense that every religionist will surely understand: decisions that are *morally*
better. Morality, we saw back in Chapter 6, is but spirituality in action. A
great nation should strive to be more spiritual than America has lately been
in deciding when to wield its most awesome and terrible power, the power
to destroy.

Not so many years ago, we actually had a rich and thoughtful and very
public debate over one aspect of the theology of war. The occasion was the
issuance, in 1983, of the Catholic bishops' pastoral letter on nuclear deterrence. The letter had three basic themes: that morality did not permit
the use of nuclear weapons at any time; that morality did permit their possession for purposes of deterrence; but that morality did not allow their
permanent possession, so that even while existing for deterrence, they
must be phased out.[16] The National Council of Churches endorsed the
document, as did some other religious groups. But several opposed it—
some on the ground that it allowed the possession of nuclear weapons at
all, others on the ground that it forbade their use even in self-defense. The
debate was lively and the God-talk flew. Was it moral to threaten, as Father Robert F. Drinan put it, "to annihilate the whole world with nuclear
weapons?"[17] On the other hand, did not just war doctrine allow the
enemy to be threatened with as much force as he himself used in his own
threats? The Reagan administration, through its secretary of defense, Cas-
par Weinberger, agreed with the bishops' right to enter public dialogue but
disagreed with their analysis. The talk shows and op-ed pages invited
clergy and theologians to state their positions. Whatever might be the correct Christian answer to the underlying question of nuclear deterrence, I
would insist on this much: It was a grand time to be a religious American.

10

Measurism

IN THE SUMMER OF 1999, which purists and Christians know was not the final summer of the twentieth century, my wife and I experienced a heart-wrenching rite of passage for middle-class parents in the United States. For the first time in their young lives, our two children went off to summer camp. Not day camp, but sleep-away camp, as it is sometimes known. The camp we chose was a performing arts camp in New York, because both our children have expressed an interest in acting.

At the end of the camp session, parents were invited to come and watch the performances the children had been rehearsing for the previous three weeks. Our son, eleven years old that summer, was in a production of the 1950s Broadway musical hit *Damn Yankees*.

Damn Yankees is an updated version of the Faust story, in which a man named Joe Boyd, a middle-aged diehard fan of the old Washington Senators baseball team, sells his soul to the devil in return for a chance to be a major league baseball star who will assist the team he loves in finally beating the hated New York Yankees for the pennant. Although I do not want to spoil the ending, I suppose I can say that the Faust story does not play out in its entirety; the devil's scheme is thwarted in part because Joe Boyd's love for his wife never quite dies, no matter what temptations the devil places in front of him.

Toward the end of the play, after complaining about how "wives have ruined more good men than the Methodist Church," the devil—he is called Applegate in this particular fable—turns to the audience and begins to talk about how easy it used to be to capture souls. Applegate, who has all the best lines in the show, then breaks into one of the better-known tunes from the musical, "The Good Old Days." (The lyrics are on the level of "I was burning with pride / The day Bonnie met Clyde"—not particularly clever but sufficient to make the point.) "The Good Old Days" is a subversive song, in the sense that it inverts common meanings. The title suggests a habit all too common among adults, whether of the current era or of the world in which *Damn Yankees* was written: looking into the past through the rosy glow of middle-aged memories and supposing that the old days must have been better. We all know, in our secret hearts, just why adults do it: In the old days, when we were children, our worries were generally more confined. As painful as adolescence, say, may seem when it is happening, it is the custom of adults, shouldering adult problems, to look back on those years and ponder with amazement, asking ourselves, "I was worried about *that?*"

When Applegate sings "The Good Old Days," he looks into the past and decides that the good old days were *worse*—which means, for him, better. For Applegate, remember, is Satan. He means that the good old days were morally worse; in the good old days, people were more corrupt, more easily tempted to evil, more vicious in how they treated one another.

Now, in theory at least, the premise that people are becoming morally better than they were in the old days is an empirical claim: Either people are becoming morally better or they are not. The claim is one about which we might have a spirited and enjoyable debate—except, of course, that nobody would ever win, because, at some point, one of us—whoever was losing, I suspect—would fall back on that absurd but mundane bit of postmodern tomfoolery: "Well, that's just your opinion."

And, because we are all happily postmodern, and therefore perfectly capable of asserting moral positions and hewing to them strongly, but utterly incompetent at defending them in ways that are persuasive, we would have to give up the argument at that point. Applegate could be right—maybe human beings are morally better than in the past—or he could be wrong—maybe human beings are worse. The trouble is that we seem to lack any common tools with which to make a decision. My concern is that if the devil were to appear tomorrow in the middle of Central Park and demand to know, on pain of eternal torment, whether we humans were prepared to prove that we are, as a community, morally better than the several hundred generations that preceded us in recorded history, we would stand helplessly before him, muttering, "Well, on the one hand . . . but on the other hand," all the way to Hell.

This development is both remarkable and sad. We live in an era of fantastic scientific progress, standing on the verge of mapping the human genome, able to hold intelligent spoken conversations with computers, and confident that we possess the mathematical tools to explain how the Big Bang could have resulted from a previous condition of nothingness. But, somehow, we have let moral progress slide, or, rather, we have let the development of tools to measure it slide. We are so infatuated with our technology and its close cousin, our economy, that all we really seem to want to hear about right and wrong is that neither one of them matters very much.

As a culture, we have become uncomfortable with moral discussion, both in public and in private. This is a cost, not a benefit, of life in America. We live in a nation that provides us with an astonishing range of freedoms. But our freedoms are morally meaningless, neither good nor bad, because our culture offers little guidance in how to use them. Not only do we tend to lack moral guidance, but we have made it our national habit to resent anybody who tries to supply it. So if you and I happen to disagree over a question of right and wrong, it is quite possible that you will not settle for telling me that my opinion is just my opinion—you might well tell me that the way you behave is none of my business. And, of course, you would presumably fight for my freedom to tell you that the way I behave is none of your business.

There is, of course, little if any substantive content to the phrase "none of your business"—because it seems less an argument than an excuse for not offering one. The words proclaim no moral position; they simply state that the speaker lacks one. One reason that we nowadays prefer not to offer moral arguments is that our culture has encouraged us to forget the skill of constructing them. Alasdair MacIntyre was absolutely right when he warned at the beginning of his well-known book *After Virtue* that "in the actual world we inhabit the language of morality is in [a] state of grave disorder."[1] MacIntyre believed that the disorder of moral language stemmed from the collapse of the Enlightenment consensus that had replaced the Aristotelian notion of moral absolutes. In other words, we lack a moral common to which we can appeal; it is not that we lack moral consensus but that we lack the linguistic skills to discover whether one exists or not. Unsurprisingly, then, we often find moral arguments offered by those with whom we disagree literally incomprehensible.

As the reader will by now be aware, I basically share MacIntyre's concerns. Religion, in particular, is often derided in our cultural language for its adherence to absolute standards of morality. But it has never been clear why standards of other sorts are sensible. And, for millions, the idea of the absolute—of the finite moral claim—remains central to faith. Yet some

Protestant denominations have abandoned traditional moral rules, which is fine if it is done on the ground that the traditional rule was wrong, but terrible if it is done on the ground that moral rules are themselves a problem. Certainly we should find it unsurprising, in a culture that insists on denying all moral absolutes, that our children grow up insisting on their right to make their own choices on everything from cheating on examinations to using drugs. We adults, after all, often insist on our rights to abandon our marital vows the instant somebody more attractive comes along and to drive at any speed we want as long as nobody gets killed.[2]

Part of the problem, in short, is that we simply do not like having rules imposed upon us. But I also think that the collapse of moral language has another cause, one less talked about but more dominant, and one that our religious traditions should be battling with all their might. The name we might give to that cause is *measurement*. Measurement might not seem, at first blush, the enemy of morality. Explaining why it sometimes is, is a useful place to begin.

I
====

When I use the term *measurement,* I mean something very specific—I mean the process by which we evaluate the significance of something by assigning it a number. We are generally aided in that task by what we might call *measurement technologies,* which are just what the name suggests. A ruler is a measurement technology. So is a public opinion poll. So is the speedometer of a car. So is an intelligence test.

Measurement technologies do not pose any problems in and of themselves. A ruler, after all, is only a tool; it possesses no moral content. A speedometer, in the absence of an external judgment (such as a speed limit), provides no information about right and wrong. Even an intelligence test, for all the understandable derision heaped upon it, is, like a loaded gun, most dangerous to those who do not know how to use it. No individual measurement technology, by itself, poses any social problem.

The trouble is that America is awash in measurement technologies. We rank the "best" colleges and universities and the "best" towns to live in, we evaluate the success of health care by how long people live and which diseases they survive, we scrutinize scores on standardized tests to decide how public schools are performing, we study murder rates to decide whether the police are doing their job. Not only do we see measurements everywhere, but we have built an ideology around them. This ideology, which we might call *measurism,* has a single, very simple dictum: That which can be measured is of greater importance than that which cannot.

All of us like to deny that this is true. As individuals and as members of society, we will surely insist that measurism is not our ideology, that we value many things that have no numbers attached to them. We might say that we value honesty—or love, and other family ties—or tradition—or nationhood—or ethnic attachment—or God. None of these concepts, we will loudly insist, can be measured; and all of this, we will add, is what we value most.

We are, for the most part, talking pleasant and comforting nonsense.

Our gentle words are nonsense not because they are insincere but because, even when we accept a set of concepts as being beyond measurement, somebody, someplace, inevitably tries to find something in the concept to measure—and, when the measurement becomes known, we begin to attach importance to it, simply because it *is* known.

Take honesty. There is plenty of empirical work showing that the overwhelming majority of us lie, and we do it pretty often—at least twice a day, by some sophisticated estimates.[3] We may tell ourselves that our lies are in good causes, and we may well be right, but they are still lies.

Indeed, there is reason to think that measurism influences our choice to lie. One of the most commonly cited reasons for our daily lying is that it makes other people feel better.[4] The dichotomy between feeling bad and feeling better might not seem to have a number attached, but it certainly implies one: Better is "more" than bad, bad is "less" than better. We justify our lying, in other words, by pointing to something we believe we can measure—the well-being, or self-esteem, or confidence, of another person. We want to increase that self-esteem or confidence rather than make it less. We are guided by the measurable.

Family ties fair little better, much as I wish they did. The divorce rate in the United States is high and not dropping much. The often-mentioned 50 percent figure is an exaggeration, but for relatively recent marriages—those since about 1980—the figure seems to be very close to 40 percent. Why do we divorce so often? One obvious reason is that the spouse who leaves falls in love with somebody else, and therefore believes that his or her happiness will be increased by the divorce. If the true goal in modern marriage turns out to be each spouse's pursuit of happiness, then we discover at its heart something that is, in principle at least, measurable—

namely, happiness. So the spouse who leaves says to the spouse who protests, "You and I will both be happier," almost always a self-serving lie. Or it is, rather, a literal half-truth, for the "I" is true and the "you" likely false. And even if the assertion is true, it remains a claim about measurement. If the old marriage continues, the argument proclaims, the happiness meter registers **H;** if the old marriage is dissolved, the happiness meter registers at least **H + 1,** possibly more. So, guided once more by the measurable, we destroy the sanctity of marriage.

Now, I am not asserting that we are awash in utilitarianism, that the ghost of Jeremy Bentham has returned to wreak a horrible vengeance on us by reducing us to human versions of Robert Nozick's "utility monster." Bentham thought that all moral argument could be reduced to an assessment of utility and that the correct moral course to pursue was that which maximized the net utility of the group. I am no fan of Bentham, but, in this case, Bentham is not the problem. What I call measurism is not directly related to mere utility, either the utility of individuals or the net utility of the society that we are measuring. It may seem that the examples I have given illustrate the very Benthamite proposition that people act in ways they think will make them or others better off. But I am not. Let me offer another example to show why.

Suppose that you want your child to attend a very competitive private high school. You learn that the only admission criterion is the score on a particular test that will be administered on a particular date. Naturally, you will do what you can to prepare your child for the test—you will buy all the right books and, if you can afford it, you will send your child to a preparation course. You might, if you possess the resources, even engage the services of a tutor. You will do all these things not to maximize your child's utility, or your own, or the school's, or society's—you will do it to maximize your child's test score.

And therein lies the problem. Measurism as an ideology assumes that because a thing can be measured, it must be more important than things that cannot be measured. Standardized tests, of which I will say more in a moment, were once used by colleges and universities because they were helpful; now, I believe, they are used because they exist. At Yale Law School, where I teach, we require applicants to sit for the Law School Admission Test, the dreaded LSAT. The score the applicant receives is boldly printed on the application form, usually more than once. In promoting ourselves, we like to talk about the high test scores of our students. But here is the curiosity of the whole thing. thing: It is no easy task to explain precisely what the test measures.

We know very little, for example, about how a Yale student's test score correlates with classroom performance, grades, or subsequent success in the legal profession. We do not know what the test does. We do not know what, if anything, it tests. But the number is available . . . and so we assign it a significance. We use it because it is there, and, if the records of students actually admitted to the law school are any indication, we rarely offer a place to anyone who fails to score very high on the test. We do not know what it is testing but we do know that we want to create a class comprising mainly those who tested well. And that is the essence of measurism.

Yale is not unique in this regard. Most colleges and universities love to claim, in their admission materials, that they consider many indices other than grades and test scores—background, extracurricular activities, and so forth. But, when it comes time to tell the alumni about the entering class, most college presidents and deans probably do the same old thing: They stand up and cite the outstanding grades and test scores of those who have recently matriculated. We measure what we can measure, and what we cannot measure we claim to value but, in practice, we discard.

Now the application of measurism to the problem of moral language should be a bit clearer. The ideology of measurism suggests that in order to make a successful argument, one must present something measurable. This explains why, in the never-ending battle over abortion, both sides point ceaselessly to studies about everything from the peace of mind to the future health prospects of women who obtain abortions and women who do not—as though the correct answer to this moral question can best be found by burrowing in the dimly lighted tunnels of statistical significance. But there are no right moral answers down there in the tunnels, just shadows and wrong turnings and fool's gold . . . and lots and lots of accidents waiting to happen.

II

It would be pleasant to imagine that America's bold religious traditions, historically the guardians of our moral understandings, would present to us a potential source of immunity, or at least resistance, to measurism. Sadly, they too often do not. Steven Goldberg, a legal scholar at Georgetown University, has recently authored a book entitled *Seduced by Science: How American Religion Has Lost Its Way*. Goldberg argues that more and more religions have hitched their wagons, as it were, to the star of science, trying to make claims that are scientific—or at least that are scientistic—as a way of rescuing themselves from the scientific age. In so doing, Goldberg warns, they are losing their best and most distinct selves.

Perhaps he is right ... and certainly he is right for the religions that have come to embrace measurability as crucial to their claims of truth.

Consider: Most Americans probably know someone who suffered from a disease that was supposed to be fatal, then experienced a recovery so complete that the physicians were unable to explain it. In the common parlance, we often refer to these recoveries as miraculous cures. The phrase also carries an obvious theological significance: A miracle has occurred, it suggests, the direct intervention of God. Not many physicians suggest to their patients that God might heal them, although I suppose some doctors must believe it. Yet there is something vaguely unscientific—which, as we will see, is also taken to mean un-American—about saying so openly.

Surveys tell us that a strong majority of Americans—around three out of four—believe that God *can* cure diseases; I believe it myself. Indeed, it would be bizarre indeed to posit an omnipotent Creator who lacks the power to cure diseases of his own creation. For the religious, then, the interesting question is not whether God is able cure diseases, but whether God *does* cure diseases—in particular, whether God ever actually does intervene, through supernatural rather than natural means, in the course of an illness that would otherwise devastate the human body.

Here again, most Americans believe—and I agree with them—that God sometimes does. In fact, about 56 percent of American adults believe that God has, at some point in their lives, healed *them*.[5]

But what does this mean? And how can we know if it is true?

Once upon a time, the answer would have been delivered in one word: faith. Today's answer, as you might have predicted, is a rather different word: measurism. Over the years, a number of medical researchers have struggled to find empirical support, or disproof, for the proposition that God sometimes intervenes to cure diseases. Now and then some very well-designed experiments have been attempted, including a famous 1984 double-blind experiment at San Francisco General Hospital in which nearly 400 coronary patients were divided randomly into two groups—one of which was prayed for by devout Christians and the other of which was not. It was a double-blind study because neither the patients nor the medical staff knew which patients were being prayed for. This study, according to its author, Randolph Byrd, as well as some, but not all, reviewers, showed slightly better outcomes in the patients for whom prayers were offered. The Byrd study became famous a few years ago as the centerpiece of Larry Dossey's best-selling book *Healing Words,* and it is frequently discussed—at times accurately—in the general press.

Critics, as might be expected, have poked holes in the Byrd study, and some of the holes are big ones. Some skeptical researchers, for example, have argued that the study purported to measure health outcomes principally by examining only such factors as pain or infection or need for medication, and that although the study did consider rates of congestive heart failure, it omitted a general discussion of death rates, which were about the same (so the critics charge) in both groups.

However, although nobody has repeated the Byrd study, a significant body of additional research has purported to find a link between prayer and health outcomes. For example, researchers published in the *Western Journal of Medicine* a study on the effects of what is nowadays known as DH (for Distance Healing) on patients with advanced AIDS.[6] As with the Byrd study, the researchers randomized their patients into a control group and a group receiving DH assistance, and neither the doctors nor the patients knew which group was which. (The groups were equalized for a variety of factors related to the severity of the disease.)

The researchers concluded that the DH group—that is, the group receiving prayers—had (at statistically significant levels) lower rates of hospitalization, shorter hospital stays, fewer doctor visits, and a reduced likelihood of contracting additional AIDS-related diseases. Moreover, whereas the Byrd study had only Christians offer prayers for the DH group, the AIDS study used the services of healers from a variety of religious backgrounds.

Here again, the study has its flaws. The sample size was very small: only 40 patients, compared to 383 in the Byrd study. In addition, although the course of the disease seemed less severe after DH intervention, the AIDS study, like the Byrd study, did not make any claims of actual healing. In particular, the researchers found no statistically significant difference between the DH group and the control group in the incidence of CD4 cells in the blood. In other words, just as the Byrd patients remained heart disease sufferers, the patients in the AIDS study remained AIDS sufferers.

Other recent studies face similar challenges. A widely reported 1998 study on the benefits of prayer for arthritis sufferers was not double-blind; the patients knew they were being prayed for, which means that it is impossible to exclude the placebo effect.[7] Another widely mentioned study, published in 1998 in *The Gerontologist,* found positive health outcomes among patients who themselves prayed following coronary artery bypass graft surgery.[8] But since the patients themselves were doing the praying, the possibility of a placebo effect is even greater.

None of this means that what the studies claim is false; I only assert that what they are able to prove is considerably less than what the media (and occasionally the authors) insist that they prove. But the entire enterprise of seeking God through measuring the health outcomes of patients suffering from illnesses, whether severe or chronic, raises troubling questions, mainly theological ones. Consider the concern raised by Professor Goldberg. He tosses out a different and, to my mind, very serious challenge to this line of research:

> Suppose prayer with a chaplain is shown to help 75 percent of patients who are recovering from heart surgery. We might ask why God would help 75 percent rather than 80 percent or 100 percent. And we might wonder why prayer works more often with people recovering from heart surgery than with people who have been shot through the heart.[9]

I would recast Goldberg's criticism this way: Even if studies of the efficacy of prayer do indeed show a statistically significant difference in outcome between those patients who receive the benefits of Distance Healing and those who do not, we cannot suppose, in the absence of a suitable theology, that we have actually discovered any facts that are particular to God. We can always say, in response to Goldberg's criticism, that it is simply God's will that 75 percent rather than 80 percent of patients receive help; or we can posit other explanations, such as that those who are helped the most received the prayers of the most devout among our pray-ers.

But none of that is what is truly important. What is truly important is the way that the studies of the efficacy of prayer seem to reduce God's majesty to the level of that which can be measured; to set up a syllogism in which the crucial evidence for what God wishes us to take on faith turns out to be a set of numbers spewing from the computer. For me, as a believing Christian—and, in particular, as one who certainly does believe that God sometimes heals the sick—the results of these studies seem implausible almost to the point of absurdity. Christians are instructed by the Bible with rigor: We are told to believe by faith, not by sight. If we find ourselves searching for scientific evidence of God's work in the world, we are struggling against the very heart of the Christian faith.

The God that is, and has been, and will be, the God of the great Western traditions, is not a God who answers every prayer with a *Yes*—thus disappointing a post-virtue world that tries to evaluate not only the efficacy but in some sense the very *justice* of any system or entity or idea by how efficiently it fulfills the needs or desires of the individual. (Which explains, to take a parenthetical example, why we are more than willing to tolerate the death of the small, local, family-owned business—often the heart of a local community—in order to save a few dollars a week over at Wal-Mart or Super Stop 'N Shop. The free market, for all its virtues, is one of the great triumphs of measurism.)

Not only does God refuse to fulfill our every desire, he also declines to leave the tracks of his existence along the interstices of recorded data, so that the apostles of the new and frightening god of the technological age—the god of measurism, appearing here in the guise of statistical inference—these new apostles declare that if the One Eternal God who has sustained us all these many centuries is nowhere found within their sacred texts, God therefore must not be real. For God, like virtue, cannot be perceived through any means known to the technological mind—cannot be measured—and therefore must become, by necessity, by the iron rules of measurism, "private." But this "private" God is private in a particular sense; this private God, not measurable, is actively irrelevant, if not actually impossible. The technocratic culture refuses to believe in what it cannot measure.

Many a church, recognizing how measurism reduces God to myth, has, just as Goldberg suggests, turned its traditions upside down in order to win the measurist battle. I think this is what the studies of faith and healing reflect—a kind of desperate need to fit our old God to new rules, to proclaim to the world that if all the world believes in is numbers, well, it is numbers that we will provide. So we tell ourselves that if God really does heal diseases, he must leave measurable tracks when he does so—even though there is no reason to imagine that this is true, and even though it concedes to the ideology of measurism a patch of sacred ground technocracy should not be permitted to touch.

God could heal diseases and hide his healing work in the crevices of the data, where no amount of inference would discover it. An omnipotent God could heal and decline to heal at any rate he chose—even at the same rate at which the disease might of its own accord go into remission.[10] The statistician might object that if God heals a disease at the same rate as the disease disappears on its own, he is not healing at all, but that is very much a measurist point of view—all the statistician can safely assert, with the authority of his training, is that if God heals at the same rate as the disease goes into remission, then there is no way to use numbers to *prove* that God heals.

In short, God could remain unmeasurable and yet remain God. In fact, it may be that God must remain unmeasurable in order to remain God. This would suggest that those who search for him in data on healing, like those who search for him by hunting out errors and omissions and contradictions in the dominant biological theories of the origin of humanity, are searching in the wrong places. To be sure, the search for the God whose existence shines forth from what secular science cannot adequately explain is a very old religious tradition, and it has, especially in recent years, produced some marvelously elegant literature.[11] But I remain a skeptic. I believe in God, but I do not believe in God's provability.

Here, the reader will perhaps say, my Christianity biases me. Fair enough. I assume that it does. After all, a religion that makes no difference is not a religion. So let me offer what I would call a Christian answer to the measurism inherent in the efforts to assess God's healing power through the construction of double-blind scientific studies. God may be in the details—but if we are to come to Him in faith, he would leave no evidence that was not susceptible to a different explanation. God, in this theory, might reveal Himself to the faithful, but the revelation would not necessarily be something that could not be explained away by others who disbelieved. Indeed, for a Christian to say to one who did not believe "Come and become a Christian because God healed my cancer" would send a woefully un-Christian message: "Believe because of the neat stuff God will give you," sort of like a large and wealthy corporation hiring a new employee by offering more money.

There is a story that preachers have used for years to make the same point. It seems that a certain very pious man was trapped in his home as a flood approached. As the water entered the front door and engulfed the first floor, a boat showed up outside. "We're here to rescue you!" the people in the boat shouted. "No need," said the man. "God will save me."

Pretty soon, the water was up as high as the second floor, and the man was hanging out a window. A second boat showed up and, once more, the people on board tried to rescue him. "No need," he called back. "God will save me."

Now the water inundated the interior of the house and the man was forced to crawl out onto the roof. In due course a helicopter flew over, spotted him, and tossed down a ladder. The pilot shouted for the man to climb up before he drowned. Again the pious man declined the offer of assistance. "No need," he shouted up to the pilot. "God will save me."

The helicopter flew away.

The waters closed in, the pious man drowned, and, upon reaching Heaven, he sought out God and demanded to know what went wrong: "I've lived a pious life. I put my faith in you. Why didn't you save me?"

And God said: "What did you want me to do? I sent two boats and a helicopter."

III

The studies that I mentioned that try to determine whether prayer or faith has a role in healing are therefore doomed to failure—but failure of a most interesting kind. The studies will fail because they seek measurable proof of the unmeasurable, they seek to confine the infinite within the calipers wielded by the mortal; ultimately, they reduce God's mystery to a set of numbers on a page.

John Updike wrote a novel on this subject. The novel, entitled *Roger's Version,* traced the adventures of a divinity professor at an unnamed school apparently modeled on Harvard. The professor and his wife began interacting with a student who was seeking a grant to buy computer time to perform a lengthy series of calculations and transformations aimed at proving the existence of God. The student's name was Dale. Dale believed that God must have left evidence of his existence, hidden in the laws of physics or some other part of the knowledge of the scientific world. In due course, Dale received his grant, and proceeded, night after night, to put the computer through its paces, searching for evidence. After what might have been the one true answer or a single false alarm, a face that appeared briefly on the computer monitor, never to be seen again—random noise? an error? a mistake in interpretation? or the real thing?—Dale concluded his investigation with the dreary statement that "Zero is also a number."

I am not denying the healing power of prayer. I am not denying—in fact, I commend to the reader's attention—the considerable work that has been done on the positive role of one's own faith in maintaining general good health and, sometimes, in overcoming otherwise debilitating conditions. Physicians who choose to pay no attention to the spiritual side of the lives of their patients are missing what is at the heart of many, probably most, of those lives—and are therefore weaker physicians for their omission. In all of these small corners of life as it is lived, God remains where he has always been—in the details.

Why should this matter to a healer?

Consider the example of the Jehovah's Witnesses. Many Witnesses will refuse to receive blood transfusions on the ground that (so they believe) God forbids it. How is a physician, or a hospital, to respond? Many institutions once followed, and some, I fear, still do, an absurd and bigoted protocol that required referral of all patients who refused medical care on religious grounds—but not patients who accepted it—to psychiatrists. The only way to explain this protocol is to propose that a religious choice at variance with what medical science recommends has a high probability of being the product of a not-quite-stable mind. But all the protocol really is . . . is measurism. We can measure the results of the treatment recommended by the doctor. We can even assign a probability of success—that is, a number. We cannot, on the other hand, measure the likelihood of divine intervention, and we certainly have no measurement technology that would allow us to assess the underlying claim about the content of God's will. Therefore we must not only ignore the claim but deride and discourage it.

But if we are able to understand that God leaves his tracks in the details, and that the tracks are more likely to be noticed in the details of the lives of those who seek him, then we can fit the refusal to agree to the blood transfusion into the context of a life lived in accordance with a specific set of rules, believed rightly or wrongly to be God-given. In this complex and richly detailed life, the prohibition on receiving blood probably forms a relatively small part of day-to-day living. It is simply one of the details.

The lives we live are full of details, and the details of those lives are full of God. The details I have in mind are the interstices of life, the tiny spaces in which we find the tiny beauties and the tiny truths of existence. We can see evidence of God, if we look, in the blue of the afternoon sky or the fury of the afternoon rain; in the cry of the newborn infant and in the tears of parents who must bury one; in the musculature of the winner of the marathon and the musculature of the sufferer from dystrophy. God has left his tracks through all creation, and those who see by faith will find him.*

---

*I am not advocating pantheism. My suggestion is not that God exists in all things but rather than God has, throughout creation, left evidence of his work, evidence that those inspired by faith will constantly discover . . . and that those who are not inspired by faith will constantly misunderstand.

But, for the faithful, God's tracks do not exist in any one set of details specially. That is why I remain skeptical of the search for God in the numbers, including the numbers that are yielded from carefully constructed double-blind studies on the efficacy of distant healing. I think that those who search for God with the tools of statistical inference, whether they search for evidence that God heals or evidence that God destroys, are likely doomed to the same dreary conclusion as poor Dale, the hapless student in Updike's novel: Zero is also a number. And if the faith of the searchers somehow requires a nonzero result, they may be doomed to lose their faith—not because faith is an error, but because the search for support in measurism is an error. The God who allows himself to be captured by our poor mortal tools, who allows his influence to be measured in numbers, would seem to be a God who is living by our rules, rather than the other way around.

IV

There is a Midrash teaching to the effect that God, when he created man, grew angry at the angel of Truth and briefly banished Truth ("dashed truth to the ground") for daring to suggest that man, if created, would lie. But after creating man, the story goes on, God picked Truth up from the ground again, thus assuring us that created man and created truth could coexist.

The burden of this story I take to be an affirmation of a very old tradition in both Jewish and Christian thought holding that there is no conflict between the evidence of our senses and what God has revealed through his prophets and messengers. Nothing I have said is meant to disparage that tradition, which, in fact, is one I accept. What the tradition implies is that science and religion should, ideally, exist in harmony, so that when they do not—when their conclusions are inconsistent—one or the other of them is in error.

One way to understand the continuing appeal of this tradition is to think for a moment about the 40 percent or more of American adults who tell pollsters that they believe the creation story in Genesis to be literally true.[12] In 1999, the Board of Education of the state of Kansas created a great brouhaha when it decided to remove evolution from the list of subjects on which the state's schoolchildren would have mandatory testing. I want to emphasize that Kansas did no more than this. In particular, despite the hysterical voices in the media, the state did not ban the teaching of evolution in its public schools and certainly did not adopt any devices for punishing teachers who decide to talk about it in the classroom. To be sure, the net effect of removing evolution from the list of tested subjects might well be to remove it from the local school curricula, but that is simply another mark of the absurdity of our educational system in the era of measurism—the tendency for every classroom to become a standardized test preparation course.

Now, what has the Kansas decision to do with our subject? Well, why is it that anybody is interested in banning the teaching of evolution?

The easy answer—but an imprecise one—is that sectarian interests are trying to use the schools to propagate their own religious beliefs. A more accurate answer is that the triumph of measurism is actually incomplete, that the nation holds within its borders what the sociologist Peter Berger refers to as "cognitive minorities"; that is, subcultures for whom knowledge itself is of a very different nature than it is within the majority, or the dominant, culture.[13] We have already discussed our difficulties as a society in agreeing on the content of our shared moral knowledge. It turns out that we as a society have difficulty in agreeing on the content of our shared scientific knowledge as well.

The correct way, I think, of understanding both those who wish to ban the teaching of evolution and those who wish to press the teaching of what has come to be called scientific creationism is that they are part of a cognitive minority—albeit a large one—in which the index of all truth is God's Word. I use the phrase "all truth" because within the epistemology of biblical literalism, there is no useful distinction between God's will regarding morality and God's will regarding what we might think of as scientific fact. The Enlightenment idea of the distinction between the two is hardly one that has gained universal acceptance, and America's religious traditions are among the major dissenters. For evangelicals in particular, all the Bible is encompassed within a single heading, and that heading is truth.

This analysis implies that the supporters of creationism, and the opponents of evolution, are motivated by precisely the same impulse that motivates the opponents of creationism and the supporters of evolution. Both groups want the public schools to teach the truth, the whole truth, and nothing but the truth. Their sharp disagreement is not over the mission of the public schools, then, but over the content of the truth—or, to be more precise, over the proper method of discovering the truth, that is, epistemology.

I will confess that despite the vehemence on both sides of such issues as this one, I see no value-free way of determining which epistemology we *as a society* ought to prefer. To march under the slogan "only science belongs in the science classroom," for example, only confuses what is at stake. For what the debate is most deeply about is not what should or should not be included in the public school curriculum but who should get to decide, and when, and how. (I have discussed this topic elsewhere in considerable detail.)[14] I am not as unhappy as many observers seem to be that people guided by faith are trying to build a cocoon of knowledge for their children—I think that is the parents' job. What interests me more, and distresses me more, is the departure of many supporters of creationism from the epistemology of the Word to try instead to demonstrate their thesis through the epistemology of modern science.

I am not arguing that people of religious faith should never test their truth-claims against the evidence of science; such a position would run sharply counter to the tradition of harmony I mentioned earlier. What troubles me, rather, is the apparent belief of many creationists that they *should* search the evidence of natural science for confirmation of their beliefs, as though, somehow, the biblical truths they assert are not valid unless the evidence of the fossil record or cosmology or biochemistry confirms their validity. And here, once more, we face the temptation of measurism.

In an earlier era, many creationists were content to say that evidence running contrary to their thesis was nothing but a series of traps set by the devil for the unwary—a proposition that is impossible to disprove. For earlier creationists, resisting the lure of science was a sign of faith. Trying to adduce evidence in the sense in which the scientific method understands evidence was a deviation from the proper epistemic path; scripture was deemed true and unassailable, and no alternative paths were invited to apply. Here I think that Steven Goldberg is at least half right: He is wrong to suggest that creationists should not be expressing views about what really happened, but he is right to suggest that they might be speaking the wrong language. America needs its diverse religious voices and needs to hear from them, regularly, on issues of public moment; but, when the religionist speaks on a proposition, the religionist's purest voice will always be the voice that convinced him in the first place. If, for example, it is faith in the Word that persuaded the creationist that the evolution of human beings from lower forms is a myth, then it is faith in the Word that the creationist should present to a skeptical world. The reason for this is not that religion and science cannot mix; the reason is that religion should be the last of our institutions to fall down and worship the graven image of measurism.

V

I should say a final word about standardized tests, for our overreliance on them is, I believe, another cultural point that the religious should resist. Standardized tests, the designers always tell us, are merely a tool . . . but nowadays, it seems, we are not using the tool. The tool is using us.

Critics of the tests point to purported cultural bias, an attack supported by evidence that is thin, and to doubts about whether the tests actually measure what they say they do, an attack supported by evidence that is more substantial. But I am less concerned with whether the tests measure what they say they measure than I am with the way that they have come to occupy so central a location in our weak, fearful national psyche that there is little room for anything else. Our religious traditions teach us to understand the human other than by achievement in the secular world, but our celebration of testing—and our worship of high scores—suggests a very different understanding.[15]

When I was a high schooler, review courses for the Scholastic Aptitude Test (SAT) were frowned upon, not only because we still believed the myth that the courses were useless but because we still believed the myth that the motivated and talented individual could triumph. Today's parents, today's educators, and, most important, today's students, believe neither of these myths. High standardized test scores are, in effect, a corporate achievement, earned by committee, the committee consisting of the home in which the child is raised, the schools the child attended, the experience of the child in taking standardized tests, and the extra training the child has received in how it is done. All of these components cost money, and when we discover, to our astonishment, the very high correlations between standardized test scores and parental income, we are left with two possible conclusions: Either all that money and the things it buys make a difference in how well children perform on tests, or we are afflicted with a genetically determined ruling class that owns the most resources by virtue of its inherited superiority and has the wealth and the test scores to prove it.

Most of us, if challenged, would no doubt say that the first conclusion is the correct one—that money does make a difference—but I also think that most of us secretly believe, or at least believe that others believe, the second, that there is something in our genes that causes these differences in test scores, that some among us just cannot do it, just cannot measure up, no matter how hard we try, and that precious educational resources should be reserved for those we believe will do the best with them . . . because of the tests.

One reason for my cynicism stems from, well . . . more statistics . . . in this case, the data on the support of or opposition to vouchers to help poor parents purchase private educations for their children. According to the annual Phi Delta Kappa survey of opinion on education, most poor people—and, in particular, most black people—are in favor of vouchers. Most well-to-do people—and, in particular, most white people—are against them.[16] But here is the single most interesting bit of data, culled from the 1998 survey. One demographic group tilts particularly hard against vouchers, and that group, that source of solid, overwhelming, implacable opposition to assistance to poor children to attend private schools is . . . parents of private school children!

Parents of children already attending private schools oppose vouchers to help poor parents purchase the same thing for their children by a margin of nearly 2 to 1.[17] It is as though they are saying, nearly in so many words, *Private education is fine for our children, but your children, well, they just belong . . . someplace else! But not among ours! Not among the achievers, the leaders-to-be, those selected by statistics and genes and money to be the future! You go your way and we'll go ours!** I hope this does not seem unfair. Private education [18]has become a rather odd duck, with some schools requiring entrance examinations for seventh grade, or even for grade school. A few years ago, I wrote a letter of recommendation for the child of a friend, who needed references in order to apply to . . . well, kindergarten.

There is a desperate cultural sickness in our reliance on standardized tests, the profound pessimism of a people who are spiritually empty, a people who do not know their purpose and, just as important, do not know *how* to know their purpose. The religious should bear witness against the enterprise of entrusting the future to professionals—in this case, statisticians and test designers—who will measure for us that which is measurable, whatever it is, and trumpet the results of that measurement to a culture all too ready to accept the notion that the thing that can be numbered with precision is more important than the thing that cannot. Thus do we allow the measurable, the precise, the number to become the crucial factor in determining the future, for we as a culture are far too morally unconfident to stand and insist that the emperor has no clothes.[18]

---

*Another possible explanation is that the consumers of private education tend to be significantly more liberal than the consumers of public education. I am aware of no data on this point, but I hope it is not true, given liberalism's traditional and honorable support of public education.

·   ·   ·

The obvious but time-consuming alternative (and the one the religious, I believe, should work to establish) is a culture that tries, whether admitting students to college or hiring adults for jobs, to do the hard work of reaching more sensitive understandings of who we are, who our children are, and what sort of future we would like to construct. We might begin by trying to reward goodness instead of test scores—although the cultural dominance of the idea that the tests must matter because they are there is huge. A few years ago, I am told, an Ivy League college came up with the bright idea of including an ethics question on its application form. Potential students were presented with a moral dilemma and asked how they would resolve it. Alumni howled. So did students, parents, and faculty. How can anybody, the protesters complained, judge anybody else's moral judgment? In the face of this moral nihilism, the college backed off.

I guess the devil still has all the best lines.

11

The Primacy of
Religious Liberty

Whilst we assert for ourselves a freedom to embrace, to profess and to observe the Religion which we believe to be of divine origin, we cannot deny an equal freedom to those whose minds have not yet yielded to the evidence that has convinced us. If this freedom be abused, it is an offense against God, not against man.

—*James Madison,* Memorial and Remonstrance Against Religious Assessments, *1785*

IT IS DIFFICULT TO ENVISION A RELIGION that does not believe in its own freedom to worship and follow God as it chooses. Indeed, from the point of view of the religious, there is probably no freedom more precious. For it does the believer little good to possess the right to vote, or send a letter to the editor of the local paper, or avoid discrimination, if he cannot, through the exercise of these liberties, do the things that God requires.

Yet to say this is already to run into the blank wall of societal complacency. Most of us, it very often seems, are concerned primarily with our own right to worship and follow God—not somebody else's. It simply is not possible to muster enthusiastic support for the right of Native Americans, in religious ceremonies older than the laws of this nation, to use peyote, a controlled substance under our drug laws.[1] Or for the right of prison inmates who happen to be Muslims to attend services required by their faith when those services are held in parts of the prison to which they have no access under the rules.[2] A leading evangelist, a man I much admire, once told me that Muslim inmates have all the same rights as Christian inmates. No doubt they do. But they would prefer to have the rights they need as Muslims. The right to do everything that Christians are allowed to do is not the same as the right to follow God in their own way.

One subject around which all the religious should be able to unite is the near-absolute right of every other religion to worship and follow its own God.* This principle has a pragmatic aspect: If Muslims do not help Buddhists when their freedom is threatened, if Hindus do not help Jews, if Christians do not help Native Americans, then there is little reciprocity on which to draw if the threats ever run the other way. (Christians, who tend to consider their position in the United States unassailable, should ponder how little excitement they have been able to demonstrate among non-Christians on the subject of mistreatment of Christian missionaries in the Third World.) The principle that each religion should fight for the freedom of all religions also has firm theological grounding. The Western religions—Christianity, Judaism, and Islam—all rest on principles discouraging or even forbidding coercion in persuading nonbelievers to believe. These principles, to be sure, have often been honored in the breach, although a good deal less often than some may think. Even the Inquisition, to take a prominent example, was never aimed at nonbelievers, only at Christians considered heretics.[3] Most Eastern religions, too, abhor coercion and violence. The fact, for example, that violence has often marked the politics of predominantly Buddhist Sri Lanka does not alter the fundamentally nonviolent teaching of that tradition.[4] It means only that the teaching of Buddhism, like similar teachings in other faiths, is sometimes disobeyed by morally frail humans.

In sum, there are good reasons, both theological and practical, for all religions to honor the freedom of nonmembers to follow other religions—or to follow no religion at all. This might seem a decoration, a mere fillip, had the Supreme Court built a better foundation of constitutional law on religious freedom. Unfortunately, the foundation is shaky, because the courts, like most of us, are having trouble with the tricky part: figuring out not where religious freedom starts, but where it ends.

In this chapter, I will sketch the outlines of an improved doctrine of freedom of religion, one broad enough to allow the religious to follow the

---

*I say "near-absolute" for the obvious reason that a well-ordered society might have trouble functioning were the right to worship (or any other right) treated as subject to no exceptions. I would not go as far as some theorists who would argue that a society could not function at all with complete religious freedom. That judgment depends a great deal on what one imagines humans with complete religious freedom would do. The result might be anarchy. The result might be improvement.

path of resistance that I have counseled throughout the book. At the same
time, I will express some caution about faith traditions that come to rely too
heavily on the goodwill of the state–rather than the providence of God–for
their nurture and survival.

I
=====

Over the years, the Supreme Court has had trouble deciding between two
competing theories on how the courts should interpret the religion clause.[5]
One strand, which survives in popular discourse and in the courts but is in
serious danger of vanishing from the academy, is the view that the state must
be neutral, neither choosing among religions nor choosing between religion
and nonreligion. Unsurprisingly, this is known in the literature as *neutrality*.
The second strand, thriving in academic discourse but remarkably difficult
to express in popular discourse, holds that the state must take steps to accommodate religious believers whose practices are burdened by otherwise
neutral state laws. This strand, predictably, is known as *accommodationism*.

I confess that I have somewhat oversimplified a vast and often intricate
literature. There are any number of carefully nuanced middle positions. Yet,
in the end, nearly all theorists lean toward one or the other of these two positions, simply because legal theory (unlike, say, literary theory) must finally
guide the decisions by actual judges of actual cases. Consequently, legal theorists quite understandably feel impelled to tell us in the end how the cases
should come out. And, in the end, just about everybody who presents a theory–no matter what the theory is called–winds up favoring something that
looks an awful lot like either neutrality or accommodationism.

The problem is this: Neutrality is a theory about freedom of religion in a
world that does not and cannot actually exist, whereas accommodationism, although a theory about the real world, is not really a theory about freedom of
religion. Accommodationism is certainly to be preferred, at least if one takes
religion seriously. But one must also be careful. Although a theory of religious
freedom is plainly necessary to the proper function of the state (because the
state's courts must decide actual cases), a theory of religious freedom may be
unnecessary to, and might even prove dangerous to, religion itself.

Why do I say that neutrality is a theory about a world that does not and
cannot exist? Because neutrality supposes that it is possible for the state to
act without taking any account of religion generally, or of the specific reli-

gious beliefs of constituent groups. No religion is to be favored over any other, nor is religion generally to be favored over nonreligion. The metaphorical wall of separation of church and state (which is only a metaphor, although we sometimes pretend it is a rule of our constitutional law) seeks to capture this idea: There is the sphere of religion and the sphere of the state, and a mighty wall protecting each from the other.

But none of this is possible.

In the first place, what we are bold to call neutrality means in practice that big religions win and small religions lose. When the Supreme Court decreed in *Lyng v. Northwest Indian Cemetery Protective Association*[6] that three Indian tribes in California could not prevent the Forest Service from allowing road building and logging on their sacred lands, I suppose the justices believed they were acting neutrally: The tribes had no more right than anybody else to protect the lands. But from the point of view of the tribes, whose religious tradition, as the justices admitted, would be "devastated" by the government's action, there was nothing neutral about the destruction of the forest. With the forest gone, their religion also would be gone: a neutral result without any remotely neutral consequences.[7]

A more powerful religion would not suffer so from neutrality. To take what might seem a painfully obvious example, nobody proposes to build a road through the Cathedral of St. John the Divine in Manhattan. My own Episcopal Church, although our numbers are dwindling, remains sufficiently powerful that nobody would even dream of so absurd a notion. (And, lest you object that the federal government "owns" the national forests and not the cathedral, let me add that nobody would dare try to take the cathedral through eminent domain either.) To be sure, neutrality governs this result: The Cathedral is not safe because it is a religious building—it is safe because it is a building valued by a politically powerful constituent group. But that only illustrates the point. Neutrality is a blueprint for the accidental destruction of religions that lack power.

The reason neutrality fails is that it imagines an impossible world. No true wall of separation is possible. Religion and the state, the two great sources of control all through human history, will never be fully separate from each other. Each will always shade into the other's sphere. Schoolchildren learn this truth in their science classes: All containers leak. The only interesting question is how fast. In the case of religion and the state, the leakage is rapid, and constant. How could matters be otherwise? Religion, by focusing the attention of the believer on the idea of transcendent truth, necessarily changes the person the believer is; which in turn changes the way the believer interacts with the world; which in turn changes political outcomes. Although there have been some clever moves in political philosophy to explain why the religious voice should not be a part of our public debates, such theories wind up describing debates from which deeply religious people are simply absent.[8]

Besides, in a nation in which the great majority of voters describe themselves as religious, religious belief will usually be the background—even if frequently unstated—of our policy debates. A widespread religious conviction that we must aid the poor will inevitably find its way into legislation, and so the nation will create welfare programs. A widespread religious conviction that long-term help is no substitute for hard work will inevitably find its way into legislation, and so welfare will evolve into workfare.

Once one recognizes that the wall of separation leaks, and leaks badly, the case for neutrality disappears. Neutrality seeks to impose an artificial order on a naturally chaotic relationship. By so doing, it cloaks hard truths about our society. Some of the truths are pleasant—for example, the happy truth that religion matters deeply to most people, even in politics. And some of the truths are unpleasant—for example, the tragic fact that other people's religions often matter less to people than their own. (One recalls Ambrose Bierce's definition of a Christian: "One who believes that the New Testament is a splendid guide for the life of his neighbor.") This truth, too, works its way into policy, which is why the "neutral" result in *Lyng* is able to stand. The state is permitted to devastate a religion, as long as it doesn't do so on purpose.

The bureaucrats who decided to build the road and level the sacred forest were not wicked people, but fallible humans, engaged in the fallible human task of governance. Yet none of them, I suspect, would have considered for a moment allowing the destruction of whatever physical symbol their own religions held to be sacred. Neutrality encourages this willful ignorance of the religious views of others. Neutrality's ideal world, in which all of us rigorously separate our religious and secular selves, simply is not the world in which most Americans live.[9] Nor would many people want to. So although neutrality is certainly a theory about religion and law, it is not a theory about a world that exists.

But that is the easy half of the argument. Neutrality theory has had its critics for thirty years, and many of them have now become accommodationists; that is, they believe that the right approach is for the state to make itself quite intentionally aware of the religions of its constituents, and then, if necessary and possible, to adjust its legal requirements, offering special exemptions so that its constituents are able to exercise their religions freely. To the accommodationist, a decision like *Goldman v. Weinberger*[10] is risible, although the neutralist defends it—*Goldman* being the case in which the

Supreme Court allowed the air force to discipline Major Simcha Goldman, an Orthodox Jew, for wearing a yarmulke while in uniform, a violation of military regulations. If you think the punishment was right, on the ground that the same rules should apply to everybody, you are a neutralist; if you think the case was wrong, that a special exception to uniform regulations should exist for religious apparel, you are an accommodationist. (And if you think the whole idea of military uniform regulations is risible, you are interestingly quixotic but, when it comes to the resolution of concrete cases, not actually helpful.)

Ever since I began writing about religious freedom over a decade ago, I have counted myself as an accommodationist.[11] I suppose that I still am—and yet I have started to wonder. Accommodationism remains, I believe, the best constitutional rule. Yet at its heart lies a difficulty sufficiently severe to threaten the entire project of protecting religion through the Constitution. It bears a strong resemblance to a similar problem in public theology, identified long ago by Søren Kierkegaard. But rather than describe the problem directly, I prefer, for the sake of clarity, to come to it by what might seem to be the longer route.

II

The problem I have in mind is a subset of a larger problem: our evidently hopeless passion for statism. When I say statism, I do not simply mean, as the formal definition would suggest, a preference for state solutions; I have in mind a sense of the state's rightness, or goodness—an empirical belief that the state is less likely than the individual to make a moral error. Since the Enlightenment, the entire liberal political project has often seemed to rest on this idea. The rightness of the state is the source of the state's authority to use force to coerce individuals.[12] That we elect our government by majority vote and call our system a democracy does nothing to change the statist truth that the democratic majority, when certain that it is right, can coerce the dissenting individual.

But, wait, you say—that is why we have constitutional rights. They are designed to avoid precisely the problem of statism. They carve out a sphere, we like to say, within which the individual is sovereign, and thus is not subject to state coercion. Free speech, for example: Here, we might say, no state, no matter how great its democratic majority, may interfere. And the same for equal protection and for due process . . . and, of course, for religion. All of these rights are set out in the constitutional text. And so statism is turned back—isn't it?

Would that it were so! There is, unfortunately, a catch. The catch is that the engine of protection for constitutional rights is the judicial branch. If I believe that the state is interfering with my sovereign sphere, I go to court and try to persuade a judge that I am right. If I lose, I make the same argument to some more judges. If I lose again, but am nevertheless very lucky, I make the argument a final time to a set of nine judges—justices—who have the final word. They tell us, authoritatively, what the Constitution means, in the process also telling me, authoritatively, what I may and may not do. If they say I have the right I claim, I have it. If they say the state may coerce me, the state may coerce me.[13]

Why is this a problem? It is a problem because the judges are themselves a part of the state. They are not (despite what law professors like myself tell our students) a *check on* the state—they are a *part of* the state.[14] We think of rights, nowadays, as proceeding from the state. That is the precise meaning, today, of the phrase "constitutional right": a right that is protected in the foundational document of the state, and that the state is obliged, *because of that protection,* to respect.

But this is just a long way of saying that the state grants the right. We have grown accustomed to this rhetoric in America—the idea that rights are protected by judges—but the ubiquity of the idea should not blind us to the fact that to file a lawsuit before a judge is the analytical equivalent of asking state permission to exercise a constitutional right.

Perhaps this does not matter for most claims of right; in any case, they are not my subject.[15] I do think this matters, deeply, when we consider religion. If we take religion seriously, as a force in the human spirit and as a connection to the transcendent, we can see at once why it matters. The three great Western religions, Christianity, Judaism, and Islam, all propose the existence of a Creator-God whose will is superior to any human construct, including human law. The demands this Creator-God places on humans—who are among the created, or creatures—are absolute. The Bible as well as the other narrative traditions of these faiths is full of stories of God's people practicing God's rules in the face of human disapproval, even human punishment. How, then, can God's people go to the state and seek permission to do what God requires?

For, again, this is what happens when a constitutional right is asserted. In the case of *Church of Lukumi Babalu Aye v. City of Hialeah,*[16] the city adopted an animal-rights ordinance with the sole apparent purpose of ridding itself of the practitioners of Santería. The Santería faith teaches that each of us is assisted by a personal God, an *orisha,* which must be nourished, lest it die and our fate be sealed. In their religious ceremonies, the *santeros* sometimes sacrifice live animals to the *orishas.* In their cosmology, they have no choice: They cannot allow the *orishas* to die, and the blood of animals killed ceremonially is crucial to the survival of the *orishas.* The Supreme Court struck down the ordinance on what amounted to a discrimination argument: It was not enforced against anybody but the church.

Now, suppose instead the case of a neutral animal-rights ordinance, not one aimed only at shutting down Santería. The neutralist would enforce it. Many (not all) accommodationists would allow an exemption. But in either case, the *santeros* have no choice about what to do. If they truly believe the teachings of the faith, they *must* make the sacrifices, whether the state allows it or not. In other words, if the state refuses permission, that does not change their obligation to follow what they take to be the will of God.[17]

Of course, the obligation to God does not always survive the threat of state punishment. The willingness of the state to punish behavior *B* effectively pressures religionists who believe that God requires *B* to change their faith. As the late Robert Cover pointed out in his classic article "*Nomos* and Narrative," religions often discover their own true and best selves in the dialectic with the awful reality of the coercive power of their fellow citizens, acting as the state.[18] So the Mormons, harassed and brutalized by state power, yielded their insistence on polygamy (more accurately, polygyny). This demonstrates the awesome force the state can wield, but it also may suggest that polygamy was not truly at the heart of the Mormon religion.

Such discoveries are useful for a religion that prefers its doctrine pure. This does not mean that oppression is good. Even if one believes that even the worst evil, in some mysterious way, serves God's plan, that answer is not quite adequate to the present point. Rather, I would say that although oppression of the religious (like other forms of oppression) is evil, when it does occur, it helps us to learn who we truly are.

In the end, the what-we-truly-are that religion *R* discovers of itself might involve behavior *B,* no matter how the state tries to discourage it. Sometimes, heroically, adherents of *R* will do *B* even when doing so means arrest, and worse. (The Bible is thick with examples, from Jeremiah suffering in prison to the Christian martyrs suffering torture and execution rather than recant.) Sometimes adherents of *R* will do *B* even when most of us are quite convinced that *B* is actively wicked. Indeed, I will admit to a sneaking admiration for the Christian racists of Bob Jones University—the subject that sparked Cover's article.

In the early years of the Reagan administration, the Justice Department joined forces with Bob Jones University to challenge the power of the Internal Revenue Service to deny tax-exempt status to schools that discriminate on the basis of race. The university, citing principally the Tower of Babel story, did not allow interracial dating (it allowed very little dating of any kind) and did not admit as students people married to people of other races.[19] Bob Jones University lost its appeal in the Supreme Court,[20] at which point just about everybody expected the school to abandon its discriminatory policies rather than lose its tax exemption. But just about everybody was wrong. The school decided to stick with its version of Christianity and give up tax exemption.[21]

There are happier examples—civil rights activists and abolitionists going to prison rather than recanting what their God has taught them—but we must not, in our celebration of their heroism, be ahistorical. The state imprisoned them not because a few nasty racists had their hands on the levers of power but because the side the protesters took was, at the time they took it, not a popular one. Their mythic character depends on our belief today that the protesters had it right, but the heroic character of their resistance does not depend on whether we agree with them or not. Antiwar protesters, not popular in the early Vietnam days and pretty much ignored if the war happens to involve Saddam Hussein, are also resisters of state power; so are protesters who fight abortion. It is our habit to sort the resisters depending on what we think of the side they take on controversial issues, and this is a very human, as well as quite sensible, response: As Oscar Wilde noted, the fact that a man dies for a cause does not mean the cause is right. But even when the cause is wrong, we should not overlook the heroism of those willing to be punished for their belief in its rightness.

To be sure, not all religionists will be heroic in the face of official pressure, and not all religions demand martyrdom of their followers. Adherents of R, faced with the threat of state punishment if they do B, sometimes will not abandon their belief that God requires them to do B but will decide nevertheless not to do it. This is not a sign that they do not "really" believe they are required to do B. It is a sign only of human frailty.

Those religions that will back off when threatened with pressure pose little threat to the state that tries to create a dominant meaning, for the hegemonic state naturally counts on human frailty as an ally. Those religions that refuse to back off are more threatening. Sometimes, the inability of the state to rout the resisting religion leads to deep and fundamental alterations in the state itself, as when the Roman Empire was transformed by Christianity. (Not that either Christianity or the empire benefited much.) So the state will work harder to achieve its goal.

What goal? The simplest way to put it is *standardization*—in particular, standardization of the people. For the modern Western democracies, whatever their pretensions to diversity, often seem to desire most a nation in which all citizens are essentially the same.[22] This tendency is a characteristic of nationhood, not of democracy as such. Totalitarian and religious states standardize, too, and far more ruthlessly than democracies. But democracies still do it. The literature is full of assertions that it is a commonality of values and outlook, in short a shared sense of meaning, that makes a people a people and, thus, a nation a nation.

The temptation, however, is one that the just state will resist. Indeed, the strongest argument in favor of the accommodation of religion is the preservation of genuine diversity—not simply people who *look* different, but people who in deep ways *are* different. As we have seen earlier, a religion that makes no difference in the lives of its adherents is not a religion at all. The accommodationist believes in religion as something that actually changes the way that people are; nurturing religion, then, also nurtures a plurality of nomic communities, communities that assign to existence meanings different from those of the dominant culture.[23] The accommodationist, therefore, argues that the state should back off whenever possible—formally, whenever a compelling state interest is not served by the effort to rein in religions that would otherwise press for meanings of reality that the state abhors.[24]

These are already dangerous words, because they can invite oppression: The state, after all, might reasonably conclude that many different ends are compelling. Indeed, the immediate difficulty for the accommodationist is that it is the state that is doing the accommodating. The problem facing the religionist is deeper than the struggle between the ideal of neutrality and the reality of accommodation. The accommodationist, at the very beginning of the analysis, is faced with two crucial problems that necessarily limit religious freedom. First, the accommodationist must define religion, which already narrows the universe of what counts. One saw evidence of this, for example, when the Massachusetts Supreme Judicial Court decreed in the *Needham* case that when religious counseling is informed even in part by secular psychology, it ceases to be religious and is entitled to no free-exercise protection.[25] The problem is plain: If the religion seeking an accommodation must first prove to the state (through the state's courts) that it is indeed a religion, it is already under pressure to meet a test that might have nothing to do with the religion's teaching.

The courts might try to avoid this difficulty, for example by adopting Kent Greenawalt's proposal that we define religion analogically.[26] Greenawalt suggests that we begin with what we know to be religions, search out their common elements, and then compare other claimants by looking for similar (but perhaps not identical) elements. This approach (which is, I think, more impressionistic than analogical) would have the advantage of not forcing all religions into a single, narrow mold, a point to which I shall return. But it would have the disadvantage of beginning with the religions with which our culture is most familiar, which at once makes potential outsiders of religions that may look very different. Besides, like all definitional approaches, this one still says to people of faith that they must ensure that they come within the approved definition if they want, in a legal sense, to be free.

Second, the accommodationist must indicate a limit beyond which no claim of religious freedom will be recognized—to resolve, for example, the problem of religiously mandated murder. Most accommodationists place the limit at "compelling state interest"; but even after setting compellingness as the standard, and handling it correctly, the courts in the end will be centering their concern on the needs of the state, not the needs of the religionist. This became painfully clear in 1996, when the Supreme Court refused to hear an appeal of the Alaska Supreme Court's *Swanner* decision, which held that the state's interest in preventing discrimination against unmarried heterosexual couples is sufficiently great that it trumps the objections of landlords who believe they are forbidden by God to permit "fornication" on their property.[27] It is not easy to discern what made the interest compelling, except that the state had decreed it to be so.

The simple problem is that the accommodationist must ultimately draw some lines; and every line divides those religions that will be privileged from those that will be demoted. The mere existence of these dividing lines creates pressures on religions to twist themselves into shapes that the state (through its courts) will recognize. Perhaps were we mortals sinless, the problem would not arise, for we would readily resist state pressure to be different. But that asks too much of weak flesh. We search for ways to ease our path through life: That is our nature. No religion picks a fight with the state if it can be avoided, and few religionists are able to resist the lure of state assistance. And so, precisely because the rules of constitutional law create some faint possibility of gaining special consideration, the question the religion must ask itself becomes (to take *Needham* as our example) not *What form of counseling does God require?* but *What form of counseling will the state allow?* Thus does constitutional protection of religion threaten to undo the specialness of religion itself.

The trouble all arises because our theories of religious freedom are not theories about religion; they are theories about the state and its needs. If the religious freedom claimant loses, it is because the state's interest is too strong—not because religion's interest is too weak. Although the tests are referred to as balances, they are not, for they suffer from the well-understood deficiency of such inquiries: The tests fail to tell us the weights to be given to the different variables. Indeed, the tests do not even tell us what all the variables are. In *Swanner,* what in the world was a fair-minded court to weigh—and against what else—in deciding whether the state's interest in protecting unmarried couples from discrimination is sufficiently compelling to trump the religionist's interest in following God's ban on allowing fornication? The test does not say, and probably cannot say, and so the judges, tossed upon the stormy seas of their own resources, seek the safest harbor they know: They are creatures of the state, and so is the Constitution, and so what comes to matter most is quite naturally the interest of the state. And that is where the problem centers: The religion that makes a legal claim for religious freedom is petitioning a functionary of the state for permission to worship and follow God. But what sort of religion can (or should) comfortably do such a thing?

Suppose the state says *No?* Is the follower of R then to decide that B is not required after all—because the state will punish him if he does it? In principle, this outcome is no more appealing than the notion that the state should decide to allow the follower of R to do B because he is going to do it anyway, even if punishment follows. But no such symmetry exists. We seem to expect that the sensible religionist will take into account state response in making a decision whether to break the law or not; yet we evidently suppose it to be absurd that the sensible state should take into account religious response in deciding whether to enforce the law or not. The religionist who persists in doing B after it is deemed to carry no constitutional protection is a fanatic, but the state that puts him in jail is only doing its job. As a formal matter, this result is possible because the state possesses the legal authority to enforce its decrees and the religionist does not. As a practical matter, the result is possible because the state, not the religionist, has the guns.

In a nation that properly prides itself on religious pluralism, we certainly do not want to put the guns in the hands of the competing religions instead.

Yet the same pride should help us to recognize that the asymmetry of religious freedom is mischievous. Although the compellingness test (which only accommodationists believe in anyway) gives us a standard for determining which state interests are so vital that a claim of religious requirement cannot overcome them, we have no test for determining which religious interests are so vital that no state interest—*not even a compelling one*—can overcome them. In other words, the balance is struck in a way that creates only two sets of cases: those that are hard and those in which the state automatically wins. There may be no set of cases in which the religion automatically wins.[28]

The asymmetry is also unstable. The neat separation assumed by the model does not survive. The result is not chaos; the result, rather, is a steady leakage in our separation cylinder, but leakage in only one direction, so that the state wins more and more and the religionist wins less and less, precisely the trend line of the cases over the past twenty years. This does not mean that there is a point at which accommodation and neutrality converge (although there may be); it means only that as time and cases go by, the state-centeredness of what we are bold to call religious freedom is more and more apparent, and the pressure on religionists to conform to the expectations of others grows and grows, with the inevitable complicity of the judges who supposedly protect religion's "right" to be free.

III

But the phenomenon I have been describing, the reader might object, is simply the way the world works. For me to accuse the courts of being state-centered on religion issues, the reader might argue, smacks of sophistry. After all, the judges must decide the cases properly before them.[29] To decide cases, they must draw lines. That the lines judges draw are occasionally a little bit arbitrary is a very old critique of judging. Unless we are to adopt a standard under which the religious freedom claimant always wins, then we must pick a point, by some method, at which the claimant loses. Whatever that point turns out to be, it will invariably be the point at which the losing claimant will accuse the judges of statism.

And besides (so the counterargument might continue), trade-offs are a necessary part of life in society. Of course religions will sometimes feel themselves pressured to change; everybody is pressured to conform; that is a fact of life, not of law. If a religious belief is sufficiently strong, it will survive the pressure. I have already mentioned that Bob Jones University refused to yield to state pressure to abandon its religious belief in racial separation after losing in the Supreme Court in 1983. Imagine, however, that the Internal Revenue Service had been after Bob Jones to abandon faith in Jesus Christ as Son of God and Savior, the bedrock on which Christianity rests. In that case, nobody would have been surprised by the school's refusal to back down.*

Neither one of these objections disturbs the theory. Yes, judges must decide cases and draw lines; but it is the fact that *judges* must draw lines—not the place where the lines happen to be drawn—that creates the risk for religions that go to court to seek protection. And, yes, religionists should ideally be strong enough to resist state pressure; but the state itself has created layer on layer of purportedly neutral pressures that combine to weaken the ability of the religions (or, rather, religious people) to resist. Among these layers are a variety of tax benefits, which, as we saw in Chapter 5, encourage religions to reshape themselves so as to be eligible; and the recent legislative efforts, certainly constitutional but perhaps of dubious value to religion, to allow religious groups to share in the rather substantial largesse of the programmatic side of the welfare state.

A principle of accommodation will not eliminate the tension that pressures the religious to change for the sake of society, but it will at least create a space in which the religions can organize their resistance. Moreover, if combined with a healthy respect for the role of the religious voice in politics, the accommodation principle might at least create some pressures for society to change for the sake of religion. A democracy that believes in religious freedom should be willing to live with the tension; so should a religion that believes in democracy.

---

*One might distinguish the two cases on the ground that faith in Jesus Christ does not raise any moral or social questions, but, from the Christian point of view, the distinction fails. The Christian does not read the Bible to hold that what we are to believe about God falls into a different category than what we are to believe about other things. Moral rules, because they derive in the Christian understanding from the will of God, are simply facts.

12

Religion, Community, and Resistance

THROUGHOUT THIS BOOK, I have argued that religion is, at its best, subversive of the society in which it exists. Religion's subversive power flows from its tendency to focus the attention and, ultimately, the values of its adherents on a set of understandings often quite different from the understandings of the dominant forces in the culture. The larger culture, as we have seen, will always try to impose a set of meanings on all of its subcultures; of all the subcultures in a society, religion is almost always the one best able to resist. That resistance, in turn, is the source of diversity, of dialogue, and, ultimately, of change.

A simple example is the continued insistence of tens of millions of Americans, most of them evangelical Christians, that the Genesis story of creation is literally true and the theory of evolution, to the extent that it is inconsistent with Genesis, is false.[1] Biologists, paleontologists, and other academics deride the believers who refuse to accept what modern science wants to teach. In the face of much derision, it is religious community, and nothing else, that sustains these believers in their certainty. To answer by saying that we would be better off if they believed something else is imperialism, not argument, for it presupposes a cultural monopoly not only on truth but on the range of permissible belief about truth. And the same answer could have been offered to the abolitionists, who were also sustained by their faith communities in their certainty that the biblical injunction to love our neighbors meant that slavery was impermissible. Abolitionists, creationists, pacifists, pro-lifers: What religion at its best supplies to the larger society is a veritable cornucopia of difference.

I have always liked the way that the theologian David Tracy puts the point in his book *Plurality and Ambiguity:* "Despite their own sin and ignorance, the religions, at their best, always bear extraordinary powers of resistance. When not domesticated as sacred canopies for the status quo nor wasted by their own self-contradictory grasps at power, the religions live by resisting."[2] The culture may press the religions to change; but the religions, at their best, press back, often in surprising places. And they press back in a way that no other force does, for the transcendence of religious belief proposes an answer higher than mere human striving. The Western religions in their traditional forms all share the model of transcendence: The answers to the most profound questions are found not in human argument but in the will of God, which exists in the world in written form and sometimes in an oral heritage as well.[3]

When religion presses back against the dominant culture, both are changed as a result of the encounter. One reason that the culture changes may be that we are constructed in a way that causes our souls to resonate to religious language, even when we prefer to avoid it. The spirituality of religion, for most Americans, fills a hole in the human soul that the more material aspects of our world leave agape. Of the theistic religions this is particularly true, but a nontheistic faith, such as the more refined forms of Buddhism, can play the same role. We might, of course, take the totalitarian view that we should allow no forces that press us to be other than we are; but then we would not be either genuinely democratic or religiously free, and, indeed, we would not be American.

Consider once more the puzzle of creationism. In Chapter 10, I mentioned the 1999 decision by the Board of Education of the state of Kansas to remove evolution as a mandatory subject of instruction in the public schools. A horrified scientific community rushed to the barricades, insisting that students not taught the theory of evolution are not really prepared for life in the modern world. I am not sure this proposition is true—plenty of people somehow manage to have rich and productive adult lives with little understanding of science—but let us assume that it is. The evangelicals who fought to rid the classrooms of evolution might respond that students not taught about the life and ministry of Jesus are not really prepared for life in the world either. If the answer is that parents, not schools, should decide what religion to teach their children, I suppose one could respond that parents, not schools, should decide what science to teach their children, too. If the answer is that the public schools are a place for teaching science, not religion, one could respond that they are not a place for science that interferes with the teaching of religion. And if the answer is (as it seems to be for many) *Oh yes they are!*–then we have reached a point on which many religionists are likely to resist. The result is an ideological struggle in which victory rests as much on power as on reason.

Religious resistance is part of its power and part of its danger. In either case, resistance is often necessary for religious survival. If a religion is indeed to be free, one of the things it must be free to do is to reinforce itself–that is, to strengthen itself against the inevitable incursions of state power. If we focus our understanding of free exercise on the needs of religion rather than on the needs of the state, especially on the need for religion to create meaning in the lives of the faithful, we can see at once the necessity of carving out a sphere in which religion is immense, not only in its ability to teach or even in its authority, but in its scope, its ability to fill a life–all in an effort to balance the subduing immensity of the state.

These spheres are particularly important if we view the subversive power of religion as something to be valued rather than controlled. The late Supreme Court Justice William Brennan seemed to have a particularly sensitive understanding of this point. The case that makes the point most sharply may be *Corporation of the Presiding Bishop of the Church of Jesus Christ of Latter-Day Saints v. Amos,* decided in 1987.[4] The decision upheld an amendment to Title VII of the Civil Rights Act of 1964, the federal statute that prohibits employment discrimination on a number of grounds, including religion. The amendment exempts religious groups, in most of their nonprofit activities, from the prohibition on religious discrimination. Without this protection, the Court explained, the state might be too free to interfere with "the ability of religious organizations to define and carry out their religious missions." This conclusion is quite sensible, and not only was the statute a good idea–it is hard to imagine religious freedom without it. If religions are not allowed to engage in what would otherwise be illegal religious discrimination, they would, for practical purposes, cease to exist.

Justice Brennan wrote a concurring opinion, joined by Justice Thurgood Marshall. This is what he said: "For many individuals, religious activity derives meaning in large measure from participation in a larger religious community. Such a community represents an ongoing tradition of shared beliefs, an organic entity not reducible to a mere aggregation of individuals."

Let us stop for a moment. Brennan is here taking a side–and the right side–in the continuing debate over whether religion is an individual or group activity. Although he carefully hedges his bets, his sympathies seem to lie with those theologians who contend that it is the very groupness of religion that gives it its meaning–that religion is a narrative activity, a story a people tells itself and its issue about its relationship to God over time. This in turn suggests that a brand new religion, one founded yesterday, say, is not a religion at all, but simply a set of ideas about God, until it stands the tests of time and community; and that the phrase "a religion of one" is an oxymoron.[5]

To say that a religion becomes a religion by virtue of its ability to extend itself over time–into the future and into the past–is not to suggest that any religion is unchanging, for the very passage of time may help the people of God to gain a richer understanding of God's will. As the historian Jaroslav Pelikan has written, "[T]he demonstrated ability to sustain and eventually to accept the development of doctrine is witness to the vitality of a tradition."[6] This is self-evidently true even of religions that often seem to critical outsiders to be hidebound, such as Orthodox Judaism and Roman Catholicism, both of which moved into their most orthodox phases only in the late nineteenth century, in response to cultural trends that touched the lives of believers. If Pelikan is right–and I believe he is–then the very ability of a religion to accommodate itself to the world is crucial to its survival; those that cannot evolve, die.

Evolution does not, however, mean the surrender of sacred truths. To say that a faith must change its most precious values because the values of the world have changed–a claim heard, for example, in the mainline Protestant churches from the end of the nineteenth century up to the present day–invites the skeptic to conclude that the moral lessons a church tries to teach emerge not from the mind of God but from the imagination of fallible humans. Unfortunately, a growing number of religious leaders write and speak as though they view religious truth in precisely this way. For example, the theologians who constitute the so-called Jesus Seminar argue that we must begin our understanding of the Gospels by excluding all claims that are supernatural.[7] The retired Episcopal bishop Shelby Spong of my own Episcopal Church, author of a book claiming that Christianity must "change or die," has suggested, among other ideas, that Jesus may have been married and that Mary did not become pregnant with the baby Jesus as a result of the intervention of the Holy Spirit but was, perhaps, a victim of rape.[8] It may be that Bishop Spong was merely engaging in theological speculation, peculiar speculation though it may be, and that the members of the Jesus Seminar were merely offering helpful hints to non-Christians who might nevertheless gain from a study of Christ's moral teachings. I certainly hope so. Otherwise, Christianity is already changing, in ways that might ensure its death. When leaders of a faith decree, in effect, that their faith is a human invention, they have lost the right to call their activity religious, for they have surrendered the transcendence that marks religion as distinct among human activities. After that point, there is no longer a reason for anybody to pay attention to them.

Nowadays, with our secular culture so drenched in money and sex and self-seeking, all religions face the temptation to yield to the world's call to celebrate human desire, in many cases because their seduced adherents demand it; and many religions are giving in. As long as they are giving in because they believe that surrendering their traditions is what God wants them to do, then they are doing what they should, even if they are wrong. If on the other hand they are giving in to ensure that they keep the pews full—or in order to be invited to the right dinner parties—or so that their leaders will not have to feel guilty or be called names—then they are doing what they should not. The space carved out for religious liberty by the separation of church and state as it should be understood is a space for the religious, working in community, to engage in prayer and discernment about God's will, and to strengthen each other to stand against the cultural forces trying to breach the wall. If religions simply surrender, remaking themselves in the image in which the world is comfortable, they squander the freedom that exists to protect them. The religions that surrender to the world lose their souls just as surely as the religions that rush to enter electoral politics, for both equally lose the power of prophetic witness. A religion cannot call the world to account once it has decided that its own traditions are wrong and the world is right.

II

In practice—that is, in the practice of constitutional law—the construction of the space of religious freedom, the garden protected from the wilderness, remains a rather tricky proposition. In the *Amos* case, upholding the right of religious groups to hire, in most of their activities, only coreligionists, the Supreme Court gave rare and much-needed judicial recognition to the notion that the garden must be protected. I have already adverted to Justice Brennan's concurring opinion, joined by Justice Marshall. Brennan continues:

Determining that certain activities are in furtherance of an organization's religious mission, and that only those committed to that mission should conduct them, is thus a means by which a religious community defines itself. Solicitude for a church's ability to do so reflects the idea that furtherance of the autonomy of religious organizations often furthers individual religious freedom as well.

Maybe it does, maybe it doesn't—I think Brennan is right, although the last point is not perhaps so obvious as to need no argument. Although many Protestants believe that God's call to grace is irresistible (for those few who are called), the constitutional understanding of religious freedom is surely motivated in part by the sense that followers of a faith possess an absolute power to exit. This understanding, in turn, meshes with our cultural attachment to liberty. We mistrust what we sometimes call "cults" precisely because we believe that their leaders have somehow overwhelmed the ability of followers to reason, so that the followers lack that freedom to exit. (Some theorists, unfortunately, mistrust the family for the same reason: Parents are perceived as possessing too much influence over their children, who possess only limited rights of exit from that influence.)[9]

But Brennan's principal suggestion is not about individual liberty at all. His perfectly sensible concern is with the liberty of the group—including its liberty to exclude. If the religious community cannot define itself, cannot set rules for membership, including rules of behavior, then it is not, in any realistic sense, a religious community. This implies that protection of religious freedom requires a high degree of deference to the definitional process within the community, that a religion must possess a large sphere within which to undertake the activities of worship and following God. Within this sphere—within the walls of the garden—a religion might well teach and preach moral lessons that the larger community would dispute. But the state nevertheless must stay out, for it is only through the process of defining, creating, strengthening, and, sometimes, reinventing itself that the religion gains the power to resist not only the competing meanings proposed by the larger society but the inevitable incursions of the state, which will, more often than is probably comfortable, pressure the religion to change. As we have seen since Chapter 2, it is in the nature of religion to resist. It is in the nature of the state to battle against that resistance. A just state will therefore allow a broad range of religious freedom to ensure that its own hands are tied.

III

This understanding of religious resistance helps explain why the battles over the education of children are so intense. A religion exists, as we have seen, by resisting the meanings pressed on it by the state and by projecting its narrative of the people's relationship to God into the future. It will be impossible to do so if the religious community does not have significant control over the upbringing of its children. This is the point the Supreme Court understood in its much-maligned decision in *Wisconsin v. Yoder*,[10] which permitted the Old Order Amish to remove their children from public school after the eighth grade. The justices noted, correctly, that "[t]he impact of the compulsory attendance law on respondents' practice of the Amish religion is not only severe, but inescapable"—that is, that the law hurt the religion and there was no way around the law unless the courts carved out an exception.

Critics of the decision have cast it as an abandonment of the children's "right" to an education different from what their parents prefer; but language of this kind only obscures what is at stake. On the one side is a religious view of the world, on the other another view—maybe religious, maybe not—held by the state. Both the claim that the children are being harmed and the compulsory attendance law itself simply represent the state's way of looking at the world. To conclude that it is superior to the parents' way of looking at the world is an extension of the state-centeredness of religious freedom that I discussed in the previous chapter. In particular, to lift the individual child from the context of the family, the place where the religion's set of meanings is most closely inculcated, is a coercive act that is very likely to destroy, in the long run, those religions with which the state is unhappy. The state will place few obstacles in the path of domesticated religions that seek to project their narratives into the future but seem supportive of the state itself; it is only religions that are subversive, particularly those that are radically so, that are at risk . . . if, as many scholars believe, *Yoder* is wrong.

The separation of an individual child from family is a dangerous staple of the contemporary understanding of education. The state requires all families (with the exception of families with the resources to make a different choice) to send their children for education for six to seven hours a day, 180 days a year, for at least a dozen years of the child's life. Many parents complain that parts of the content of the public-school curriculum interfere with their ability to raise their children in their religion—what we have been calling, more formally, the ability of their religious community to project its meanings into the future. Elsewhere, I have argued for very strong deference to the judgment of parents who object to the curriculum, at least those who want to remove their own children from certain classes,[11] but that is not to the present point. Rather, I wish to show how our assumptions about the role of family and state in raising children not only retain the state-centeredness that is always poison to religion, but largely (although, of course, not entirely) originate in religious, not secular, visions of education.

It is hornbook constitutional law that the religious training of the young is a responsibility of the family and must take place outside the bounds of the public-school day. Where does this understanding come from? It has emerged, at least in part, from the nation's complicated religious history.

First, consider public schooling itself, including the rather extraordinary fact that education is compulsory, which, for roughly half the nation's history, it was not. Why the change? Some might credit the ideology of Progressivism, which held that important tasks should be performed by trained experts. The elevation of schoolteachers into well-regarded if undercompensated professionals is one outcome of Progressive social theory. In the late nineteenth century, moreover, industrial capitalism began to demand a better-prepared workforce, and educational theory began to make important strides in understanding the proper building blocks for learning. At the same time, a jingoistic vision of Americanism grew in popularity and seemed to most a perfectly sensible component of a compulsory school curriculum. In short, there are plenty of solid, secular explanations for the swift and sudden rise of compulsory public schooling in the years between the Civil War and World War I.

But what we have come to accept as the given form of public schooling also represents the outcome of a fierce battle in late-nineteenth-century America between nativist Protestants and Roman Catholic immigrants. The Catholics, arriving on these shores from a Europe in which there were few common schools, saw religious instruction as pervasive, something to which youngsters should be exposed all day, every day. America's Protestants saw religious instruction as something easily confined to that odd invention of theirs, Sunday school.[12] The idea that children needed any more religion than they could get at home and in Sunday school was, to the Protestant mind, simply ridiculous—not least because such public schools as existed in nineteenth-century America were designed to further the dominant Protestant ethic of the day. The Protestants won the battle, which is one reason the school day is shaped the way it is, without formal religious instruction. They won by inventing a constitutional principle against state aid to religious education, which nobody discovered until this battle was joined.[13] And that is why there are so many Catholic schools.

Indeed, there is some reason to think that common school was at least partly *designed* to make it harder for Catholic parents to raise their children as Catholics. Certainly the early-nineteenth-century movement to create, as Horace Mann called it, "universal, free, public education" generated little support until later in the century, after the great post–Civil War wave of European immigrants. The movement that might have prevailed in solid liberal fashion under the banner of equality prevailed instead under the banner of nationalism: The children of the immigrants had to be "Americanized," supporters of compulsory schooling argued, meaning that they had to internalize the norms of American culture—in short, that they had to be assimilated. In its historical context, the movement to Americanize the immigrant children meant to Protestantize their religious beliefs—particularly their Catholicism.[14]

The same religious battle created our strange American tradition barring state aid to religious schools. When I say that the tradition is strange, what I mean is that it is difficult to explain. The tradition is shared by few other countries, not even those, like France, that zealously separate church and state. Most countries—and all western European countries—consider direct aid to religious schools as part of a portfolio of pro-family policies, like generous family leave for workers and, for those governments that can afford it, a regular stipend for parents. All these programs together are aimed at supporting families by supporting the choices that families make—the choice, for example, whether to stay home with a child or send that child to a religious school.

In America, we have gone our own way—or rather, we have lost our way. So parents who stay home with their children are penalized in the employment market. Parents who send their children to religious schools are penalized in the pocketbook. Both American policy failures have the effect of channeling parental choices in the direction the state presumably wants them to go: Parents should spend less time with children and more time in the paid workforce, and, instead of educating their children in the close-knit, nurturing environment of the religious school, should send them to the bureaucratized, often impersonal, and aggressively secular public school. Although these may appear to be liberal values, they are, in practice, merely the values of capitalism.

Well, we Americans have always been the wonders of the world, and we are what we are. Still, even in the United States, the tradition against public aid to religious schools is of relatively recent vintage; it is only, perhaps, a century old. During the first century of the nation's history, such "public" schools as existed were for all practical purposes Protestant parochial schools, supported by local communities. (Whether we should think of local communities in the late eighteenth and early nineteenth centuries as "the state" raises tremendous risks of anachronism.) The schools of the day, supported by local assessments, featured both prayer and formal religious instruction.[15] As the common-school movement spread, instruction in Protestant values, along with school prayer, spread with it. Nobody doubted that government funds could be used to pay for these schools. For all the virtues of the movement, the schools it produced often amounted to little more than state-supported efforts to preserve Protestantism and kill the "un-American" religions before they could take their pernicious hold on the immigrant children. Unsurprisingly, Roman Catholic and Jewish immigrants quickly denounced the schools as what they were.

Yet the climate of the times was such that nobody bothered to hide any of these facts. On the contrary: It is hardly an accident of history that the first compulsory education law in the country was adopted in Massachusetts during the period when its legislature and state house were in the hands of the rabidly anti-Catholic Know-Nothing Party. And Governor William Seward, during his two decades of running New York, fought for state money to pay for separate Catholic and Jewish schools, on the interesting ground that immigrants should not be forced to send their children to schools where they would encounter prejudice. In New York City, the plan was partly adopted, as the municipal government, for a time, paid the salaries of teachers at the Catholic schools.

Supporters of compulsory education laws in the late nineteenth century were quite explicit about their goals. From politicians to schoolteachers (including the head of the fledgling National Education Association), they argued that it was the task of the schools to wean immigrant children from their foreign religions; and, under this banner, compulsory public education triumphed. At the same time, the nativists suddenly discovered—*invented* might be a better word—the principle that prohibits the use of state funds to support religious education, a mischievous idea that killed federal legislation that would have benefited the Catholic schools, while allowing local governments to continue to pay for their Protestant "public" schools.[16]

But look at the result. We inherit from this battle the shape of the school day, which we take as a given, notwithstanding its ridiculous assumption that parents struggling to offer one set of meanings can easily compete with the state, which prefers another. Yet it is not obvious that we have correctly calculated the number of hours children must attend school, and educational theory, although hunting around the margins in search of an hour more or an hour less, also begins with the baseline that we have: Six hours of classroom instruction a day, or thirty hours a week, is always the starting point.

I am not against the public schools; I am a product of public schools. I am, however, against the reckless continuation of policies and principles designed to make it difficult for families to teach their children moral principles with which the dominant culture disagrees. The millions of parents who choose religious education for their children, as well as the millions more who say they would make the same choice if they could afford it, evidently feel the same way. If we do not protect the space for the religious teaching of children, we are not really protecting religious freedom at all. Instead, we are preserving a system that began as an effort to domesticate religions that were seen as un-American, and, however more noble our rhetoric than the rhetoric of the nativists, there is every reason to think that it plays that role even today.

There are theorists who defend the role. Amy Gutmann, in *Democratic Education,* is quite explicit in urging that the schools be used to limit the ability of parents to raise their children in intolerant religious beliefs.[17] Stephen Macedo calls for a liberalism prepared to do battle, including through its schools, with religions that teach "illiberal" ideas.[18] Suzanna Sherry warns that educational policy must be crafted to limit the effect of the bad choices that religious parents will inevitably make for their children.[19] Quite apart from its totalitarian bent—America is envisioned as the land of the single true meaning, which the state, distinct from the people it governs, alone decides—this literature seems to assume that the purpose of the schools is to minimize the aggregate cost of parental error. The error is defined as raising children who do not approach problems the way the state wants them to. The family, in this vision, becomes a little baby-making factory, whose purpose is to create children for the benefit of the state.

This is also the unspoken message of much of the criticism of *Yoder*—including, I would say, Justice Douglas's famous dissent, in which he explains why the parents' liberty to choose a religious education for the child is not

unlimited: "Where the child is mature enough to express potentially con-
flicting desires, it would be an invasion of the child's rights to permit such
an imposition without canvassing his views." The image that comes to
mind is of a state bureaucracy charged with determining, each time a "mature" child is sent to a religious high school, whether the child objects; the
fact that we might call the bureaucrats judges does nothing to alter, from
the point of view of the religiously resisting family, the totalitarian implications of the idea itself.[20]

The case that here comes to mind is of course the Sixth Circuit's rather
controversial 1987 decision in *Mozert v. Hawkins County Public Schools*.[21] The
case involved religious parents who objected on religious grounds to a curriculum aimed at teaching what school officials described as "tolerance."
(The official title of the course was "critical reading.") The parents believed
that the contents of the course were actively at odds with the teachings of
their faith. The court, siding with the school, responded that learning the
tools of tolerance would not be harmful to the children and would not force
them to reject their parents' beliefs. As Nomi Maya Stolzenberg has pointed
out, however, the judges actually rejected not only the parents' legal claim,
but their religious claim. The panel simply did not believe that teaching
"tolerance" could be religiously objectionable.[22]

The *Mozert* decision represents what I hope will be the zenith of judicial
endorsement of the idea that we as individuals should lead unsituated lives,
or lives that are situated only by a choice informed by the analytical methods of liberalism, with emphasis on self-expression and self-satisfaction—in
other words, on the self. In this model, we are, or should be, able to create
and re-create ourselves constantly according to the new theories to which
we are exposed, so that our convictions, such as they are, are ever open to
challenge. Nothing constitutes us but our ability to think and choose. This
approach treats humans as consumers in the world of values, encouraging
us to live our preferences, whatever they are, simply because we prefer
them.

The view more common among traditional religions is that we are, each
of us, deeply connected to a community, and that the community and its
norms are as constitutive of our selves as anything else.[23] These norms,
moreover, are given, not chosen, for they are God's norms, not our own.
The fact that many critics would not want to be bound by norms that are
not freely chosen does not justify the imposition of that philosophy on
everyone else. The very question of the givenness of norms is one on
which religious communities are likely to dissent from the values of the

elite; to insist that children spend most of their young lives attending schools that teach the opposite is simply another way of limiting religion's ability to subvert the dominant culture.

The *Mozert* court, for example, in rejecting the parental objection to teaching "tolerance," implicitly accepted the proposition that being exposed to new things is always good. Many Christian parents, however, insist that their faith requires them to make distinctions, relying instead on such New Testament passages as the injunction to keep the mind focused on "whatever is true, whatever is noble, whatever is right, whatever is pure, whatever is lovely, whatever is admirable" (Phil. 4:8). We flout the ideal of genuine diversity when we strip mothers and fathers of the freedom to limit the exposure of their children to what is not, according to the judgment of the parents, true and noble and right.

I am not, quite, arguing that vouchers, or other forms of state support for parents who choose private education for their children, is another issue around which the religious should all rally. There are strong reasons for religions not interested in vouchers to support them for other parents, especially poor ones: in order, for example, to maximize the ability of dissenting faiths to survive in a culture often hostile to them. But there is also the common objection: Why should my tax money go to assist a religion I not only do not follow, but may actually consider dangerous? This argument is far from unanswerable, and there is plenty of literature answering it, but taking on that task is not to the present point.[24]

I do believe that the religious should unite behind a very strong norm elevating parental interest above the interest of the state (except in extreme cases, such as physical abuse), so that dissenting religious communities have the chance to survive and thrive rather than drowning in the cultural sea that, if left unchecked, will eventually overwhelm them all.

IV

I would not want the reader to imagine that my argument represents the mainstream view in constitutional law or philosophy. *Mozert* has plenty of academic defenders; I suspect that its academic defenders outnumber its academic critics. The strongest form of their argument might be summarized, in formal terms, this way: The family holds the potential to exercise enormous power, and power, in the liberal understanding, must always have a liberal justification. Arming the children with the tools of critical inquiry, then, might be seen as a way of limiting the power the family would otherwise be able to exercise.[25]

But the student of religion as resistance cannot help but be troubled by the degree of trust this approach places in the state. By positing a right of the children to gain sufficient critical insight to allow them the possibility of rejecting the religious community of their parents, *Mozert*'s defenders risk undermining the ability of the community to resist state domination. Once we concede the authority of the state to set up its own schools and compel attendance except for those wealthy enough to make other choices, we already give the state an enormous advantage in deciding which meanings to inculcate in children, and so we reduce the likelihood that dissenting religions will successfully project their subversive meanings into the future. We domesticate the religions through the simple device of taking their children.

We can justify this, of course, by following the lead of the icons of the public-school movement, Horace Mann and John Dewey, who argued with some force that the state needs citizens raised to respect certain democratic values if it is to function—in principle, a very good idea.[26] Yet now our state-centeredness becomes simple statism, for the argument assumes, on the basis of what evidence one can only guess, that the state, as an empirical matter, will make better judgments than the parents about what the children need to know. Or, more formally, it assumes that the aggregate costs of the errors the state will make if it is the central source of meanings will be smaller than the aggregate costs of the errors the parents will make if the family is the central source of meanings.

Moreover, the very idea that we can aggregate these costs—or, for that matter, that we have measured them correctly—rests on the assumption that the dominant paradigm will remain undisturbed, that no subsequent shift, perhaps led, as so often, by a radically subversive religious vision, will undo what we have thought to be settled moral and even scientific knowledge. Once we kill off the ability of the religious to create centers of meaning in serious opposition to the meanings of the state, we are left without the possibility of future prophets calling us to righteousness. Perhaps some would prefer an America without any truly subversive, and truly effective, prophetic voices. But how do we know that the system established today to promote liberal hegemony by wiping out opposing centers of meanings will not be captured tomorrow to promote racist or fascist hegemony? How do we know, in other words, that the good guys will always, or even usually, be on top?* Nothing in the history of the state as an entity, or of humanity as a species, justifies so extraordinarily optimistic an assumption.

V
═══════

To be sure, even if we create these spaces for the nurturing of religious re-sistance, they will, in the long run, be useless, unless religions resist. So much of American religion today has become so culturally comfortable that one can scarcely find differences between the vision of the good that is preached from the pulpit and the vision of the good that is believed by the culture. If a religion wants to be just like everything else, it needs no guarantee of reli-gious liberty. After all, both breakfast cereal manufacturers and automobile companies manage to transform themselves constantly into images accept-able to the culture without the benefit of a constitutional right to do it.

If the Constitution or the culture or the two in combination do manage to carve out the spaces in which religionists can freely build communities preaching meanings sharply at odds with those that dominate our era, reli-gion must take advantage of that opportunity.[27] In America today, so many traditions are politically identifiable. In the Protestant churches, the prob-lem is especially acute. Denominations that make common cause with the Right have learned to mute the Gospel message about the dangers of wealth. Denominations that make common cause with the Left have learned to cast aside New Testament teachings about sex. As we have seen in earlier chapters, the pull of political involvement, if it is heeded, invari-ably alters the content of the message. The Integrity Objection holds firm.

American religion needs more time in the garden, less in the wilderness, more time for prayer and discernment, more time for renewal, more time for community, more time to discover what it is that God is calling it to be. Prophetic witness, the distant, transcendent voice that calls on the nation to repent and return to righteousness, is impossible if religion is comfortable. The religious voice is destroyed when religion yields to the temptation to be important, to shape the outcome of elections, to fit snugly into the cul-ture, to make filling the seats on the Sabbath day the highest goal. And

_____

*As a believer in actual diversity of opinion, I leave it to the reader to decide whether the good guys are on top now.

without the religious voice, our politics will be nothing–which means, in a democracy, that our nation will be nothing.

And religion: Without renewal, without a retreat from the wilderness and a return to the garden, without more time spent listening to the voice of God and less time spent drafting position papers or fighting over who gets to be in charge of what–without these necessities, religion will be nothing too.

AFTERWORD

The Multicultural Difficulty

What does the Lord require of you? To love mercy, act justly, and walk humbly with your God.

—Micah 6:8

AND WHAT OF RELIGION'S FUTURE IN AMERICAN politics? Is there, somewhere, another Charles Finney, teaching at a major university, training the leaders of the future, explaining to them why some particularly objectionable aspects of the culture are against God's law, as Finney did from his Oberlin base in the days of slavery?

Unlikely.

On America's elite campuses, today, it is perfectly acceptable for professors to use their classrooms to attack religion, to mock it, to trivialize it, and to refer to those to whom faith truly matters as dupes, and dangerous fanatics on top of it. I have heard some of the wisest scholars in the country deride religious beliefs and religious believers in terms so full of stereotype and of—let us say the word—bigotry that we would be appalled were they to say similar things about just any other group. Sometimes these stereotypes show up in scholarly articles, visions of the religious as narrow-minded, irrational, and subject to manipulation.[1]

Antireligious slurs have become a commonplace of intellectual discourse, so much so that scholars are not expected to cite any authority when, in their academic work, they refer to the religiously devout as narrow-minded, irrational, or poorly educated. We have grown comfortable with the idea that the classroom is the proper forum in which to insist that true believers are dangerously undemocratic.

By way of useful contrast, imagine the reaction were a professor at an Ivy League school, say, to use the classroom as a pulpit from which to evangelize, urging students to march out and fight the good fight because God demands it of them—following, in short, in the footsteps of Finney and his protégés. We would be shocked and offended and deeply angry. Because attacking religion is fine. But being openly religious, allowing one's students to know that one is religious—well, that is a problem. Which might help explain why it was a private lawyer rather than the American Association of University Professors or the American Civil Liberties Union that came to the defense of a professor at the University of Alabama who was prohibited by the school from telling his students of his Christianity and how it shaped his views.[2]

Do not misunderstand the point. I am not calling for professors to evangelize. But I see no reason why trying to further a religion in the classroom is worse than trying to destroy it. I am pointing out the disequivalence. The campuses are not necessarily the future of America, but it does not pay to bet against them; so if religion is more easily attacked in our colleges than defended, we might indeed have a clue to what the future holds. If our great universities teach, in effect, that there is nothing to learn from religion and every reason to dislike it, many students are bound to take those teachings to heart. Perhaps, in the future, there will be less worry about religion in politics because there will be fewer religious people. And that would be a tragedy.

Yet, as we have seen from the opening chapters of this book, it is in the nature of religion to resist, to fight back against attempts to limit its sphere. It is in the nature of the truly religious to resist, too, for efforts to wall in the faith will often be antithetical to what believers think God wants of them. The death of religion has been declared many times. It is said to be a spent force, no longer relevant to matters of genuine human concern, a superstition that cannot survive our technological times. It is said to fall to pieces under the scrutiny of our trained faculties of critical rationality. It is said to be outmoded, misogynistic, arrogant, irrational.

But it never quite goes away.

II

How strange to be a committed black Christian, increasingly evangelical, teaching at a traditionally white and aggressively secular academic institution. One of Yale's virtues is that it has a place for somebody like me—not me in particular, but somebody *like* me. But not a lot of spaces.

We live in a purportedly multicultural era, when colleges and universities, in the face of the assault on affirmative action, continue to try to recruit with an eye toward what they like to call diversity. Admissions officers are always ready with relevant statistics—we have so many of this color, so many of that sex, perhaps some number from the other side of the continent, and so on. What they never talk about—not almost never, but actually never—is how many different religions are represented. This omission is understandable, but it is also strange. If one truly wants diversity, it might be useful to look for people who are truly different—and religion, if it is sincere, is one of the forces that can make us so. Let me repeat what I wrote in Chapter 2: A religion that makes no difference in the life of the believer is not a religion worthy of the name.

III

There is much talk in America about the so-called Religious Right but very little about the Religious Left, even though there clearly is one. (The reader will know by now that I do not like the term Religious Right, and I do not like the term Religious Left either, but, in this case, I will use both in order to make my point.) If the Religious Right comprises the organizations of conservative religionists trying to influence policy in the direction they prefer, then the Religious Left must be the organizations of liberal religionists trying to influence policy in the direction *they* prefer. If the Christian Coalition and the Traditional Values Coalition are emblematic of the Religious Right, then the National Council of Churches and the Southern Christian Leadership Conference and the Interfaith Alliance are emblematic of the Religious Left.

And it is a peculiar artifact of our era that the history books already mention the Religious Right as a force in the 1980s (which it wasn't really), but few of them refer to the Religious Left when discussing the (successful) antiwar movement of the Vietnam era or the (moderately successful) civil rights movement of the 1960s—both of which might be painted as great triumphs for the Religious Left, if we ever admitted that one existed. We do not admit its existence, I suspect, because the word "Religious" in "Religious Right" is used pejoratively. The very term "Religious Right" has become an insult on many lips, which may be why it is now disdained by some of the very conservatives who coined it and gave it meaning back in the 1970s and 1980s.

Unlike some critics of the extremist version of separation of church and state, I have not argued, and do not believe, that people of deep faith are oppressed in America. Some prominent Christian conservatives have made a similar point, urging others in their movement not to speak of Christians as though they were some victimized minority. (Ralph Reed, former executive director of the Christian Coalition, has been particularly outspoken on this point.)[3] I do believe, however, that there exists in much of the nation's elite culture—particularly the legal and media cultures—at least a moderate bias against religious devotion in general, and evangelical Christianity in particular.[4] We cannot understand the emergence of an antireligious politics in America since the early 1970s without understanding that this bias exists. "Religion in public," Father Richard John Neuhaus has written, "is but the public opinion of those citizens who are religious."[5] Absolutely. But, among intellectuals, public opinion of religious citizens is public opinion of a decidedly inferior sort. A peculiarity of our age is that we proclaim our respect for diversity except when the diversity is religious. And adding diversity by adding Christianity is evidently worst of all. That is why a federal appellate court in Colorado had no trouble approving a public school's decision to bar a Christian teacher from leaving his Bible where students might see it, even though he taught in a classroom where religious materials from other traditions were on the bookshelves.[6]

One answer that is offered in the literature and in public commentary is that Christianity is already the dominant religious faith in the country, so there is no need to look for more of it. A nicely nuanced proposition, too—except that it is false. Or, rather, such meaning as it has is not relevant to the question. More than four out of five Americans call themselves Christians, but they do not all profess the same things, and sometimes the differences are vast. If Christianity is dominant, there should be a single, clear Christian view on such divisive issues as abortion or same-sex marriage. There is not. There are people who in all sincerity call themselves Christians on both sides of such issues, as there are on both sides of more vital theological questions, such as the salvation of non-Christians or the justification of the sinner by faith alone and grace alone or by faith, grace, and good works. That these debates might make little sense to most people who are not Christians, and even to many people who are, simply illustrates the point: The diversity of the Christian community is vast and, for too many intellectuals, unmined.

There often seems to be, at the heart of our purported celebration of diversity, the image of a museum. Elites want to celebrate cultures different from their own as long as the elites themselves can remain unaffected by the contact. It is not, ever, elite culture that should be altered by these encounters, except in ways that, secretly or not so secretly, it already wants to change. It is, rather, the others who should change, the members of the different cultures, so obviously primitive, perhaps even savage, in their understanding of such crucial human activities as sex. And, certainly, members of these other cultures should not be allowed to impose their moral understandings on their own children. Teaching moral truth is the job of the culture, and multiculturalism cannot be allowed to get in the way.

Does this seem overstated? I wish it were. But consider: Every four years, the many churches of the worldwide Anglican Communion meet for an international gathering known as the Lambeth Conference. My own Episcopal Church is a member of the Communion and sends delegates. At the 1998 Lambeth Conference, Western representatives were shocked when bishops from Africa and Asia forced the adoption of resolutions approving traditional Christian understandings of family life. And did these fine Western liberals, doubtless supporters of diversity, go away determined to learn from the socially conservative clergy of the Third World? Heaven forbid! Instead, they went away muttering at the foolishness, the backwardness, the intellectual immaturity of these bishops, and determined to find a way to bring the Third World churches around to a more Western point of view.[7] (I have heard some of the muttering myself.) When the old-style missionaries did the same thing, elites derided it as cultural imperialism; but now it seems that the justice of imposing Western ideas on the rest of the world is a matter of whose ox is being gored.

About the time I completed this manuscript, I encountered a young seminary student, an Anglican from East Africa. She expressed her concern about the American response to both Lambeth and the continuing efforts by traditionalists from the Third World to press their case. She did not come out and use the word "racism," but I think it lurked just beneath the surface of her complaint. Americans, she argued, do not take the claims of non-Americans seriously. I do not think she was suggesting that what I took to be her side was entitled to prevail. She objected, rather, to the ready American assumption that, when it comes to matters of morality, there is nothing to learn from traditions that are different.

The infuriating truth of the elite celebration of diversity is that the celebration is limited by a staggering, absolutely staggering, moral arrogance.

Our cultural elites believe they have much to teach but nothing to learn. Multiculturalism is the cloak behind which they hide this truth. The true reason school vouchers are ultimately bad in the elite view is that they might give parents—*parents, imagine that!*—too much authority over what their children learn. Naturally, vouchers must be unconstitutional, for they interfere with the steady onward march of the dominant culture. If parents can choose their children's education, there is a terrible risk that their children will grow up with ideas radically different from the cultural norm. They might even counsel resistance. This genuine diversity would be a threat to elite values and must therefore not be allowed. Sometimes it seems that the point of multiculturalism is to make sure all cultures are basically the same, except, of course, for singing and dancing and sampling exotic food and the occasional recitation of a famous speech. (If you disagree, think not about Black History Month but about Lambeth.)

Yet I would not want to be taken as suggesting that the moral arrogance of the Religious Left is greater than the arrogance of the Religious Right. That competition would, I suspect, be a very close and depressing one. On the right, too, are religious leaders who believe that they already know all the answers, who want no new arguments, who refuse to accept the possibility that traditions other than their own might possess a piece of the truth. Of those who choose to get involved in electoral politics, this is particularly true—for politics seems to provoke many faithful believers to remarkable feats of theological certainty, so that they know, for certain, where Jesus stands on the capital gains tax. Long-time conservative Christian activist George Weigel, writing during President Clinton's first term, put the point forcefully:

> A partisan Gospel is an ideological Gospel, and as many of us insisted against the claims of liberation theology in the 1970s and 1980s, an ideologically driven Gospel is a debasement of the Gospel. 'Christian voter scorecards' which suggest that the Gospel provides a 'Christian answer' to President Clinton's economic stimulus package, to the administration's tax proposals, to questions of voting rules in the House of Representatives, and to increasing the federal debt ceiling demean the Gospel by identifying it with an ideological agenda.[8]

Hubris, always, is the risk the activist assumes, and the activist who chooses to battle on the field of politics, hoping to change the nation by changing its laws, faces all the temptations of the insider.

Still, the Religious Right's hopeless efforts to fiddle with the law pale beside the Religious Left's successful efforts to fiddle with the culture. The Religious Left is not necessarily better than the Religious Right, only smarter . . . and it has cooperated with elite efforts to fix the rules so that nobody else can win. Which is why clergy who endorse political candidates are condemned but clergy who destroy traditional values are lionized. And why the barbed wire on the wall of separation of church and state faces inward, keeping religion imprisoned. And why so many churches have lowered their sights, no longer trying to work in God's creation, worrying only about filling the seats. And why continued prosperity is so crucial to the culture's survival, for our nation's wealth buys off many religionists who might otherwise be sufficiently discontented to try to make things different.

Some, of course, are discontented anyway. And many of them continue, as they always have, to turn to politics. I have not argued in these pages that it is usually or even frequently a mistake for the religious to try to influence the course of policy; I have argued that it is usually wrong for the religions, as institutions, or religious leaders, as representatives of their traditions, to endorse political candidates. In either case, however, the matter is one for each religion to decide for itself—for it is to God's rules, not the rules of the secular state, that the faithful must look for guidance.

Yet I believe that the religious should rarely opt for coercion (which is all that policy is, no matter who creates it) as a means of awakening a cranky and reluctant world to the higher truth that nearly every religion believes it can teach. The biblical tradition of prophetic witness, being forceful in criticism of the sovereign but doing it from without rather than from within, still seems to me to represent religious activism at its best. Religion, as we have seen, can inspire people to do great things. It can also inspire them to commit great crimes. Those who fear religion, like those who love it, have reasons for their sentiments . . . which is another reason for religionists who are seized by great ideas to be prayerful in their activism and to proceed with care.

Nevertheless, taking care or not, it is vital to proceed. Over the centuries, many religions have chosen to retreat from the contagion of the world. Some of these have thrived, but many others have withered. In recent years, many evangelical Christian activists have returned to their dissenting roots, calling for disengagement from culture, the (temporary) abandonment of politics, and the development of "parallel institutions" for the raising of their families . . . and the living of their lives. Others have questioned this call, determined not to surrender in a struggle they believe vital to the nation's future.

The abolitionists chose the path of work in God's creation rather than standing back and concentrating only on personal salvation. But so did the prohibitionists. So did Mrs. Fannie Lou Hamer. What matters, surely, is that religionists contemplating public activism spend most of their time in the garden, to be sure of what it is that the Lord requires. If the ultimate decision is to enter the wilderness, they must not make the mistake of lingering there too long—not because they might lose a battle, or even a war, but because they might lose themselves, along with any serious sense of a God-given mission. To engage with the culture is to strike an awkward balance, straddling the wall of separation that protects the garden without yielding to the temptations of the wilderness. The risks of either course are plain. In the end, a religion that believes in its own truth should move as that truth directs. If God calls the believer to witness, then the believer must go into the wilderness and witness.

IV

The simple and clear message that the religious generally—and Christians particularly—must not allow the world to forget is this: God is present. God has not died or gone off on vacation or lost interest in his creation and the human beings he created. There is no direction in which we can turn, no philosophical shield behind which we can cower, no constitutional judgment we can assert, to evade God's exacting gaze. There is no structure we can erect that God cannot topple, no physical law we can discover that God could not change, no ethical argument we can design that God could not refute. From God's eternal presence, we should learn humility.

The religious must not retreat before the evangelizing armies of the secular. We should neither settle for reducing our faith to the "God of the gaps" condemned by Bonhoeffer, nor accept the bizarre proposition that religion is wholly private, thus not entitled to a place at the democratic dinner table where we squabble over serious matters. We should resist the pressure to "translate" the teachings of our faith into a less powerful and untranscendent secular language that is designed to forestall the radicalism of the outsider's ideas. By insisting on God's presence, the religious can become conscientious objectors to the burgeoning effort to conscript the en-

tire nation into the service of the bland yet dangerous ethic of self-fulfillment, an ethic that long ago claimed both major political parties. Consider:
When was the last time the presidential nominee of a major party, instead
of promising to give us what we want, at no charge, instead said to us
something like: "We have important work to do together. It is hard work.
It is going to cost us. It will demand sacrifices. But it is work that must be
done." The answer is that no candidate would dare talk to us that way, not
in this era that celebrates the fulfillment of the self above all.

Whereas the great Western religious traditions call for (or used to call
for) the *denial* of the self. Life in God's presence means, fundamentally, life
lived in the knowledge that we owe the very fact of our existence not to accident but to Divine Will. The obligations that knowledge creates we can
never fulfill, which is why the religious life is a life of striving. In the United
States of the bold new century, few people want to strive, and everybody
wants to be fulfilled; we are, in short, morally lazy. The real reason, I think,
that so many are so fearful of the religious voice in our public affairs, even
the voice of prophetic witness, is that religionists have a stubborn little habit
of pointing this out. As the United States grows more and more complacent, fewer and fewer people want to listen, for the defining ethic of our politics has become a simple rule: We should all get what we want.

The ethic of self makes the religious task more difficult ... but also
more necessary. With a more vibrant religious voice in our politics, we
should be able to do better. We could, indeed, hardly do any worse.

Please, God—bless America.

NOTES

Introduction

1   I am well aware of the scholarship in the field of religious studies criticizing
    the indiscriminate use by Westerners of the term "religion," when the cultural
    phenomena concerning transcendence and ritual are so varied. See, for ex-
    ample, Jonathan Z. Smith, *Imagining Religion: From Babylon to Jonestown*
    (Chicago: University of Chicago Press, 1982). But I do not think my usage
    is likely to confuse.

2   According to a 1997 Gallup survey, 44 percent of American adults believe in
    the literal truth of the Genesis creation story, 39 percent believe that evolu-
    tion was guided by God, and 10 percent do not believe that God played any
    role. Women are far more likely than men to be creationists. See the data
    cited in George Gallup Jr. and D. Michael Lindsay, *Surveying the Religious
    Landscape: Trends in U.S. Beliefs* (Harrisburg, Pa.: Morehouse Publishing,
    1999), pp. 36–38.

3   In a survey taken a few weeks before the 1996 presidential election, the Pew
    Research Center asked 1,938 registered voters: "How much influence do
    you think churches have on who becomes the president: too much, too little
    or about the right amount?" The responses were: too much, 15 percent; too
    little, 29 percent; right amount, 45 percent; don't know or refused to answer,
    11 percent. Pew Research Center survey, published October 25, 1996 (from
    Polling the Nations CD-ROM). But, if the question is phrased differently, the
    results are different, too—that is, the clear majority in favor of religious ac-
    tivism shrinks a bit. In June 1996, just after the primaries but well before the
    general election, Pew asked: "In your opinion, should the churches keep out
    of political matters—or should they express their views on day-to-day social
    and political questions?" The responses were: keep out, 43 percent; express
    views, 54 percent; no opinion, 3 percent. Pew Research Center survey, pub-
    lished June 25, 1996 (from *Polling the Nations*).

4   See Frederick Mark Gedicks, *The Rhetoric of Church and State: A Critical Analy-
    sis of Religion Clause Jurisprudence* (Durham, N.C.: Duke University Press,

1993), pp. 16–20. Professor Gedicks is following the usage of Mark deWolfe Howe, whose work I discuss in Chapter 4.

5 I heard Stanley Hauerwas deliver this bon mot when both of us spoke at Middlebury College in the winter of 1996.

6 Jim Wallis, *The Soul of Politics: A Practical and Prophetic Vision for Change* (New York: The New Press and Orbis Books, 1994), p. 32.

7 See Ralph Reed, *Active Faith: How Christians Are Changing the Soul of American Politics* (New York: The Free Press, 1996).

8 C. S. Lewis, "Meditation on the Third Commandment," in C. S. Lewis, *God in the Dock: Essays on Theology and Ethics,* ed. Walter Hooper (Grand Rapids, Mich.: William B. Eerdmans Publishing Company, 1970), p. 196.

Chapter One

1 See the data discussed in Clyde Wilcox, *God's Warriors: The Christian Right in Twentieth Century America* (Baltimore, Maryland: The Johns Hopkins University Press, 1992). The data discussed in text rely on self-identification to determine who is a fundamentalist.

2 Some 84 percent of Americans say they believe in God, and another 10 percent say they believe in a higher power. See George Gallup Jr. and D. Michael Lindsay, *Surveying the Religious Landscape: Trends in U.S. Beliefs* (Harrisburg, Pa.: Morehouse Publishing, 1999), pp. 23–25. The data are for 1997.

3 See William James, *The Varieties of Religious Experience* (1902; reprint, New York: The Modern Library, 1929).

4 See Max Weber, *The Sociology of Religion,* trans. Ephraim Fischoff (first English translation 1963; reprint, Boston: Beacon Press, 1993) (originally published 1922).

5 Sebastian de Grazia, "Under God? Religion and the US Presidency," *Times Literary Supplement,* June 4, 1999.

6 See generally the discussions in Donald M. Shriver Jr., *An Ethic for Enemies: Forgiveness in Politics* (New York: Oxford University Press, 1995); and Lewis Smedes, *The Art of Forgiving: When You Need to Forgive and Don't Know How* (Nashville: Moorings, 1996). Note that Professors Shriver and Smedes both published their excellent books well before the Lewinsky scandal.

7 Smedes, in *Art of Forgiving,* makes this point with some eloquence.

8 "Declaration Concerning Religion, Ethics, and the Crisis in the Clinton Presidency," reprinted in *Judgment Day at the White House: A Critical Declaration Exploring Moral Issues and the Political Use and Abuse of Religion,* ed. Gabriel Fackre (Grand Rapids, Mich.: William B. Eerdmans Publishing Company, 1999), p. 1.

9 Lewis Smedes, "On the Other Hand," in *Judgment Day at the White House: A Critical Declaration Exploring Moral Issues and the Political Use and Abuse of Religion,*

ed. Gabriel Fackre (Grand Rapids, Mich.: William B. Eerdmans Publishing Company, 1999), p. 128. In the interest of full disclosure, I should explain that I, too, was invited to sign the letter but declined to do so.

10 For a rather dispassionate catalogue, see Paul Johnson, *A History of Christianity* (New York: Atheneum, 1976).

11 See, for example, the discussions of religion in Stephen Macedo, *Diversity and Distrust: Civic Education in a Multicultural Democracy* (Cambridge: Harvard University Press, 2000); and Kathleen Sullivan, "Religion and Liberal Democracy," *University of Chicago Law Review* 59 (1992): 195.

12 See John R. Noonan Jr., *The Lustre of Our Country: The American Experience of Religious Freedom* (Berkeley: University of California Press, 1998), p. 43.

13 See Orlando Patterson, *Freedom in the Making of Western Culture* (New York: Basic, 1991).

14 Nathan O. Hatch, *The Democratization of American Christianity* (New Haven: Yale University Press, 1989), p. 136.

Chapter Two

1 Both here and elsewhere in the book, my account of the relationship between religion and meaning is influenced by the work of the sociologist Peter L. Berger, especially *The Sacred Canopy: Elements of a Sociological Theory of Religion* (New York: Doubleday, 1967).

2 I defend the definition of religion as narrative in my Oliver Wendell Holmes Lecture. See Stephen L. Carter, "Parents, Religion, and Schools: Reflections on *Pierce,* Seventy Years Later," *Seton Hall Law Review* 27 (1997): 1194. Obviously, the consequence of this view is that there is no such thing as a religion of one— or a religion founded just yesterday. Until the belief system develops both facets of the definition, a people and an extension over time, it may be an interesting set of ideas about God, those ideas may even involve a strong faith commitment, they may even be *true*—but it is not a religion.

3 For an argument that the free exercise clause of the First Amendment should be explicitly understood to foster a plurality of meanings, in order to avoid state hegemony, see Bette Novit Evans, *Interpreting the Free Exercise of Religion: The Constitution and American Pluralism* (Chapel Hill: University of North Carolina Press, 1997).

4 For two quite different accounts of the process of that change, see Harold Bloom, *The American Religion: The Emergence of the Post-Christian Nation* (New York: Simon & Schuster, 1992); and Nathan O. Hatch, *The Democratization of American Christianity* (New Haven: Yale University Press, 1989).Bloom believes that the strange workings of American individualist ideology have reduced almost all of religion to a form of gnosticism. Hatch argues that the

tug of democracy has altered the hierarchical structures that characterized most European religions, greatly enhancing the importance and the power of the lay member. Although Bloom's polemic is, as always, fascinating, and what he says is surely true of many mainline Protestant churches, my scholarly sympathies lie with Hatch.

5 I discuss the problem of domestication through the granting of rights in greater detail in my Brennan Symposium Lecture. See Stephen Carter, "Religious Freedom As If Religion Matters: A Tribute to Justice Brennan," *California Law Review* 87 (1999): 1059.

6 This account is drawn from Charles Marsh, *God's Long Summer: Stories of Faith and Civil Rights* (Princeton: Princeton University Press, 1997), pp. 39–40. For a shorter version of the same story, somewhat more sympathetic to Hubert Humphrey, see Taylor Branch, *Pillar of Fire: America in the King Years, 1963–65* (New York: Simon & Schuster, 1998), pp. 465–466. Branch's account has both Humphrey and Hamer in tears as she promises to pray for him. Marsh sees the two of them as adversaries, with Humphrey's eye fixed rigidly on the main chance.

7 Before President Clinton's supporters get too excited about this story, it is worth remembering that although David repented and kept his throne, the Lord still exacted punishment. The child born of his illicit affair with Bathsheba grew ill. Despite David's desperate prayer and fasting, the Lord took the child's life. Because David had truly repented, he accepted the Lord's hard justice. When his son died, David worshiped the Lord (2 Sam. 12:11–20).

8 The image of religion as subversive of the state it inhabits I borrow from the work of the liberation theologians, especially David Tracy. See David Tracy, *Plurality and Ambiguity: Hermeneutics, Religion, Hope* (San Francisco: Harper & Row, 1987).

9 Alfred Wesley Wishart, "Religion in Industry" (sermon delivered at Powers' Theatre, October 23, 1921), p. 6.

10 See Jeffrey K. Hadden, "Clergy Involvement in Civil Rights," *Annals of the American Academy of Political and Social Science* (January 1970): 118. See also the discussion in Taylor Branch, *Parting the Waters: America in the King Years, 1954–1963* (New York: Simon & Schuster, 1984).

11 Quoted in Juan Williams, *Eyes on the Prize: America's Civil Rights Years, 1954–1965* (New York: Penguin, 1988), p. 244. For background on Mrs. Hamer, including her relatively radical stances on everything from redistribution of wealth (pro) to abortion (anti), see Kay Mills, *This Little Light of Mine: The Life of Fannie Lou Hamer* (New York: Dutton, 1993).

12 Although the prediction of the voting behavior of individual politicians is quite difficult, most political scientists now seem to agree that the desire to be re-elected is the dominant variable. In deciding how to vote, politicians who

are eligible to serve another term evidently place re-election above what is sometimes called principle but what might be better described as personal ideology. See, for example, the model developed in Linda R. Cohen and Roger G. Noll, "How to Vote, Whether to Vote: Strategies for Voting and Abstaining in Congressional Roll Calls," *Political Behavior* 13 (1991): 97. See also Joseph B. Kalt and Mark A. Zupan, "The Apparent Ideological Behavior of Legislators: Testing for Principal-Agent Slack in Political Institutions," *Journal of Law and Economics* 33 (1990): 103. The incumbent who ignores or at least submerges personal ideology might seem unprincipled but is actually behaving rationally because of another well-known phenomenon, that voters are more likely to base their decisions on what the incumbent has done in office than what they expect him to do if re-elected. See Morris P. Fiorina, *Retrospective Voting in American National Elections* (New Haven: Yale University Press, 1981).

13   For a critique of this ideology, which might be called "measurism," see Chapter 10.

14   For discussions of the de-radicalization of the religious power of the civil rights movement, see Anthony E. Cook, *The Least of These: Race, Law, and Religion in American Culture* (New York: Routledge, 1997); James H. Cone, *Risks of Faith: The Emergence of a Black Theology of Liberation, 1968-1998* (Boston: Beacon Press, 1999); and Michael Eric Dyson, *I May Not Get There with You: The True Martin Luther King, Jr.* (New York: Free Press, 2000). The sociologist Orlando Patterson argues that the King era saw Christianity re-invigorated by a return to its activist roots, an emphasis on justice in this world, and a rejection of the Pauline emphasis on self-denial and salvation. See Orlando Patterson, *Rituals of Blood: Consequences of Slavery in Two American Centuries* (Washington, D.C.: Civitas/Counterpoint, 1998), pp. 224–232.

15   Martin Luther King Jr., "An Address Before the National Press Club," in *A Testament of Hope: The Essential Writings and Speeches of Martin Luther King, Jr.*, ed. James Melvin Washington (San Francisco: HarperSanFrancisco, 1986), pp. 99, 105.

16   Martin Luther King Jr., "The American Dream," in *A Testament of Hope: The Essential Writings and Speeches of Martin Luther King, Jr.*, ed. James Melvin Washington (San Francisco: HarperSanFrancisco, 1986), p. 208.

17   Martin Luther King Jr., "Our God Is Marching On," in *A Testament of Hope: The Essential Writings and Speeches of Martin Luther King, Jr.*, ed. James Melvin Washington (San Francisco: HarperSanFrancisco, 1986), pp. 227, 229.

18   See the data discussed in George Gallup Jr. and D. Michael Lindsay, *Surveying the Religious Landscape: Trends in U.S. Beliefs* (Harrisburg, Pa.: Morehouse, 1999), pp. 52–54. The assertion that black Americans may be the most religious group in the Western world is a commonplace of the sociology of religion and is, in this case, taken from an earlier Gallup study. See George

Gallup Jr. and Jim Castelli, *The People's Religion: American Faith in the 90's* (New York: Macmillan, 1989), pp. 122-123.

19   Even black Roman Catholics tend to be on the evangelical end of the Catholic spectrum. See the data discussed in James C. Cavendish et al., "Social Network Theory and Predictors of Religiosity for Black and White Catholics: Evidence of a 'Black Sacred Cosmos'?" *Journal for the Scientific Study of Religion* 37 (1998): 397.

20   Actually, the voting patterns of evangelicals are significantly more complicated than what my text may seem to imply. In presidential elections this is particularly true. The NES data show that the notion that white evangelicals overwhelmingly vote Republican is an artifact of two campaigns: 1984 (Reagan vs. Mondale) and 1988 (Bush vs. Dukakis). In 1976 (Carter vs. Ford) and 1992 (Clinton vs. Bush), they split Democratic. In 1980 (Reagan vs. Carter) and 1996 (Clinton vs. Dole), they split more or less down the middle. The journalist E. J. Dionne suggests that if one looks further back in history, the voting behavior of white evangelicals grows even more complex, but points out that in the fifties and sixties, racial animus contributes as much as religious sentiment to their votes. See E. J. Dionne, *Why Americans Hate Politics* (New York: Simon & Schuster, 1991). On the other hand, as Dionne further notes, many evangelicals did not even vote until the 1970s. Ibid., pp. 209-210.

21   See, for example, the data discussed in Venise Wagner, "Black Republicans Call for New Focus on the Inner Cities," *San Francisco Examiner*, September 19, 1999, p. C1; and Ralph Z. Hallow, "Gore, Bradley Do Well in Wide-Ranging Poll," *Washington Times*, August 31, 1999, p. A1.

22   See Cornel West, *Race Matters* (New York: Vintage Books, 1994), pp. 43-70. West argues that black leadership has lost its spiritual power in part because the "vibrant tradition of resistance" has largely vanished. Ibid., pp. 56–57. There is merit to his contention, but one might also say of Professor West what Rousseau said of Aristotle, that he takes the effect for the cause. Perhaps the problem is not that the leaders are weaker because the tradition of resistance has ended; perhaps the problem is that the tradition of resistance has ended because the leaders are weaker. More to the point, the leaders may be too secure. As West puts it: "[M]ost present-day black political leaders appear too hungry for status to be angry, too eager for acceptance to be bold, too self-invested in advancement to be defiant." The earlier generation "made sense of the black plight in a poignant and powerful manner," he writes, but the current leadership "appeals to black people's sense of the sentimental and sensational." Ibid., p. 58. Professor West does not criticize black leadership alone. He argues that white liberals and conservatives have essentially abandoned the spiritual needs of black Americans, a point with which I strongly agree.

23   See Dietrich Bonhoeffer, *Ethics*, trans. Neville Horton Smith (New York: Touchstone, 1995), pp. 125–132. (Originally published in German in 1949;

first published in English 1955.) I omit this argument in the main text because he was using the term "radicalism" differently than I, and I do not
want to confuse the point.

24   The classic statement of the proposition that the black churches should be
     communities of resistance remains James H. Cone, *Black Theology and Black
     Power*, rev. ed. (Maryknoll, N.Y.: Orbis Books, 1997) (originally published
     1969).

25   James H. Cone, "White Theology Revisited?" in *Risks of Faith: The Emergence
     of a Black Theology of Liberation, 1968–1998* (Boston: Beacon Press, 1999), pp.
     130, 136.

26   See, for example, the surveys discussed in Terry M. Neal, "The Black Vote: A
     Turnout You Shouldn't Stereotype," *Washington Post*, November 8, 1998, p. C2.
     The tendency of black adults to take more "conservative" (I would prefer the
     term "traditional") positions than white adults on social and family issues is
     nowadays a commonplace of social science. At the same time, black adults
     rarely identify themselves as conservative, doubtless because the conservative
     movement in America has tended to be on the wrong side of most civil rights
     issues. (I am not singling out conservatives for special abuse: from the point of
     view of more traditionalist African Americans such as myself, liberals have
     tended to be on the wrong side of most social and family issues.)

27   See the data discussed, for example, in Siobhan Gorman, "Desperate Mea-
     sures," *National Journal*, December 18, 1999; and Peter Schrag, "The Voucher
     Seduction: The Issue Liberals Can't Ignore," *American Prospect*, November 23,
     1999, p. 46.

28   For an interesting discussion of the move among black activists away from
     the politics of persuasion, see Glenn Loury's essay "Two Paths to Black
     Progress" in his collection *One By One from the Inside Out: Essays and Reviews on
     Race and Responsibility in America* (New York: The Free Press, 1995), p. 63.
     Loury points to, but does not emphasize, the fact that the Christian tradition
     favors persuasion rather than coercion.

29   James H. Cone, "New Roles in the Ministry: A Theological Appraisal," in
     Risks of Faith: The Emergence of a Black Theology of Liberation, 1968–1998
     (Boston: Beacon Press, 1999), p. 111.

30   The roots of black Christianity go back, obviously, to slavery. The classic
     study of the transition from traditional African faiths to Christianity is Albert
     J. Raboteau, *Slave Religion: The "Invisible Institution" in the Antebellum South* (New
     York: Oxford University Press, 1978). Chapter 2 is particularly to the point—
     and particularly poignant.

31   The black clergy, even though they probably rescued Christianity, as Cornel
     West says, during the middle years of the twentieth century, are as prone to
     any other clergy to fall victim to the temptations of worldly power—not only
     political power but also economic and social influence. An excellent study of

the clergy, which lauds where laud is earned and criticizes where necessary, is C. Eric Lincoln and Lawrence H. Mamiya, *The Black Church in the African American Experience* (Durham, N.C.: Duke University Press, 1990). See especially chapters 9 and 13.

32 My comments on the state of the black clergy are not intended as "piling on." For black intellectuals, heaping criticism on the black church was something of an insider sport throughout the twentieth century, beginning with the outright rejection of the traditional faith in the Harlem Renaissance, and reaching its zenith in 1957, with the publication of E. Franklin Frazier's *Black Bourgeoisie*, which dripped contempt every time he mentioned the churches. In truth, I hold the black clergy, as a group, in enormous respect. My family and I attend a black church. I agree with James Cone that in many ways the black clergy have rescued Christianity in America. At the same time, I worry that the politicization of the clergy—and here I refer to involvement in electoral politics, not policy debates—is robbing the nation of what has been, since the 1950s, perhaps its most important source of prophetic voices.

Chapter Three

1 Quoted in Paul Rolly, [untitled article], United Press International, BC Cycle, February 16, 1983 (available on LEXIS/NEXIS).

2 Quoted in John M. Leighty, [untitled article], United Press International, PM Cycle, July 12, 1984 (available on LEXIS/NEXIS).

3 As Ralph Reed, former executive director of the Christian Coalition, has pointed out, when Moral Majority's inflated membership claims came to light, opponents "turned on it with a vengeance, pronouncing it a paper tiger." Ralph Reed, *Active Faith: How Christians are Changing the Soul of American Politics* (New York: Free Press, 1996), pp. 109–110.

4 C. S. Lewis, "Meditation on the Third Commandment," in C. S. Lewis, *God in the Dock: Essays on Theology and Ethics,* ed. Walter Hooper (Grand Rapids, Mich.: William B. Eerdmans Publishing Company, 1970), p. 196.

5 For a discussion of the Christian Nation Amendment, see Mark Silk, *Spiritual Politics: Religion and America Since World War II* (New York: Simon and Schuster, 1988), pp. 99–100. Silk's book is one of many sources giving the lie to the notion that our politics have traditionally been secular and only lately has the religious voice entered in.

6 See "Campaign Notes," *Washington Post,* March 5, 1980, p. A9.

7 Alan Brinkley, "The Problem of American Conservatism," *American Historical Review* 99 (April 1994): 425. Another factor often ignored by liberal analysts is the spiritual seeking of many members of the Baby Boom generation, large numbers of whom, across lines of class and education, seem to be hunting for a deeper meaning than the one the materialistic culture can offer. See, for ex-

ample, the discussion in Wade Clark Roof, *A Generation of Seekers: The Spiritual Journeys of the Baby Boom Generation* (San Francisco: HarperSanFrancisco, 1993).

8 In fact, this unfortunate (and demographically false) anti-evangelical slur by the *Post*, although it was made in 1993, continues to serve as a successful applause line for the Christian Coalition and many other organizations of conservative religionists, who cite it as evidence of media bias. See the discussion in Justin Watson, *Christian Coalition*, pp. 132–135.

9 In a survey by the Pew Research Center just after the 1996 election, 91 percent of respondents said that neither clergy nor any other religious group urged them "to vote a particular way" in "the presidential race, congressional race, a state race, or a local race." Only 5 percent answered yes for the presidential race, 3 percent for each of the other races (November 10, 1996). In a survey taken two weeks earlier asking whether "information on parties or candidates for the upcoming election" was available in the respondent's place or worship, 22 percent said yes, 75 percent said no (October 25, 1996). (All data are taken from *Polling the Nations* [CD-ROM].)

10 The abortion decision is *Roe v. Wade*, 410 U.S. 113 (1973).

11 See, for example, Dallas A. Blanchard, *The Anti-Abortion Movement and the Rise of the Religious Right* (New York: Twayne Publishers, 1994). Professor Blanchard makes a number of questionable claims, especially his insistence on linking the theology and worldviews of Protestant fundamentalists and those he calls "fundamentalist Catholics." He insists, moreover, that turning back the gains made in the fight for women's equality is an important motive for those who oppose abortion. Like many opponents of conservative Christian groups, he supports such points as these by ascribing to everyone with whom he disagrees the public statements of some.

12 See Stephen L. Carter, *The Culture of Disbelief: How American Law and Politics Trivialize Religious Devotion* (New York: Basic Books, 1993), pp. 56–58.

13 The term "culture war" came into popular use following the publication of James Davison Hunter's *Culture Wars: The Struggle to Define America* (New York: Basic Books, 1991). Nowadays, the phrase has become ubiquitous in conservative social commentary. Its German equivalent has even crept into a Supreme Court opinion, albeit a dissent. But not all conservatives agree that the culture war in fact exists. For a thoughtful dissenting voice, see Jeremy Rabkin, "The Culture War That Isn't," *Policy Review*, August-September 1999. For sharp responses to Rabkin, see James Neuchterlein, "Culture War No More?" *First Things*, October 1999, and peruse the letters to the editor published in *Policy Review* in the December 1999-January 2000 issue.

14 For a recent example of the argument, see Daniel P. Moloney, "Sex and the Married Missileer," *First Things*, February 2000, p. 45.

15 I discuss the "creation versus evolution" debate in greater detail in Carter, *Culture of Disbelief*, chap. 9. I am not a supporter of the teaching of creationism in

the schools, but I do not think it more troubling than much that is taught there now. Indeed, to the extent that the schools reinforce the cultural message that the child's world should revolve around the self and its desires, they are already teaching something that does enormous damage, not only to the children but to the nation. I should add that I consider the argument between creationists and evolutionists an argument about the source of knowledge—that is, about epistemology—and, therefore, well outside the purview of courts. In other words, although I do not consider either the banning of evolution or the teaching of creationism in the public schools to be particularly good ideas, I certainly do not consider either choice to be unconstitutional. Thus, I think the Supreme Court erred when it struck down both. See *Epperson v. Arkansas,* 393 U.S. 97 (1968), and *Edwards v. Aguillard,* 482 U.S. 578 (1987).

16   David Frum, *How We Got Here: The 70's: The Decade That Brought You Modern Life (for Better or Worse)* (New York: Basic Books, 2000), p. 155 and elsewhere.

17   For scholarly discussions of the reasons traditionalists join Christian Coalition and other politically active groups, see, for example, Watson, *The Christian Coalition,* pp. 89-121; Brinkley, "Problem of American Conservatism"; and Robert Wuthnow, "The Future of the Religious Right," in Michael Cromartie, ed., *No Longer Exiles: The Religious New Right in American Politics* (Washington, D.C.: Ethics and Public Policy Center, 1993), p. 27. The sociologist Wade Clark Roof has pointed out how the same forces and needs that lead conservative Christians to choose particular denominations can also influence their decision to become politically active. See Wade Clark Roof, *A Generation of Seekers: The Spiritual Journeys of the Baby Boom Generation* (San Francisco: HarperSanFrancisco, 1993), especially chapter 4. Careful studies have found no support for any of the more demeaning liberal explanations for the growth of the groups, such as the claim that adherents tend to be driven by irrational fears or to have adjustment problems; the claim that adherents tend to have an unusually strong, perhaps even pathological, need for authority; or the claim that it is only the forceful personalities of the leaders of the groups, or their manipulation of communication technology, that leads to adherence. See the discussion in Wilcox, *God's Warriors.*

18   This is as good a place as any for an unhappy confession. In the hardcover edition of my 1993 book *The Culture of Disbelief,* I included the Christian Coalition in a chapter entitled "Religious Fascism." I deeply regret this characterization, which was not only unfair but absurd. Perhaps I was led astray by the reporting on the group by an often hostile media or by my own incomplete understanding of the organization. My disagreements with some parts of the group's platform provide no justification for my polemic. The chapter bearing the unfortunate title actually includes no discussion of fascism of any kind. I wish there were a way to go back and change the chapter title, but there is not. I can only repeat the apology I have made elsewhere

(including the foreword to the paperback edition) and ask forgiveness from those who were quite justifiably angered.

19 See the data discussed in Clyde Wilcox, *God's Warriors: The Christian Right in Twentieth Century America* (Baltimore: The Johns Hopkins University Press, 1992).

20 See Lyman A. Kellstedt et al., "Religious Tradition, Denomination, and Commitment: White Protestants and the 1988 Election," in *The Bible and the Ballot Box: Religion and Politics in the 1988 Election,* ed. James L. Guth and John C. Green (Boulder: Westview Press, 1991), p. 139.

21 See Michael J. Avey, *The Demobilization of American Voters: A Comprehensive Theory of Voter Turnout* (New York: Greenwood Press, 1989), p. 83.

22 Ralph Reed, *Active Faith: How Christians Are Changing the Soul of American Politics* (New York: The Free Press, 1996), p. 112.

23 Ibid.

24 Unless otherwise noted, all voting data in this chapter and elsewhere in the book is compiled from National Election Studies, Center for Political Studies, University of Michigan, The NES Guide to Public Opinion and Electoral Behavior <http://www.umich.edu/~nesguide/nesguide.htm>, (Ann Arbor, Michigan: University of Michigan, Center for Political Studies [producer and distributor], 1995–1998). I am grateful to Yale law student Nathaniel Zylstra for collecting and analyzing the NES data.

25 The numbers are highly susceptible to definition. If, for example, we redefine our voting blocs so that we create a category of "white evangelicals" instead of using denominational affiliation, we find a much more heavily Republican split. See, for example, the figures discussed in Corwin Smidt, "Evangelical Voting Patterns: 1976-1988," in Cromartie, *No Longer Exiles,* p. 85. There is need for caution, however, when using anything other than denominational affiliation to rank voters, because the categories can become highly fluid and subject to error.

26 Prior to 1960, the NES figures, dating back to 1948, distinguished only four categories: Protestant, Catholic, Jewish, and "Other and None."

27 The remarks in question are by Mark Rozell of Catholic University, quoted in Mark Z. Barabak, "Bush Forges Victories in 3 States," *Los Angeles Times,* March 1, 2000, p. A1.

28 See generally the essays in Peter L. Berger, ed., *The Desecularization of the World: Resurgent Religion and World Politics* (Washington, D.C.: Ethics and Public Policy Center; Grand Rapids, Mich.: William B. Eerdmans Publishing Company, 1999).

29 This point is conceded and feared even by Dobson's critics. See, for example, Gil Alexander-Moegerle, *James Dobson's War on America* (Amherst, N.Y.: Prometheus Books, 1997).

30 Robert Booth Fowler, "The Failure of the Religious Right," in *No Longer Exiles: The Religious New Right in American Politics,* ed. Michael Cromartie (Washington, D.C.: Ethics and Public Policy Center, 1993), p. 57.

31 For example, in the 1980 Reagan landslide, the group claimed victory in forty of the forty-three local races in which it had taken sides, and nobody doubts the figures. The question is whether Moral Majority deserved a significant part of the credit.

32 See E. J. Dionne, "Response," in *Disciples and Democracy: Religious Conservatives and the Future of American Politics,* ed. Michael Cromartie (Washington, D.C.: Ethics and Public Policy Center; Grand Rapids, Mich.: William B. Eerdmans Publishing Company, 1994), p. 16. Dionne was responding to an essay by Ralph Reed, who was at the time the executive director of the Christian Coalition.The skepticism among Catholics and Jews about the motives of evangelicals has policy effects. For example, at least one observer has argued that the perception of evangelicals as anti-Semitic has hurt efforts to build a movement around opposition to abortion among traditionalist Jews. See Matthew Berke, "Jews Choosing Life," *First Things,* February 1999, p. 34.

33 Writes Judis: "Like other sectarian movements, [the Christian Coalition] found itself torn between maintaining its purity of heart—and the zeal of its followers—and winning conventional power. It could not do both, and when Reed turned the Christian Coalition into an arm of the Republican National Committee in the 1996 election, it began to crumble at the base." John B. Judis, "Razing McCain: The Conservative Campaign to Derail the Arizona Senator," *American Prospect,* March 13, 2000, p. 15.

34 According to a 1998 survey conducted by the George H. Gallup International Institute for Phi Delta Kappa, the educational organization, some two-thirds of American adults (and nearly three out of four parents of children in public schools) support a constitutional amendment to allow spoken prayers in public schools. George Gallup Jr. and D. Michael Lindsay, *Surveying the Religious Landscape: Trends in U.S. Beliefs* (Harrisburg, Pa.: Morehouse Publishing, 1999), pp. 151–152. Lest one think that American adults are unaware of the implications of classroom prayer, they understand perfectly well that somebody would have to write or select the prayer to be recited—they simply disagree on who should do it. Thus, 32 percent say that "parents" should be responsible for choosing the prayer, 30 percent would give the choice to students, and 13 percent are willing to trust the school board. Ibid., p. 153. Also, four out of five adults would not require dissenting students to join the prayer, and three out of four would welcome prayers from the Jewish, Muslim, and Hindu traditions. Ibid., p. 154. The significance of this data is that the school prayer issue, often seen as an initial wedge for a Christianization movement in public education, might, if ever implemented, prove more a device for studying comparative religion.

35 For example, a very detailed 1996 USA Today/CNN/Gallup Survey on attitudes toward abortion found that 82 percent of respondents favored a ban on all abortions during the final three months of pregnancy. See "Abortion Battles: More in Common Than We Think," *USA Today*, August 13, 1996, p. 17A. Figures of this kind can be misleading. Consider: Some 56 percent of those who say abortion should be illegal in all circumstances are willing to make an exception if they are asked directly about a threat to the life of the mother. George Gallup Jr. and D. Michael Lindsay, *Surveying the Religious Landscape: Trends in U.S. Beliefs* (Harrisburg, Pa.: Morehouse Publishing, 1999), p. 105. But there again, the answer may mislead because the question is insufficiently nuanced. The doctrine of "double effect," for example, might, for some respondents, justify taking measures to save the life of the mother, even if those measures might have the unintended consequence of killing the unborn child. Consequently, the 56 percent figure might include many who take the view that it is wrong to kill the fetus but right to save the mother. The classic invocation of this argument in the abortion context is Philippa Foot, "Abortion and the Doctrine of Double Effect," *Oxford Review* 5 (1967): 9. (Foot's essay also introduced to philosophy the famous "trolley problem." I would rather not reveal what the trolley problem is, lest I spoil the fun for those who have never read the article.) I should add that the application of double effect, which is drawn from natural law and much developed in Catholic theology, is not read by the Catholic Church as supporting abortion.

36 This is the basic argument of Cal Thomas and Ed Dobson, *Blinded by Might: Can the Religious Right Save America?* (Grand Rapids, Mich.: Zondervan Publishing House, 1999). Although the book is coauthored, it is appropriate to refer to the views of the authors as individuals because they wrote different chapters. Cal Thomas, to whom I refer in the text, makes this point most forcefully in chapters 3 and 7. Dobson makes a similar argument in chapter 4.

37 Dean Merrill, *Sinners in the Hands of an Angry Church: Finding a Better Way to Influence Our Culture* (Grand Rapids, Mich.: Zondervan Publishing House, 1997), p. 149.

38 Dietrich Bonhoeffer, *Ethics,* p. 130.

39 Ibid., p. 129.

40 Ibid.

41 Bonhoeffer is at pains to distinguish the label of radicalism, which believers should not be afraid to bear, from genuine radicalism, in the sense of a taste for radical and immediate solutions, which, he says, is as much an enemy of the Word as is compromise. Ibid., pp. 126–132.

42 Quoted in Watson, *Christian Coalition,* p. 95.

43 Lewis, "Meditation," p. 197.

44 Reed, *Active Faith,* p. 140.

45   For a journalist's detailed rebuttal of the claim of a takeover, see Fred Barnes, "Why the Nation Needs the Religious Right," in *Disciples and Democracy: Religious Conservatives and the Future of American Politics,* ed. Michael Cromartie (Washington, D.C.: Ethics and Public Policy Center; Grand Rapids, Mich.: William B. Eerdmans Publishing Company, 1994), p. 111. Barnes makes some excellent points about media exaggeration, but he is not entirely persuasive on his main thesis. He argues, for example, that only 3 of 128 speeches at the convention were religious in tone, thereby omitting, among others, George Bush's speech complaining that the Democratic platform did not mention God.

46   Reed, *Active Faith,* p. 201.

47   Watson, *Christian Coalition,* p. 73.

48   Reed, *Active Faith,* pp. 200–207.

49   See, for example, Sol Villasana, "But Beware of a Hidden Agenda," *Dallas Morning News,* July 24, 1995, p. 9A (warning that the contract conceals "the far right's hidden agenda" for schools); editorial, "Threat to Our Freedom," *Denver Rocky Mountain News,* June 12, 1995, p. 29A (release of the *Contract* transforms Christian Coalition into "a subtle and covert threat"); and Ellen Goodman, "GOP Readies a Replay of '92," *Boston Globe,* May 21, 1995, Op-Ed Section, p. 51 (suggesting that *Contract* is a "disguise" for a "move to dump the First Amendment and get official religion in the schools." For an intriguing response to some of the criticism, see Don Browning, "Contractual Problems," *Christian Century,* June 7, 1995, p. 596, which argues that critics who believe the *Contract* with the American Family to be a stalking horse for something radical and wrong should offer an alternative Contract of their own devising.

50   See, for example, Bruce Ackerman, "Why Dialogue?" *Journal of Philosophy* 86 (1989): 5; Amy Gutmann and Dennis Thompson, "Moral Conflict and Political Consensus," *Ethics* 101 (1990): 64; Stephen Holmes, "Gag Rules or the Politics of Omission," in Jon Elster and Rune Slagstad, eds., *Constitutionalism and Democracy* (New York: Cambridge University Press, 1989), p. 19; Thomas Nagel, "Moral Conflict and Political Legitimacy," *Philosophy and Public Affairs* 16 (1987): 215; and Ruti Teitel, "A Critique of Religion as Politics in the Public Sphere," *Cornell Law Review* 78 (1993): 747. Even scholars who are sympathetic to the religious voice in public discourse often conclude that translation of some sort is appropriate. See, for example, Kent Greenawalt, *Religious Convictions and Political Choice* (New York: Oxford University Press, 1988).

The late–twentieth century turn to rules of dialogue in political philosophy owes its origin to the brilliant work of the philosopher John Rawls. In his famous book *A Theory of Justice* (Cambridge: Harvard University Press, 1971), Rawls set forth a thought experiment on the derivation of the distribution of rights and resources in a just society. In his more recent book, *Political Liberalism* (New York: Columbia University Press, 1993), Rawls turns to the nature of public deliberation, and concludes that "public" reasons ("a shared public basis of justification") must be presented to justify fundamental decisions about justice. A concept of the good that rests on a comprehensive philosophical or religious understanding is, for the most part, barred from the deliberation. *Political Liberalism*, unlike *A Theory of Justice*, seems intended not as a thought experiment but as a guide to actual public conversation.

Neither Rawls nor the other theorists who have followed him explain why a religious vision, no matter how comprehensive, cannot be shared by everyone. It is true, as an actual picture of American society, that the populace is religiously diverse, and I have argued elsewhere that even people who are sure of the truth of their own religion should count this pluralism as a benefit. (See Stephen L. Carter, "The Free Exercise Thereof," *William and Mary Law Review* 38 [1997]: 627.) But it is also true, as an actual picture of American society, that we lack many widely shared political and philosophical premises. Rawls suggests that public acts must rest on reasons that we could at least *in principle* share, whether or not we actually agree with them. Yet there is no obvious reason why a religious reason could not *in principle* share a religious understanding.

The better argument for wariness in resting public policy, or fundamental arrangements of justice, on religious premises is the historical argument—that nations choosing to take that route have rarely developed into states to be admired, especially today. Two responses come to mind. First, we might conclude that in the example of the United States itself, we have a nation whose fundamental arrangements of justice do indeed rest, at least in part, on the comprehensive religious view of the eighteenth century Founders and of the nineteenth-century Abolitionists. (This argument is controversial but it is also, so far, unrefuted.) Second, we might conclude that what history really proves is that *all* comprehensive views are dangerous. Rawls, I think, would agree with this last proposition. But he is then left in the position of arguing for his own comprehensive view partly on the ground that it has not yet been seriously attempted.

51 See Carter, *Culture of Disbelief,* chaps. 2–3, 11.
52 See the account in Watson, *Christian Coalition,* pp. 73–76. Many of the attacks were aimed personally at Ralph Reed, whose strategy of "mainstreaming" the coalition came in for special scorn. See the account in Reed, *Active Faith,* pp. 203–204. So strident was the anti-Reed rhetoric that one might reasonably have wondered, when he announced his resignation in 1997, whether he jumped or was pushed. Although it is possible that some of the severe criticism of the group was a holdover from the skepticism that many fundamentalists harbored toward Robertson, a charismatic, from the start, many of the critics were Roman Catholic pro-life activists with no position on evangelical theology.

53   See C. S. Lewis, "The Shocking Alternative," in C. S. Lewis, *Mere Christianity* (New York: Touchstone, 1980), pp. 52, 55-56. (Originally published in 1943.)

54   A similar point, interestingly, is made by the philosopher Bernard Williams, who is no fan of religion. Williams disagrees with many of the familiar liberal reasons for questioning the notion that a life guided by the moral precepts of a religion could be a life well lived. Religion, says Williams, "should not be dismissed on the ground that the egoistic motive it invokes could not possibly count, nor because we supposedly could not derive an *ought* from the fact of God's power but only from his goodness." No, says Williams, there is a simpler reason: "It is rather that we know that it could not be true . . . "–precisely what Lewis would say is the right reason for rejection. Bernard Williams, *Ethics and the Limits of Philosophy* (Cambridge: Harvard University Press, 1985), p. 32. Happily for Williams's fans, he swiftly retreats to the sort of religion-bashing all too common in contemporary moral philosophy: "If God exists, then arguments about him are arguments about the cosmos and of cosmic importance, but if he does not, they are not about anything." And does God exist? Well, no, says Williams: "[I]t seems inevitable that [religion] must come to understand itself as a human construction; if it does, it must in the end collapse." He adds: "Nietzsche's saying, God is dead, can be taken to mean that we should now treat God as a dead person: we should allocate his legacies and try to write an honest biography of him." Ibid, p. 33.

55   Reed, *Active Faith*, p. 114.

56   For a polemical but still fascinating discussion of the transformation of most of the nation's religious universities into purely secular institutions of higher learning, see George Marsden, *The Soul of the American University: From Protestant Establishment to Established Non-Belief* (New York: Oxford University Press, 1995). I am far less concerned with the fall into secularism of some religious universities than with the fall into secularism of some religions. Nevertheless, I believe that religious universities serve important functions for both the sponsoring religion and the larger world. See Stephen L. Carter, "The Constitution and the Religious University," *DePaul Law Review* 47 (1998): 479.

57   The Christian Coalition, to be sure, does not represent the views of all white evangelicals. Although survey data tells us that white evangelicals tend to be politically conservative, exceptions abound. For example, Bill Clinton and Al Gore are both white evangelicals, as is John Buchanan, the former Republican member of Congress who later became one of the founders of People of the American Way. Also, the Christian Coalition evidently has relatively few black members, largely because of continued wariness about the underlying motives of conservative activists. See Watson, *Christian Coalition*, pp. 67–70. Although no figures seem to be available, the group's leaders insist that minority representation is growing. I myself once met two black women who

described themselves as political *liberals* who were also members of the Christian Coalition. The seeming paradox vanishes once we take religion sufficiently seriously that we are able to envision individuals more interested in finding a home among activists who share their faith and disdain their politics than among activists who share their politics and disdain their faith. I discuss this proposition in Stephen L. Carter, *The Dissent of the Governed: A Meditation on Law, Religion, and Loyalty* (Cambridge: Harvard University Press, 1998), pp. 9-13.

58   Reed, *Active Faith*, p. 146.

59   Thomas and Dobson, *Blinded by Might*, p. 98.

60   Peter Beinart, "Will Politicians Matter? Religion Will Increasingly Replace Electoral Politics As the Realm Where Battles for the National Soul Are Fought," *Time*, February 21, 2000, p. 68.

61   The sociologist Martin Marty suggests that people of faith, no matter how great their confidence in the rightness of their cause, should readily concede in public debate the past errors and failures of their co-believers. See Martin E. Marty, Larry Greenfield, and David E. Guinn, "To Speak and Be Heard: Principles of Religious Civil Discourse," in *Religion and Public Discourse: Principles and Guidelines for Religious Participants* (Chicago: Park Ridge Center, 1998), p. 7. I do not think Professor Marty believes that every religious argument in the public square should begin, "Now I know my faith was wrong before. . . ." Rather, the devout believer, striding boldly into politics, should carry those errors with him like weights, slowing him, warning him, and helping him to remember that the faith to which he has dedicated his life is capable of terrible mistakes.

Chapter Four

1   See *Bob Jones University v. United States*, 461 U.S. 574 (1983).

2   The ban, which the media constantly mentioned but rarely analyzed, was actually the outgrowth of the school's theological belief in God's intention that the races remain separate until Christ's return. This thesis, according to the school's web site, rested principally on a reading of the story of the Tower of Babel in Genesis 11. Thus, the ban covered not only black-white dating but dating across any racial lines (as the school defines race). The web site also proclaims that the school does not ban couples in interracial marriages from enrolling, which I assume to be true. Curiously, the school explains that the ban on interracial dating is based in Scripture but a ban on interracial marriage would not be. As an evangelical Christian myself, I do not find any biblical warrant for either ban. Moreover, even if the school is correct about Babel and I am wrong, the conclusion that students may marry but not date across racial lines does not make much analytical sense, and is not a consistent reading of Scripture: The Bible, which has much to

say about marriage, has nothing to say about dating as we now conceptualize it.

3   See the discussion in Stephen Holmes, "Gag Rules or the Politics of Omission," in Jon Elster and Rune Slagstad, eds., *Constitutionalism and Democracy*
(New York: Cambridge University Press, 1989), p. 19.

4   I do not discuss in this book the long-simmering problem of clergy as political candidates or office-holders. The question is as old as America, but re-
newed interest was sparked by the Reverend Pat Robertson's presidential
runs. As Gary Wills has pointed out, reporters covering the 1988 primary
season referred frequently to Robertson's status as an ordained minister but
almost never mentioned the similar status of the Reverend Jesse Jackson. See
Gary Wills, *Under God: Religion and American Politics* (New York: Simon &
Schuster, 1990), p. 63. The claim that Jackson talked about his faith less than
Robertson did is simply false.

The clergy-as-candidate conundrum generated considerable controversy
in the spring of 1980, when Pope John Paul II directed five-term representative Robert Drinan, an ordained Catholic priest, not to seek reelection. The
Vatican's defenders insisted that the Pope was simply enforcing traditional
Catholic doctrine. Some critics, however, saw the decision as aimed at Drinan particularly, who was seen by the Pope, they insisted, as too liberal. At
least one other Catholic priest, Father Robert J. Cornell of Wisconsin, also
chose not to run after the Vatican directive, and Haitian president Jean-
Bertrand Aristide, also a priest, was suspended from his clerical duties. Some
Latin American clergy defied the Vatican's order and remained in office. For
contemporaneous discussions of the Pope's decision, see Kenneth L. Wood-
ward, "A Key Vote Against Drinan," *Newsweek*, May 19, 1980, p. 31; and
Warren Brown, "Second U.S. Priest Quits Political Race," *Washington Post*,
May 7, 1980, p. A3. For a more extended treatment of the issues, see
Madonna Kolbenschlag, ed., *Between God and Caesar: Priests, Sisters, and Politi-
cal Office in the United States* (New York: Paulist Press, 1985).

I am not a Catholic and am in no position to interpret the traditions of the
Church. I certainly am not prescribing a general rule that clergy should not
seek elective office. Such a rule would bar from public office not only Drinan, Robertson, and Jackson, but also such notables as William Gray III, a
Baptist minister who served thirteen years in Congress and was elected majority whip, the highest congressional post ever held by an African American.
On the other hand, if, as I have argued, there are terrible temptations for the
religious when they seek political power, it may be that those who have been
lifted up as spiritual leaders should take particular pains to avoid the risks of
temporal authority.

5   Although the ban on religious tests is treated nowadays as obvious and right,
it sparked a heated argument within the Founding Generation, with many of

those now revered for their commitment to religious liberty opposing it. See Gerard V. Bradley, "The Religious Test Clause and the Constitution of Religious Liberty: A Machine that has Gone of Itself," *Case Western Reserve Law Review* 37 (1987): 674.

6   Both Abbott and Iredell are quoted in Jonathan Elliott, ed., *The Debates of the Several State Conventions on the Adoption of the Federal Constitution* (5 vols.), vol. 4 (New York: Burt Franklin, 1888), pp. 192–194.

7   See Jon Butler, *Awash in a Sea of Faith: Christianizing the American People* (Cambridge: Harvard University Press, 1990).

8   Quoted in *Torcaso v. Watkins*, 467 U.S. 488, 494 n. 9 (1961).

9   For a useful history of the Know-Nothings, see John R. Mulkern, *The Know-Nothing Party in Massachusetts: The Rise and Fall of a People's Movement* (Boston: Northeastern University Press, 1990). A very useful treatment by a historian of an earlier generation is Humphrey J. Desmond, *The Know-Nothing Party* (Washington, D.C.: New Century Press, 1905). For a slightly sharper tone, see David H. Bennett, *The Party of Fear: From Nativist Movements to the New Right in American History* (Chapel Hill: University of North Carolina Press, 1988).

Chapter Five

1   See *Abortion Rights Mobilization, Inc., v. Regan,* 544 F. Supp. 471 (S.D.N.Y. 1982), which held that the plaintiffs had standing to bring the lawsuit.

2   See *United States Catholic Conference v. Baker,* 885 F.2d 1020 (2d Cir. 1989), holding that there was no standing and ordering the suit dismissed. The stated aim of the litigation was to force the Internal Revenue Service to revoke the tax-exempt status of the Roman Catholic Church. Because the court of appeals found that the plaintiffs lacked standing to sue, it never addressed the argument that denying tax benefits because of advocacy violates the first amendment's promise of religious liberty.

3   Editorial, "IRS to Falwell: Thou Shalt Not," *St. Petersburg Times,* April 8, 1993, p. A20.

4   Arthur Kropp, quoted in David E. Anderson, "Accent on Religion and Ethics," *Portland Oregonian,* April 10, 1993 (Religious News Service; available on LEXIS/NEXIS).

5   Pope John Paul II, *The Gospel of Life [Evangelium Vitae]* (New York: Times Books, 1995), p. 104 (official English-language translation) (emphasis in original).

6   In debates on this issue, I have often heard it argued that strict enforcement of the rules against electioneering by tax-exempt religious groups is necessary to protect the purity of the churches themselves. I strongly agree that endorsing candidates is almost always harmful to religion; I strongly disagree

that it is the job of the state, acting through its tax laws, to protect religions from themselves.

7   In a striking coincidence, the publicity over the lawsuit arose at the same time as the Reverend Jesse Jackson was campaigning for the Democratic presidential nomination. Much of his campaign took place in black churches, and observers worried about the implications. See Richard Ostling, "Jesse Takes Up the Collection: A Presidential Campaign Enlists Black Churches' Support," *Time*, February 6, 1984.

8   For a suggestion that the supposed decline of "social capital" is almost entirely a phenomenon of poor, inner-city communities, see Nicholas Lemann, "Kicking in Groups," *Atlantic Monthly*, April 1996.

9   See Frederick C. Harris, "Something Within: Religion As a Mobilizer of African-American Political Activism," *Journal of Politics* 56 (1994): 42.

10 Over the years a number of bills have been introduced in the Congress to soften this provision of the tax code—for example by allowing religious institutions to retain their special tax status as long as they spend no more than 5 percent of their income on political activities. Religious groups might reasonably object to the extra scrutiny of their spending that such a rule would entail, which is why many might prefer the "all-or-nothing" approach of the current code.

This leads to a second point. Suppose a constitutional exception were crafted so that the government could not regulate speech by religious groups, regardless of their tax status. In return for freedom from regulation of their speech, religious groups might have to accept a degree of official scrutiny they would rather not face. In particular, a court (or an administrative agency) might call upon an organization to prove its bona fide religious nature in order to escape the strictures of the Internal Revenue Code. This is unavoidable. Otherwise, an entire political party—whether Democratic, Republican, or anything else—could simply declare itself a religion, thereby assuring its contributors of the deductibility of the money they send.

These objections are not offered in support of the current rules, which seem to me to violate religious freedom. They are offered, rather, as cautions, so that religious groups, if they ever find themselves free of official regulation of the words spoken from the pulpit, might nevertheless remember to be wary of accepting an apparent state "benefit." Some theologians and other observers argue even now that churches would be better off if, under the current rules, they refused any special tax status and spoke out freely without fear of official punishment.

11 For a useful discussion of both the relevant tax law and the constitutional issues, see Anne Berrill Carroll, "Religion, Politics, and the IRS: Defining the Limits of Tax Law Controls on Political Expression by Churches," *Marquette Law Review* 76 (1992): 217.

12   *McCollum v. Board of Education,* 333 U.S. 203, 247 (1948) (Reed, J., dissenting).

13   *Everson v. Board of Education,* 330 U.S. 1 (1947).

14   For harsh criticism of the Court for its reliance on Jefferson, see, for example, Frederick Mark Gedicks, *The Rhetoric of Church and State: A Critical Analysis of Religion Clause Jurisprudence* (Durham, N.C.: Duke University Press, 1995).

15   See William Lee Miller, *The First Liberty: Religion and the American Republic* (New York: Alfred A. Knopf, 1986), especially part II.

16   See Timothy L. Hall, *Separating Church and State: Roger Williams and Religious Liberty* (Urbana: University of Illinois Press, 1998).

17   Mark DeWolfe Howe, *The Garden and the Wilderness: Religion and Government in American Constitutional History* (Chicago: University of Chicago Press, 1965).

18   Williams quoted in Miller, *The First Liberty,* p. 160.

19   Hall, *Separating Church and State,* p. 83.

20   Ibid., pp. 103–111.

21   Because of the Supreme Court's consistent misreading of the First Amendment, we have come to speak of the religion *clauses* rather than the religion *clause.* But there is only one. The amendment begins: "Congress shall make no law respecting an establishment of religion, or prohibiting the free exercise thereof." The word *religion* appears only once, but theorists and judges who believe there are two separate clauses, in order to transform the "establishment clause" into an actual check on the substantive enactments of the state, are forced to insist that the word has two different definitions in this single clause. The authors of the amendment suffered from no such misunderstanding. For some historical verification of this proposition, see John R. Noonan Jr., *The Lustre of Our Country: The American Experience of Religious Freedom* (Berkeley: University of California Press, 1998); and Miller, *First Liberty.* No serious historian disputes the proposition that the antiestablishment provision in the First Amendment was included *solely* to prevent the Congress from either establishing a national church or interfering with those states that had established churches. Some supporters of the "establishment clause" worry that without its protections, the state would be free to pressure citizens to adopt an official religion. But this is not so. The religion clause, taken as a whole, protects religious liberty. Were the state to require, for example, that the public-school day begin with an organized prayer in the classroom, the requirement would be in violation of the religious liberty of families trying to raise their children without interference from the state. No "establishment clause" is necessary to reach this result. I discuss this notion in more detail in my Holmes Lecture. See Stephen L. Carter, "Parents, Religion, and Schools: Reflections on Pierce, 70 Years Later," *Seton Hall Law Review* 27 (1997): 1194.

22   Robert M. Cover, "The Supreme Court, 1982 Term, Foreword: *Nomos* and Narrative," *Harvard Law Review* 97 (1983): 61–62.

23 David Tracy, *Plurality and Ambiguity: Hermeneutics, Religion, Hope* (Chicago: University of Chicago Press, 1987), p. 83.

24 See Noonan, *Lustre of Our Country,* pp. 43–45.

25 Quoted in Hugo Rahner, *Church and State in Early Christianity,* trans. Leo Donald Davis (1961; reprint, San Francisco: Ignatius Press, 1992), p. 45.

26 Purists will point out that my metaphor refers to the wrong Lewis Carroll creation, that I have described the Looking Glass World that Alice visits when she crawls through the looking glass, not Wonderland, which she visits when she pops down a rabbit hole. Purists will be correct. But the more literary minded will also, I hope, see the purpose of my trope: By reversing the two worlds Alice visited, and using the invented reversal for my own polemical purposes, I am mimicking the move made by legal theorists and commentators who do the same with the First Amendment's religion clause.

Chapter Six

1 See Don E. Fehrenbacher, *Slavery, Law, and Politics: The Dred Scott Case in Historical Perspective* (Oxford: Oxford University Press, 1981), pp. 57 and passim.

2 See Ahlstrom, *Religious History of the American People,* pp. 648–651.

3 Charles G. Finney, "On Love to Our Neighbor," in *Principles of Love,* ed. Louis Gifford Parkinson (Minneapolis: Bethany House, 1986), pp. 195, 201.

4 Theodore Parker, *An Address Delivered by the Rev. Theodore Parker Before the New York City Anti-Slavery Society at Its First Anniversary, Held at the Broadway Tabernacle, May 12, 1854* (New York: American Anti-Slavery Society, 1854), p. 45.

5 Quoted in William Lee Miller, *Arguing About Slavery: The Great Battle in the United States Congress* (New York: Alfred A. Knopf, 1996), p. 162.

6 See Edmund S. Morgan, *American Slavery, American Freedom: The Ordeal of Colonial Virginia* (New York: W. W. Norton and Company, 1975), pp. 329–332.

7 Quoted in Richard Lovelace, "The Bible in Public Discourse," in *Christianity and Civil Society,* ed. Rodney L. Peterson (Maryknoll, N.Y.: Orbis Books, 1995), pp. 62, 72.

8 Miller, *Arguing About Slavery,* p. 83.

9 Jonathan Edwards is himself an interesting case. Edwards, who owned slaves, so emphasized personal piety over social reform that he was often quoted by pro-slavery preachers. Recently discovered private writings of Edwards, however, suggest that he was opposed to the slave trade as early as the 1740s, and so informed his correspondents. See Kenneth P. Minkema, "Jonathan Edwards on Slavery and the Slave Trade," *William and Mary Quarterly,* 3d series, 54 (1997): 823. The Quakers opposed slavery as early as 1700 and formed America's first anti-slavery society in Philadelphia in 1775. New England opposition to slavery is usually dated from the 1770s, led by Edwards's disciples, including his son, Jonathan Jr. See Ahlstrom, *Religious History of the American People,* pp.

648–651. The new findings concerning the views of Edwards Sr., if true, might require an earlier dating of the period in which New England opposition began.

10   See Miller, *Arguing About Slavery*, pp. 83–84. It should be noted that not all historians are comfortable with the idea of a Second Great Awakening. The historian Jon Butler, for example, warns that the idea of "the so-called Second Great Awakening that allegedly began in Kentucky in 1805 and lasted into the 1820s . . . obscures important religious revivals that began as early as the Revolution." Jon Butler, *Awash in a Sea of Faith: Christianizing the American People* (Cambridge: Harvard University Press, 1990), p. 221.

11   Nathan O. Hatch, *The Democratization of American Christianity* (New Haven: Yale University Press, 1989).

12   Parker, *Address Before the New York Anti-Slavery Society*, p. 39 (emphasis in original).

13   Ibid., p. 45.

14   See Miller, *Arguing About Slavery*, pp. 67–68.

15   Charles E. Hodges, *Disunion Our Wisdom and Our Duty* (New York: American Anti-Slavery Society, n.d.), p. 12. Internal evidence suggests that the pamphlet was printed in the 1860s.

16   Ezra S. Gannett, *Relation of the North to Slavery: A Discourse Preached in the Federal Street Meetinghouse in Boston on Sunday, June 11, 1854* (Boston: Crosby, Nichols, and Company, 1854), p. 15.

17   Seth Williston, *Slavery: Not a Scriptural Ground of Division in Efforts for the Salvation of the Heathen* (New York: M. W. Dodd, 1844), p. 24.

18   Henry Darling, *Slavery and the War* ([Boston]: Lippincott and Company, 1863), p. 4.

19   Nathaniel Hall, *The Iniquity: A Sermon Preached in the First Church, Dorchester, on Sunday, December 11, 1859* (Boston: John Wilson and Son, 1859), p. 8.

20   Ibid., pp. 17–18.

21   Ibid., p. 19.

22   Nathaniel Hall, *The Man,—The Deed,—The Event: A Sermon Preached in the First Church, Dorchester, on Sunday, December 4, 1859* (Boston: John Wilson and Son, 1859), pp. 31 and passim.

23   Gannett, *Relation of the North to Slavery*, p. 6.

24   Ibid., p. 16.

25   Williston, *Slavery*, pp. 12 and passim.

26   See Butler, *Awash in a Sea of Faith*, pp. 130–151. For an account of early evangelical opposition to slavery in Virginia—and its collapse late in the eighteenth century—see James David Essig, *The Bonds of Wickedness: American Evangelicals Against Slavery, 1770-1808* (Philadelphia: Temple University Press, 1982). For an incisive if occasionally polemical analysis of southern Christianity following the end of slavery, see Orlando Patterson, *Rituals of Blood:*

Consequences of Slavery in Two American Centuries (Washington, D.C.: Civitas/Counterpoint, 1998), pp. 202–224. I am constrained to add that I do not endorse many of Professor Patterson's characterizations of Christianity in his otherwise thoughtful book.

27 See Fehrenbacher, *Slavery, Law, and Politics,* pp. 55–57.

28 See Merton L. Dillon, *Slavery Attacked: Southern Slaves and Their Allies, 1619-1865* (Baton Rouge: Louisiana State University Press, 1990), chap. 7.

29 See remarks quoted in Butler, *Awash in a Sea of Faith,* p. 138.

30 See, for example, Iveson L. Brookes, *Defence of the South Against the Reproaches and Incroachments of the North* (Hamburg, S.C.: Republican Office, 1850), pp. 23–27.

31 Henry J. Van Dyke, *A Sermon Preached in the First Presbyterian Church, Brooklyn, on Sabbath Evening, December 9, 1860* (New York: D. Appleton and Company, 1860), pp. 18–19.

32 George D. Armstrong, *The Christian Doctrine of Slavery* (New York: Negro Universities Press, n.d.), p. 141. (Internal evidence suggests publication between 1848 and 1860.)

33 Nathan Lord, *Northern Presbyter's Second Letter to Ministers of the Gospel of All Denominations on Slavery* (Boston: Little, Brown and Company, 1855).

34 Forrest McDonald, *Novus Ordo Seclorum: The Intellectual Origins of the Constitution* (Lawrence: University Press of Kansas, 1985), p. 54.

35 Lord, *Northern Presbyter's Second Letter,* p. 79.

36 Ibid., pp. 80–81.

37 Van Dyke, *A Sermon Preached in the First Presbyterian Church,* p. 8.

38 Ibid., p. 21.

39 Brookes, *Defence of the South,* p. 26.

40 Van Dyke, *A Sermon,* p. 34.

41 See, for example, the discussions in Anne Loveland, *Southern Evangelicals and the Social Order, 1800–1860* (Baton Rouge: Louisiana State University Press, 1980).

42 George D. Armstrong, *The Christian Doctrine of Slavery,* p. 124.

43 Ibid., p. 129.

44 Ibid., pp. 131-134.

45 "Abolition and Anti-Abolition," *The Southern Baptist and General Intelligencer,* October 2 [?], 1835, p. 213.

46 See Mitchell Snay, *Gospel of Disunion: Religion and Separatism in the Antebellum South* (Cambridge: Cambridge University Press, 1993).

47 Senator Stephen Douglas, statement in the Senate, March 14, 1854, reprinted in *Right of Petition: New England Clergymen* (Washington, D.C.: Buell and Blanchard, 1854), p. 3.

48 Ibid.

49 Senator Mason, statement in the Senate, March 14, 1854, reprinted in *Right of Petition: New England Clergymen* (Washington, D.C.: Buell and Blanchard, 1854), p. 5.

50   Senator Butler, statement in the Senate, March 14, 1854, reprinted in *Right of Petition: New England Clergymen* (Washington, D.C.: Buell and Blanchard, 1854), pp. 5–6.

51   Ibid., p. 6.

52   Senator Houston, statement in the Senate, March 14, 1854, reprinted in *Right of Petition: New England Clergymen* (Washington, D.C.: Buell and Blanchard, 1854), p. 7.

53   See Steven Smith, *Foreordained Failure: The Quest for a Constitutional Principle of Religious Freedom* (New York: Oxford University Press, 1998).

54   See Miller, *The First Liberty*, pp. 143–190.

55   For a discussion of Backus, see, for example, Miller, *The First Liberty*, pp. 211–216. For the role of Jay, see Gerard v. Bradley, "The Religious Test Clause and the Constitution of Religious Liberty: A Machine That Has Gone of Itself," *Case Western Reserve Law Review* 37 (1987): 674.

56   The religious debate over slavery was not solely among Christians. Not counting the views of the slaves themselves or of the indigenous Americans, the only other religion of significant size in nineteenth-century America was Judaism, and Jews, it turns out, were apparently just as divided on the issue as Christians. See Sydney E. Ahlstrom, *A Religious History of the American People* (New Haven: Yale University Press, 1972), p. 666.

The unfortunate spreading of anti-Semitic nonsense about Jews and the slave trade by some black activists in recent years has made the question of Jewish opinion on slavery harder to discuss. But some have tried. For an argument that the Jewish tradition developed the theological case against slavery long before the Christian tradition did, see Yehuda Bauer, "The Impact of the Holocaust," *Annals of the American Academy of Political and Social Science* 548 (November 1996): 14, 17-18. For a deeper discussion of Jewish law on the subject of slavery, see David M. Corbin, "Beyond the United States: A Brief Look at the Jewish Law of Manumission," *Chicago-Kent Law Review* 70 (1995): 1339. Jewish slave traders, who were certainly few in number, were operating in defiance of Jewish tradition and, probably, Jewish law. See, for example, the discussion in Bertram Wallace Korn, "Jews and Negro Slavery in the Old South, 1789–1865," in Leonard Dinnerstein and Mary Dale Palsson, eds., *Jews in the South* (Baton Rouge: Louisiana State University Press, 1973). For an account of black-Jewish relations in the South in the years immediately after the Civil War, see Lee Shai Weissbach, "East European Immigrants and the Image of Jews in the Small-Town South," *American Jewish History*, September 1, 1997, 231.

57   Ahlstrom, *Religious History*, p. 649.

58   For an account of the targeting of college students by Finney and other abolitionist preachers, see Miller, *Arguing About Slavery*, pp. 83–93.

59   Miller, *Arguing About Slavery*, p. 38.

60   A lucid summary of the battle in Alabama, and elsewhere in the South, is Suzi Parker, "Gambling's Rise Splits Southern Communities," *Christian Science Moni-*

tor, December 29, 1999, p. 3. See also the brief but clear discussion in William
C. Singleton III, "An Education Gamble," *Christianity Today*, December 6, 1999.

Chapter Seven

1 Nathan O. Hatch, *The Democratization of American Christianity* (New Haven: Yale
   University Press, 1989), p. 65.
2 Sydney E. Ahlstrom, *A Religious History of the American People* (New Haven: Yale
   University Press, 1972), p. 640.
3 Ibid., pp. 640–647.
4 For an argument that the America of the nineteenth century was at least as
   multicultural, and probably more so, than the watered-down, media-soaked,
   everybody-the-same culture in which we live, see Mary P. Ryan, *Civic Wars:
   Democracy and Public Life in the American City During the Nineteenth Century* (Berkeley: University of California Press, 1997). The hyphenated adjectives in the
   previous sentence describing the culture are mine, not Professor Ryan's.
5 The text describes only the popular history. The free market of the nineteenth
   century is often overstated, as are the regulatory triumphs of the twentieth.
   The innovative regulatory forms of the Progressive Era were frequently cloaks
   for cartelization. Licensing statutes for the professions provide a typical example: Described as laws to protect the public, they had the effect (and still do) of
   limiting entry to a field, thus enabling those in the profession to raise prices.
   Moreover, the new regulatory forms were quickly subjected to another inno-
   vation known as regulatory capture–the tendency of the regulators to become
   advocates for rather than watchdogs of the industries they regulate–which has
   been studied by economists for forty years, but was known to historians long
   before. An early study is Gabriel Kolko, *Railroad and Regulation, 1877-1916*
   (Princeton: Princeton University Press, 1965). For the classic argument by an
   economist, see George Stigler, "The Theory of Economic Regulation," *Bell
   Journal of Economic Regulation* 2 (1971): 3. For a classic analysis of how licensing
   statutes can serve as a form of capture, see Edmund W. Kitch, Marc Isaacson,
   and Daniel Kasper, "The Regulation of Taxicabs in Chicago," *Journal of Law
   and Economics* 14 (1971): 285. The problem of regulatory capture is often offered
   as a justification for unusual regulatory forms less susceptible to manipulation
   by the regulated parties. See, for example, Ian Ayres and John Braithwaite,
   "Partial-Industry Regulation: A Monopsony Standard for Consumer Protection," *California Law Review* 80 (1992): 13. To be sure, regulatory capture, like
   the rest of public choice theory, is very far from the whole story of how laws
   are made. See, for example, the more complex model in Michael E. Levine and
   Jennifer L. Forrence, "Regulatory Capture, Public Interest, and the Public
   Agenda: Toward A Synthesis," *Journal of Law and Economic Organization* 6 (Special Issue, 1990): 167.

6   (Rev.) George Chalmers Richmond, *The Open Altar: The Sermon Preached Sunday Morning, November 1, 1914* (Philadelphia: [The Vestry], 1915), p. 7.

7   Ibid., p. 17.

8   Charles D. Williams, *The Christian Ministry and Social Problems* (New York: Macmillan Company, 1917), p. 7.

9   Ibid., p. 9.

10 Ibid., p. 23.

11 Ibid., p. 31.

12 Pope Leo XIII, *Rerum Novarum—Encyclical Letter on the Condition of Labor* [authorized translation] (Washington, D.C.: National Catholic Welfare Conference, 1942). (Originally issued in 1891.)

13 Here is what Reid wrote on the subject of women in the workforce: "It means the destruction of the home among the lower one-third or one-half of human society. It means the creation of a soil in which human character cannot grow. It means the growing up of children on the streets, with no mother's care or uplifting influence surrounding them." David C. Reid, *Effective Industrial Reform* (Stockbridge, Mass.: David C. Reid, 1910), p. 256. His solution was to "release these wives and mothers from work in the factory," so that they might "go where their hearts are, and where they of right ought to be—*into their own homes* with their own children; and all these evil conditions will be changed." Ibid., p. 257.

14 Reid, *Effective Industrial Reform,* p. 247.

15 Ibid., p. 221.

16 James Myers, *Religion Lends a Hand: Studies of Churches in Social Action* (New York: Harper and Brothers, 1929), p. 92.

17 (Rev.) Charles S. Macfarland, "The Opportunity of the Minister in Relation to Industrial Organizations," in *The Christian Ministry and the Social Order,* ed. Charles S. Macfarland (New Haven: Yale University Press, 1909), pp. 113, 121.

18 Williams, *Christian Ministry,* p. 55.

19 See Ahlstrom, *Religious History of the American People,* pp. 781–783.

20 Francis Greenwood Peabody, *The Social Teaching of Jesus Christ* (Philadelphia: University of Pennsylvania Press, 1924), p. 57.

21 Ibid., pp. 64–65.

22 (Rev.) George H. Ferris, *The Moral Element of Spirituality—Sermon Preached in the First Baptist Church in Philadelphia on Sunday, April 9, 1911* (n.p.: n.d.).

23 Charles S. Macfarland, "The Part and Place of the Church and the Ministry in the Realization of Democracy," in *The Christian Ministry and the Social Order,* ed. Charles S. Macfarland (New Haven: Yale University Press, 1909), pp. 13, 21.

24 Williams, *Christian Ministry,* p. 12.

25 For a list of arguments in opposition to the social reformers, see, for example, Charles Reynolds Brown, *The Social Message of the Modern Pulpit* (New York: Charles Scribner's Sons, 1906), pp. 256ff.

26 Macfarland, "Part and Place," p. 41.

27 See Matthew 16:18 ("And I tell you that you are Peter, and on this rock I will build my church, and the gates of Hades will not overcome it"). See also Matthew 18:17, on what to do when one who has sinned against you refuses to listen to the testimony of witnesses ("If he refuses to listen to them, tell it to the church; and if he refuses to listen even to the church, treat him as you would a pagan or a tax collector").

28 Sherwood Eddy, *Religion and Social Justice* (New York: George H. Doran Company, 1927), p. 94.

29 Charles Taylor, *Sources of the Self: The Making of Modern Identity* (Cambridge: Harvard University Press, 1989), p. 97.

30 See the discussion in Hatch, *Democratization,* especially Chapter 8.

31 The abortion decision, of course, is *Roe v. Wade,* 410 U.S. 113 (1973). The decisions collectively known as the classroom-prayer cases are: *Engel v. Vitale,* 370 U.S. 421 (1962) (no classroom recital of state-composed prayer); *Abington School District v. Schempp,* 374 U.S. 203 (1963) (no classroom reading of Bible verses); *Stone v. Graham,* 449 U.S. 39 (1980) (no posting of the Ten Commandments on classroom walls); *Lee v. Weisman* (1992) (no school-sponsored prayer at graduation).

32 Liberals are understandably irritated by the tendency of pro-life activists to link their protests (such as sit-ins at abortion clinics) to the Civil Rights Movement led by King. But the analogy is stronger than pro-choice advocates care to admit. Consider the argument offered by the theologian Michael Eric Dyson, who insists that the movements are distinguishable because pro-life activists, unlike civil rights marchers, "seeks to deny constitutional rights," in this case, the rights of women to choose whether to terminate their pregnancies. Dyson, *I May Not Get There with You,* p. 243. Yet the pro-life marchers would insist that they, like the civil rights protesters, want to expand the reach of the Constitution, to cover a group that should have been covered all along—in this case, unborn children. Moreover, the Civil Rights Movement might also be conceptualized as seeking to deny constitutional rights—the right, let us say, of owners of private property (lunch counters or hotels) to decide for themselves who should be allowed to use it. The verdict of morality and of history tells us that the movement was correct in seeking to override rights that might otherwise have existed, but that conclusion does not disturb the analogy.

Professor Dyson also argues that "very few" followers of the Civil Rights Movement demonized their opponents, whereas pro-life activists engage in it often. To Dyson, this matters for two reasons. First, the furious rhetoric of some pro-lifers forces them to bear a degree of responsibility for violent acts carried out in the name of their cause. Second, the rhetoric makes the pro-lifers less admirable because, unlike the civil rights activists, they are refusing "to spread love" and are returning evil for good, rather than the other way around. See Dyson, pp. 242–244. My impression, like Dyson's, is that pro-life protesters are less civil, less loving, and more angry than civil rights marchers. But I have seen no serious empirical study on this point, and it is possible that the memories of those of us who draw the distinction are confounded, first, by our romantic view of the civil rights era, and, second, by our living in an era in which the media will always emphasize the one colorfully angry protester over the thousand peaceful and loving ones. (We must bear in mind that King's carefully trained marchers were not the entire Civil Rights Movement.) More to the point, even if Dyson is correct, and pro-life marchers tend to be less civil than those who marched with King, their *cause* might still be analogous to King's, even if their conduct is not.

33 My colleague Akhil Amar has pointed out that a striking aspect of the abortion battle is that each side, pro-choice and pro-life, can plausibly claim to be the inheritor of the mantle of the civil rights movement, for each side insists that it is fighting for the freedom and equality of a person (a *type* of person) that society prefers to disdain.

34 Quoted in Carol Krol, "Pontifical Council Sets Guidelines for Making Ads: Vatican Values Leave U.S. Admen Unimpressed," *Advertising Age,* March 3, 1997, p. 37.

Chapter Eight

1 Paul Weyrich, "The Moral Minority," reprinted in *Christianity Today,* September 6, 1999, p. 44. We should not perhaps be too quick to concede Weyrich's point that electoral "success" is properly measured in whether one's candidate wins. As the legal scholar Peter Schuck points out, in a pluralistic democracy, success might better be measured by whether a candidate, in order to win, must deal seriously with the issues one raises. See Peter H. Schuck, "The Thickest Thicket: Partisan Gerrymandering and Judicial Regulation of Politics," in Peter H. Schuck, *The Limits of Law: Essays on Democratic Governance* (Boulder: Westview Press, 2000), pp. 285, 312–315.

2 See, for example, some of the comments in "Is the Religious Right Finished? An Insiders' Conversation," *Christianity Today,* September 6, 1999, p. 43.

3 George F. Will, "1999: Sort of Satisfactory," *Newsweek,* December 20, 1999.

4 Private courts are alternative forums for dispute resolution to which parties may go by choice to settle their disputes, whether or not the law allows it. An important distinction between private courts and other alternative mechanisms, however, is that the parties who go to the private courts often refuse to acknowledge the authority of the official courts—or even of the state itself. In addition, it is not unheard of for a private court to assert jurisdiction over individuals who have not chosen it as their preferred forum and, indeed, may never even have heard of it.

5 For liberal commentary on Weyrich, see, for example, Nicholas Confessore, "The Rorschach Candidate: Presidential Candidate George W. Bush," *The*

American Prospect, January 31, 2000, p. 34, mentioning Weyrich's letter in passing and labeling it "bizarre." A commentary in *The Village Voice* dismissed the
letter as "Weyrich in Wonderland." james ridgeway [sic], "Mondo Washington," *The Village Voice,* July 20, 1999, p. 37. Among prominent conservatives,
economist Thomas Sowell of the Hoover Institution pointed out that "you
can lose big battles and still win the war," and Patrick Buchanan admonished:
"We can no more walk away from the culture war than we could walk away
from the Cold War." Both quoted in Deborah Mathis, "Religious, Legal,
Moral Issues Fuel Culture War," Gannett News Service, October 4, 1999
(available on LEXIS/NEXIS).

6   This is not an ad hominem I have invented but a central theme of arguments
for compulsory schooling at least since John Dewey and arguably all the way
back to Horace Mann. I discuss much of this history in my book *The Dissent of
the Governed: A Meditation on Law, Religion, and Loyalty* (Cambridge: Harvard University Press, 1998). For a contemporary example of the argument that schooling should be a tool for weaning children from their parents' illiberal beliefs, see,
for example, Amy Gutmann, *Democratic Education* (Princeton: Princeton University Press, 1987). The commentary on religion is not Gutmann's principal concern, but it is not quite a sideshow either. See also Chapter 12 of this book.

7   See, for example, Margaret Talbot, "A Mighty Fortress," *New York Times Magazine,* February 27, 2000, p. 34.

8   For a lively, scholarly account of how Western marriage moved from the control of the church to the control of the state, see John Witte Jr., *From Sacrament
to Contract: Marriage, Religion, and Law in the Western Tradition* (Louisville, Ky.:
Westminster John Knox Press, 1997). In a recent lecture, I speculated on
what "privatized" marriage—that is, marriage without the state—might look
like. For a lightly footnoted transcript, see Stephen L. Carter, "Defending
Marriage: A Modest Proposal," *Howard Law Journal* 41 (1998): 215.

Religious traditionalists should be attracted by the image of marriage
without the state. Marriage is one of the institutions that the sociologist Peter
L. Berger had in mind when he wrote: "Religion mystifies institutions by explaining them as given over and beyond their empirical existence in the history of a society." Peter L. Berger, *The Sacred Canopy: Elements of a Sociological
Theory of Religion* (New York: Doubleday, 1967), p. 90. The point is that the
secular observer will agree that marriage exists and will then seek to find a
persuasive historical or political reason for its existence in a particular form.
The religious traditionalist, however, will posit marriage as existing for God's
purposes, and as subject, therefore, to God's ordinances.

9   See, for example, the discussions in Amy Gutmann, *Democratic Education*
(Princeton, N.J.: Princeton University Press, 1987), pp. 1-70; and Ira C. Lupu,
"The Separation of Powers and the Protection of Children," *University of Chicago
Law Review* 61 (1994): 1317.

10 See, for example, Cal Thomas and Ed Dobson, *Blinded by Might: Can the Religious Right Save America?* (Grand Rapids, Mich.: Zondervan Publishing House, 1999), esp. chap. 10.

11 See the argument in Bette Novit Evans, *Interpreting the Free Exercise of Religion: The Constitution and American Pluralism* (Chapel Hill: University of North Carolina Press, 1997).

12 For a journalistic account of our growing busy-ness, see James Lardner, "World-Class Workaholics," *U.S. News and World Report,* December 20, 1999, p. 42.

13 See Hannah Arendt, *The Life of the Mind—Part I: Thinking* (New York: Harcourt Brace 1978), p. 197.

14 See, for example, the excellent discussion in Howard Lesnick, *Listening for God: Religion and Moral Discernment* (New York: Fordham University Press, 1998). I should add that I do not by any means share all of Lesnick's views on biblical exegesis.

15 Weyrich, "Moral Minority," p. 45.

Chapter Nine

1 See Harry Dunphy, "U.S. Christian Religious Leaders Urge NATO to Stop Bombing," *Cleveland Plain Dealer,* April 2, 1999 (from Westlaw).

2 Many of the churches that did weigh in were cautious to the point of equivocation. The usually forthright National Conference of Catholic Bishops, for example, stated that "there is no substitute for a genuine dialogue between the parties" but stopped short of calling for an end to the bombing, explaining instead that the "bombing campaign poses difficult moral and policy questions on which persons of good will may disagree." National Conference of Catholic Bishops, *Statement on Kosovo,* March 24, 1999. The Southern Baptist Convention called for decisive military action to remove Yugoslav president Slobodan Milosevic from power. See Teresa Watanabe, "Crisis in Yugoslavia: NATO Campaign Poses Moral Dilemma for Religious Leaders," *Los Angeles Times,* April 4, 1999 (from Westlaw).

3 Gleason L. Archer, *Encyclopedia of Bible Difficulties* (Grand Rapids, Mich.: Zondervan Publishing House, 1982), p. 158.

4 Harold S. Kushner, *When Bad Things Happen to Good People* (New York: Schocken Books, 1981).

5 This is of course a famous problem in the practice of what is called *theodicy,* the justification of God to man. Theodicy is often criticized because of its assumption that it is necessary to justify what God does and because of its further assumption that such justification is even possible. Nevertheless, its Christians practitioners go back to Thomas Aquinas and earlier. For a recent effort, see Richard Swinburne, *Providence and the Problem of Evil* (New York: Oxford University Press, 1998).

6   Martin Buber, "Dialogue," in *Between Man and Man,* trans. Ronald Gregor Smith (New York: Macmillan Company, 1965), pp. 1, 7 (originally published 1929).

7   Archer, *Encyclopedia,* p. 158.

8   Professor Archer, it should be noted, does not think that such wars for the destruction of evil are necessary in the Christian era:

> In our Christian dispensation true believers possess resources for resist-ing the corrupting influence of unconverted worldlings such as were hardly available to the people of the old covenant. As warriors of Christ who have yielded our members to Him as 'weapons of righteousness' (Rom. 6:13) and whose bodies are indwelt and empowered by God the Holy Spirit (1 Cor. 6:19), we are well able to lead our lives in the midst of a corrupt and degenerate non-Christian culture (whether in the Roman Empire or in modern secularized Europe or America) and still keep true to God. We have the example of the Cross and the victory of the Resurrection of Christ our Lord, and he goes with us everywhere and at all times as we carry out the Great Commission.

Archer, *Encyclopedia,* p. 159. This Bible-based argument will not persuade everyone, of course, but evangelical Christians, at least, should be relieved.

9   See the various conversations reported in Ron Rosenbaum's exemplary book, *Explaining Hitler: The Search for the Origins of His Evil* (New York: Random House, 1998).

10 To gain a sense of just how horribly shared the sacrifice of war has tradi-tionally been, see John Keegan's excellent book, *A History of Warfare* (New York: Alfred A. Knopf, 1993).

11 See the discussion in Paul Johnson, *A History of Christianity* (New York: Atheneum, 1976), pp. 247–250.

12 A useful and readable summary of the doctrine may be found in Robert L. Phillips, *War and Justice* (Norman: University of Oklahoma Press, 1984), chaps. 1, 2. It must be added that Phillips seems a good deal more accepting of war than are most writers in this field. For other scholarly discussions of how Christian theology speaks to war, see, for example, Roland Bainton, *Christian Attitudes Toward War and Peace* (Nashville, Tenn.: Abingdon Press, 1980); James Douglass, *The Non-Violent Cross* (Toronto: Macmillan Company, 1969); and Paul Ramsey, *The Just War: Force and Political Responsibility* (New York: Charles Scribner's Sons, 1968).The Catholic "just war" doctrine has also formed the basis for a great deal of work in secular philosophy. Perhaps the best known is Michael Walzer's *Just and Unjust Wars: A Moral Argument with Historical Illustrations* (New York: Basic Books, 1977).

13 This raises the intriguing question in American constitutional practice of whether an order by the President as commander in chief constitutes a suffi-cient command of constituted authority to allow American forces to wage

just war, or whether the Congress must first declare war. This problem has split constitutional theorists for generations. I myself have long been of the view, based on the history and structure of the Constitution, that the President may command troops to fight without express congressional authorization. See Stephen L. Carter, "War Making Under the Constitution and the First Use of Nuclear Weapons," in Peter Raven-Hansen, ed., *First Use of Nuclear Weapons: Under the Constitution, Who Decides?* (New York: Greenwood Press, 1987); and Stephen L. Carter, "The Constitutionality of the War Powers Resolution," *Virginia Law Review* 70 (1984): 101. I doubt, however, that mine is the majority view among scholars.

14   Stanley Hauerwas, "Whose 'Just' War? Whose Peace?" in his *Dispatches from the Front: Theological Engagements with the Secular* (Durham, N.C.: Duke University Press, 1994), p. 136. Hauerwas wrote the essay in response to Christian support for the Gulf War, which he considered unjustified in Christian terms.

15   This and other contradictions of Bryan's spectacular and complex career are noted in Richard Hofstadter, *The American Political Tradition* (New York: Vintage Books, 1948), pp. 199–200.

16   See National Conference of Bishops, *The Challenge of Peace: God's Promise and Our Response* (U.S. Catholic Conference, 1983).

17   Robert F. Drinan, *The Fractured Dream: America's Divisive Moral Choices* (New York: Crossroad, 1991), p. 8.

Chapter Ten

1   Alasdair MacIntyre, *After Virtue: A Study in Moral Theory*, 2nd ed. (Notre Dame, Ind.: University of Notre Dame Press, 1984), p. 2.

2   I discuss this tendency to celebrate the desires of the self in my books *Integrity* (New York: Basic Books, 1996) and *Civility: Manners, Morals, and the Etiquette of Democracy* (New York: Basic Books, 1998).

3   See the data discussed in David Nyberg, *The Varnished Truth: Truth Telling and Deceiving in Ordinary Life* (Chicago: University of Chicago Press, 1993).

4   See ibid., especially chapter 6. See also Sissela Bok, *Lying: Moral Choice in Public and Private Life* (1978; reprint, New York: Vintage Books, 1989).

5   See the data cited in Alissa J. Rubin, "Pills and Prayer," *Washington Post* [magazine], Jan. 11, 1998, p. W12. According to the story, which cites several reputable surveys, 56 percent of adults surveyed believe that "their faith helped them recover from illness, injury or disease" and 77 percent believe that "God sometimes intervenes to cure people who have a serious illness." (Another interesting finding is that 63 percent "believe it is good for doctors to talk with patients about their spiritual health.")

6   Fred Sicher, Elisabeth Targ, Dan Moore II, and Helene S. Smith, "A Randomized Double-Blind Study of the Effect of Distant Healing in a Population

with Advanced AIDS: Report of a Small Scale Study," *Western Journal of Medicine* 169 (December 1998): 356–363.

7   "Intercessory Prayer Ministry Benefits Rheumatoid Arthritis Patients," *Journal of General Internal Medicine* 13, 1 (Supplement, April 1998): 17.

8   Amy L. Ai, Ruth E. Dunkle, Christopher Peterson, and Steven F. Bolling, "The Role of Private Prayer in Psychological Recovery Among Mid-life and Aged Patients Following Cardiac Surgery," *The Gerontologist* 38 (October 1998): 591–601.

9   Steven Goldberg, *Seduced by Science: How American Religion Has Lost Its Way* (New York: New York University Press, 1999), p. 46.

10 This might help explain why the Roman Catholic Church, when considering the record of miracles that must be attributed to a potential saint prior to canonization, has a policy of never recognizing as miraculous the alleged healing of a disease that is known to have a high rate of natural remission.

11 I here refer not to the work of so-called scientific creationists, but to the writings of serious physical scientists. See, for example, Frank J. Tipler, *The Physics of Immortality: Modern Cosmology, God and the Resurrection of the Dead* (New York: Doubleday, 1985); Dean L. Overman, *A Case Against Accident and Self-Organization* (Lanham, Md.: Rowman & Littlefield, 1997); and, particularly, any of physicist John C. Polkinghorne's elegant contributions to the debate. Two of the better known are *Belief in God in an Age of Science* (New Haven: Yale University Press, 1998); and *The Faith of a Physicist: Reflections of a Bottom-Up Thinker* (Princeton, N.J.: Princeton University Press, 1994).

12 George Gallup Jr. and D. Michael Lindsay, *Surveying the Religious Landscape: Trends in U.S. Beliefs* (Harrisburg, Pa.: Morehouse Publishing, 1999), pp. 36–38.

13 See Peter L. Berger, *A Rumor of Angels: Modern Society and the Rediscovery of the Supernatural*, exp. ed. (1969; reprint, New York: Anchor Books, 1990).

14 See, for example, Stephen L. Carter, *The Culture of Disbelief: How American Law and Politics Trivialize Religious Devotion* (New York: Basic Books, 1993), chap. 9.

15 For a discussion of Christian theology and standardized testing, see Harold W. Faw, "Does Scripture Support Standardized Testing?" *Perspectives on Science and Christian Faith* 42 (June 1990): 86.

16 See the data presented in Lowell C. Rose, Alec M. Gallup, and Stanley M. Elam, "The 29th Annual Phi Delta Kappa/Gallup Poll of the Public's Attitude Toward the Public Schools," *Phi Delta Kappan*, September 1997.

17 See the data discussed in Lowell C. Rose and Alec M. Gallup, "The 30th Annual Phi Delta Kappa/Gallup Poll of the Public's Attitude Toward Public Schools," *Phi Delta Kappan*, September 1998.

18 When we are measurist in considering the schools, all we think about are test scores. But many parents choose religious schools for other reasons. First among them is morality—that is, parents care what lessons their children learn

about right and wrong. As the sociologist James Coleman famously pointed out, the religious school teaching strong values may serve a particularly important purpose when family structures are weak. See, for example, James S. Coleman, "Changes in the Family and Implications for the Common School," *University of Chicago Law Forum 1991*, (1991), 153. A voucher program targeting the poor would largely benefit children from weak families.

Chapter Eleven

1 See *Employment Division v. Smith*, 494 U.S. 872 (1990).

2 *O'Lone v. Estate of Shabazz*, 482 U.S. 342 (1987).

3 In the officially Christian Europe of the late eleventh and early twelfth centuries, the availability of the Inquisition against heretics meant, in practical terms, its availability against nearly everyone. Those unfamiliar with the particular horrors of the Inquisition (especially in Spain and, earlier, in France at the time of the Albigensian crusades) might usefully peruse Paul Johnson, *A History of Christianity* (New York: Atheneum, 1976), pp. 250–264.

4 For an outline of this tragic history, see Stanley Jeyaraja Tambiah, *Buddhism Betrayed? Religion, Politics, and Violence in Sri Lanka* (Chicago: University of Chicago Press, 1992).

5 I explained in Chapter 5 why I am persuaded that there is only one religion clause in the Constitution, not two.

6 *Lyng v. Northwest Indian Cemetery Protective Association*, 485 U.S. 439 (1988).

7 As of 1999, the road in question still had not been built. See Jesse H. Choper, "Comments on Stephen Carter's Lecture," *California Law Review* 87 (1999): 1087. Although friends of religious freedom might rejoice that the traditional practices of the tribes have so far been preserved (as of this writing), the Supreme Court deserves none of the credit for the maintenance of the status quo. In particular, despite the forbearance of government officials, there is no constitutional guarantee that the preservation will continue.

8 Rather than bore the reader with a lengthy footnote, let me simply state that I discuss some of this important literature, and what I see as its shortcomings, in my book *The Culture of Disbelief: How American Law and Politics Trivialize Religious Devotion* (New York: Basic Books, 1993), esp. chaps. 2, 11. For an effective, book-length response to much of the literature on the role of religion in public debate, see Michael Perry, *Love and Power: The Role of Religion and Morality in American Politics* (New York: Oxford University Press, 1991).

9 The theologian Stanley Hauerwas has argued that this separation has a deeper flaw, that the very concept of the "secular" is imaginary and, to the Christian, incomprehensible. See Stanley Hauerwas, *Dispatches from the Front: Theological Engagements with the Secular* (Durham, N.C.: Duke University Press, 1994).

10   *Goldman v. Weinberger,* 475 U.S. 503 (1986).

11   The most optimistic statement of my accommodationist faith is my article "The Resurrection of Religious Freedom?" *Harvard Law Review* 107 (1993): 118.

12   Although this insight is not new, it occasionally surprises. But consider, for example, the social contract theories of John Locke and Thomas Hobbes. Hobbes despairs of what humans left to their own devices in the state of nature are likely to do, and Locke, although a little more sanguine about human instinct, winds up in the same place: We need the state for our protection. The idea that the state will protect us supposes humans as a collectivity behaving more wisely (or with a different understanding of rational self-interest) than humans as individuals. This may even be true—but it still considers the state more likely than the individual to be right.

Immanuel Kant makes the same assumption. Kantians are less worried about the source of the state's authority than the proper manner of its exercise. They believe that it is possible for humans to reason their way to right answers. But—the key Kantian move—the state has the power to enforce these right answers on dissenting citizens. For Locke and Hobbes (and Jean-Jacques Rousseau), the enforcement power exists because the state is the state. For Kant, the enforcement power exists because the state is right. Thus Kant, even more than the contractarians, ultimately derives the authority of the state from a sense of its rightness.

13   For a lively and provocative exploration of the implications of this thesis for the religious, see Robert M. Cover, "The Supreme Court, 1982 Term—Foreword: Nomos and Narrative," *Harvard Law Review* 97 (1983): 4.

14   This is another very old insight, stemming from the Critical Legal Studies movement in American legal scholarship and, before them, from the Legal Realists. But I believe it to have an often unremarked relationship to theories of civil disobedience. See Stephen L. Carter, *The Dissent of the Governed: A Meditation on Law, Religion, and Loyalty* (Cambridge: Harvard University Press, 1998), chap. 3.

15   As it happens, I do believe that an obligation to God is unlike an obligation to a strongly held secular moral view, but my analysis does not turn on this belief, and, in any case, I doubt that I possess the rhetorical tools to persuade those who disagree. But only in the mirror maze of secular discourse is the weakness of my rhetorical abilities evidence that I am wrong.

16   *Church of Lukumi Babalu Aye, Inc. v. Hialeah,* 508 U.S. 520 (1993).

17   The problem of the animal-rights ordinance helps explain why the distinction between fact and belief that is so crucial to much of Western thought is often incomprehensible within the confines of a particular religion. To the *santeros,* the notion that their futures will be destroyed should the *orishas* die is a fact, not a belief. Thus, the *santeros* can provide what we might think of as a secular reason for their sacrifices: They want to live healthy, productive lives. True, no-

body who lacks their faith in the *orishas* will accept this "secular" truth, any more than someone who lacks faith in the medicinal qualities of marijuana will be impressed by "secular" claims that its use should be normalized; but this is precisely what makes the notion of the secular so slippery.

18   Cover, "*Nomos* and Narrative."

19   The Reagan administration took the view that the case was about the separation of powers, not the right to discriminate, and that the authority to deny the exemption rested in Congress, not the IRS. This claim of high principle would have been more persuasive had the administration announced its decision to seek an amendment barring discrimination on the basis of race by tax-exempt entities before, rather than after, announcing its decision to join the *Bob Jones* lawsuit.

20   See *Bob Jones University v. United States,* 461 U.S. 574 (1983).

21   For a profile of the university a decade after the Supreme Court decision, see Kate Muir, "Majoring in Bible-Bashing," The *Times* (London), November 21, 1992 (available on LEXIS/NEXIS). Ironically, the same Bob Jones University that refused to yield to the pressure of a threat to its tax status in 1983 changed its policies on interracial dating in the face of political and media pressure in 2000, as recounted in Chapter 4.

22   The most open and obvious version in the West was the transformation of France, as set forth in Eugen Weber's wonderful yet tragic book, Eugen Weber, *Peasants into Frenchmen: The Modernization of Rural France, 1870-1914* (Stanford, California: Stanford University Press, 1976). As I shall argue, however, we Americans may only be less clumsy, not more just.

23   Both the terminology and the argumentation are borrowed from Cover, "*Nomos* and Narrative."

24   One of the simplest judicial statements of the compelling interest test for accommodation is that of Justice Sandra Day O'Connor (joined by Justices William Brennan and Thurgood Marshall) in her dissenting opinion in *Bowen v. Roy,* 476 U.S. 693 (1986): "[T]he government must accommodate a legitimate free exercise claim unless pursuing an equally important interest by narrowly tailored means." *Bowen* involved the religious objection by Native American parents to using a social security number to identify their daughter, Little Bird of Snow. The plurality opinion answered that victory for the claimants would require the government to "join in their chosen religious practice." The theorist of resistance will immediately spot the weakness of the plurality's position: The state interferes quite actively with the nurturing of the religious community when it requires parents to conceptualize their children, even for a brief time, as the impersonal objects of bureaucratic scrutiny.

25   *Needham Pastoral Counseling Center, Inc. v. Board of Appeals of Needham,* 29 Mass. App. Ct. 31, 557 N.E.2d 43 (Appeals Court of Mass., Norfolk, 1990).

26 See Kent Greenawalt, "Religion as a Concept in Constitutional Law," *California Law Review* 753 (1984): 753.

27 See *Swanner v. Anchorage Equal Rights Commission*, 513 U.S. 979 (1994), where only Justice Thomas, dissenting from the Court's refusal to review the Alaska decision, was able to spot the interference with religious liberty.

28 The Supreme Court has suggested in dicta, and at least one federal court of appeals has held as a matter of law, that the selection of clergy should be utterly beyond the scrutiny of the state. The Supreme Court, in *Kedroff v. Saint Nicholas Cathedral of the Russian Orthodox Church*, 344 U.S. 94 (1952), proposed that "a spirit of freedom for religious organizations" requires that churches retain the "power to decide for themselves, free from state interference, matters of church government as well as those of faith and doctrine." The justices added: "Freedom to select the clergy, where no improper methods of choice are proven, we think, must now be said to have federal constitutional protection as a part of the free exercise of religion against state interference." Ibid., 116. In *Rayburn v. General Conference of Seventh-Day Adventists*, 772 F.2d 1164 (4th Cir. 1985), cert. denied, 478 U.S. 1020 (1986), the Fourth Circuit applied the *Kedroff* language to hold that the provisions of Title VII of the Civil Rights Act of 1964 banning discrimination on the basis of sex cannot be applied to selection of clergy.

I obviously agree with the language and spirit of *Kedroff*, as well as with the result in *Rayburn*. But it must be noted that this approach has its critics. For example, Professor Jane Rutherford, in a provocative article, neatly turns contemporary legal scholarship on its head, pointing out that if contemporary critics are correct in asserting that the courts have erred by conceptualizing religion as a choice rather than an obligation, we have an additional reason to consider the application of Title VII to religious groups: Those who are dissatisfied with a religion's hiring policies do not, as the courts seem to think, retain the option of easy exit. See Jane Rutherford, "Equality As the Primary Constitutional Value: The Case for Applying Employment Discrimination Laws to Religion," *Cornell Law Review* 81 (1996): 1049.

29 Few scholars, and virtually no judges, seem to believe any longer in the "passive virtues" introduced into constitutional discourse by Alexander Bickel. See Alexander Bickel, *The Least Dangerous Branch: The Supreme Court at the Bar of Politics* (New Haven: Yale University Press, 1962).

Chapter Twelve

1 In a 1997 Gallup survey, 44 percent of respondents said they accept the literal truth of the Genesis creation account. See George Gallup, Jr., and D. Michael Lindsay, *Surveying the Religious Landscape: Trends in U.S. Beliefs* (Harrisburg, Pennsylvania: Morehouse Publishing, 1999), pp. 36–38.

2 David Tracy, *Plurality and Ambiguity: Hermeneutics, Religion, Hope* (Chicago: University of Chicago Press, 1987), p. 83.

3 Nothing in this argument turns on one's view of who the authentic interpreter of God's word happens to be. One can believe that God's will is eternal and unchanging, and believe at the same time that fallible human beings often get it wrong, and believe at the same time that God's will, even imperfectly understood, remains transcendently authoritative.

4 *Corporation of the Presiding Bishop of the Church of Jesus Christ of Latter-Day Saints v. Amos,* 483 U.S. 327 (1987).

5 The new set of ideas about God may thus be true and yet not be a religion.

6 Jaroslav Pelikan, *The Vindication of Tradition* (New Haven: Yale University Press, 1984), p. 59.

7 For an explanation of the seminar's method, see the notes in Robert W. Funk et al., *The Five Gospels: What Did Jesus Really Say* (New York: Macmillan, 1993). For one scholar's reaction to the Jesus Seminar, see Luke Timothy Johnson, *The Real Jesus: The Misguided Quest for the Historical Jesus and Truth of the Traditional Gospels* (San Francisco: HarperSanFrancisco, 1997). A thoughtful summary of evangelical criticism is James R. Edwards, "Who Do Scholars Say That I am?" *Christianity Today,* March 4, 1996, p. 14.

8 See John Shelby Spong, *Born of a Woman: A Bishop Rethinks the Birth of Jesus* (San Francisco: HarperSanFrancisco, 1992). The book mentioned in text is *Why Christianity Must Change or Die : A Bishop Speaks to Believers in Exile: A New Reformation of the Church's Faith and Practice* (San Francisco: HarperSanFrancisco, 1998). Despite its depressingly postmodern structure—Spong rejects inconvenient texts and amasses his reading of the remainder to support a reconstruction of the church in the image of all that Spong believes—the book does score some telling points against religious complacency. As an evangelical and an Episcopalian (Spong is a retired Episcopal bishop), I do not find his work particularly attractive—indeed, I find much of it dangerous— but I do think that Bishop Spong is correct when he says he speaks for millions who call themselves Christians. All through the history of the church, Christians have been seduced by dangerous ideas, and the present era is no exception.

9 See, for example, the discussion in David A. J. Richards, *Toleration and the Constitution* (New York: Oxford University Press, 1986), pp. 150–155. See also Ira C. Lupu, "Home Education, Religious Liberty, and the Separation of Powers," *Boston University Law Review* 67 (1987): 971; and Suzanna Sherry, "Responsible Republicanism: Educating for Citizenship," *University of Chicago Law Review* 62 (1995): 131.

10 *Wisconsin v. Yoder,* 406 U.S. 205 (1972).

11 See Stephen L. Carter, "Parents, Religion, and Schools: Reflections on *Pierce,* Seventy Years Later," *Seton Hall Law Review* 27 (1997): 1194.

12 Not even all Protestant groups accept the idea of teaching religion at Sunday school. The Mennonites, for example, who live their lives in determined nonconformity to the state, reject Sunday school as part of the "Americanized civil religion." Theron F. Schlabach, *Peace, Faith, Nation: Mennonites and Amish in Nineteenth Century America* (Scottdale, Pa.: Herald Press, 1988), p. 226.

13 For the first several decades of the nation's existence, the state governments supported religious education with public funds. Only late in the nineteenth century, as the flood of Roman Catholic immigrants began to alarm Protestant nativists, did the nation withdraw aid from religious schools. See Warren A. Nord, *Religion and American Education: Rethinking a National Dilemma* (Chapel Hill: University of North Carolina Press, 1995), pp. 71–74, as well as the history discussed in Charles Leslie Glenn Jr., *The Myth of the Common School* (Amherst: University of Massachusetts Press, 1988). For a more specific study, see Diane Ravitch, *The Great School Wars, New York City, 1805–1973: A History of the Public Schools as Battlefield of Social Change* (New York: Basic Books, 1974). General background on anti-Catholicism (including the school controversy) may be found in Jay P. Dolan, *The American Catholic Experience: A History from Colonial Times to the Present* (Garden City, N.Y.: Doubleday, 1985). A more polemical but quite readable review of some of the same history is Andrew M. Greeley, *An Ugly Little Secret: Anti-Catholicism in North America* (Kansas City: Sheed Andrews and McMeel, 1977). It is important to bear in mind that the anti-Catholic Blaine Amendment to the U.S. Constitution, which would have barred the use of public money to fund religious schools but would also have allowed the use of the Bible in public schools—the Protestant Bible, that is—failed to pass in the Senate by only a small margin in 1875. A number of states subsequently adopted "Blaine" amendments to their own constitutions, and some are still in force. The Blaine movement was fired not by constitutional principle but by anti-Catholic animus. A thoughtful discussion of this history, by a scholar who generally advocates a high wall of separation between church and state, is Douglas Laycock, "The Underlying Unity of Separation and Neutrality," *Emory Law Journal* 46 (1997): 43. See also Kurt T. Lash, "The Second Adoption of the Establishment Clause: The Rise of the Nonestablishment Principle," *Arizona State Law Journal* 27 (1995): 1085.

14 I discuss some of this history in Stephen L. Carter, *The Dissent of the Governed: A Meditation on Law, Religion, and Loyalty* (Cambridge: Harvard University Press, 1998).

15 Although this evidence has been much picked over, one of the most enduring commentaries on the constitutional significance of these early practices remains Jesse Choper, "The Establishment Clause and Aid to Parochial Schools," *California Law Review* 56 (1968): 260.

16 The purportedly secular educational theorists of the twentieth century did not improve matters very much. John Dewey, for example, the twentieth century's

great apostle of educating for democracy, huffed that parents should not be allowed to "inoculate" their children with beliefs that they "happen to have found serviceable to themselves." Quoted in Steven C. Rockefeller, *John Dewey: Religious Faith and Democratic Humanism* (New York: Columbia University Press, 1991), p. 250. Religious education, he wrote at a moment when many states were deciding whether to outlaw it, was simply a form of segregation. Ibid., p. 267. Dewey's words should not be lifted from their context. He wrote at a time when the only schools formally considered religious were Catholic and Jewish schools aimed at the children of immigrants. Dewey believed that the immigrant children should attend the Protestant public schools.

17 Professor Gutmann insists, without citing any evidence, that many religious parents teach their children "disrespect for people who are different." Amy Gutmann, *Democratic Education* (Princeton: Princeton University Press, 1987), p. 31.

18 See, for example, Stephen Macedo, "The Politics of Justification," *Political Theory* 18 (1990): 280. Professor Macedo proposes educating children for what he calls "situated autonomy," a status in which "quiet obedience, deference, unquestioned devotion, and humility" become practically impossible. Ibid., 278. One can easily see how many religious families would view such state action as totalitarian—and perhaps downright wicked.

19 See Sherry, "Responsible Republicanism," pp. 160–161. See also Ira C. Lupu, "The Separation of Powers and the Protection of Children," *University of Chicago Law Review* 61 (1994): 1317, 1353, arguing that "compulsory education laws reduce the risk of totalitarian control or abuse of children."

20 One wonders whether Justice Douglas would have had the same solicitude for a child whose parents prefer public school but who would rather attend a parochial school—always assuming, for the sake of the example, that the parents have the means to pay. If, as I suspect, the answer would turn out to be that the ratchet turns only one way, then the state, through its courts, would be evidencing a quite open and obvious antireligious bias.

21 *Mozert v. Hawkins County Public Schools*, 827 F.2d 1058 (6th Cir. 1987), cert. denied, 484 U.S. 1066 (1988).

22 Nomi Maya Stolzenberg, "'He Drew a Circle That Shut Me Out': Assimilation, Indoctrination, and the Paradox of Liberal Education," *Harvard Law Review* 106 (1993): 581.

23 The leading academic defenders of this vision of the communal self are Alasdair MacIntyre and Charles Taylor, even though their understandings of its significance are quite different. Compare MacIntyre's *After Virtue: A Study in Moral Theory*, 2d ed. (Notre Dame, Ind.: University of Notre Dame Press, 1984) with Taylor's *Sources of the Self: The Making of Modern Identity* (Cambridge: Harvard University Press, 1989).

24 For a thoughtful answer, see Michael W. McConnell, "The Selective Funding Problem: Abortions and Religious Schools," *Harvard Law Review* 104 (1991): 989.

25 See, for example, the sources cited in notes 17–19, above.

26 See the discussion in Carter, *Dissent of the Governed,* pp. 35–47.

27 Frederick Mark Gedicks, in his very fine book *The Rhetoric of Church and State: A Critical Analysis of Religion Clause Jurisprudence* (Durham, N.C.: Duke University Press, 1993), argues that religious freedom can be saved only if the courts begin to conceptualize religious liberty as a communitarian or group right rather than merely as an individual right. In this he is surely correct. It would help, however, if religions themselves were able more often to behave like groups rather than collections of self-seeking individuals.

Afterword

1 The proposition that there is much hostility to religion on campus is a point well picked over but never refuted. See, for example, the discussion in George Marsden, *The Soul of the American University: From Protestant Establishment to Established Non-Belief* (New York: Oxford University Press, 1995). I discuss some of the antireligious stereotypes in the literature in my book *The Culture of Disbelief: How American Law and Politics Trivialize Religious Devotion* (New York: Basic Books, 1993).

2 See *Bishop v. Aronov,* 926 F.2d 1066 (11th Cir. 1991).

3 Ralph Reed, *Active Faith: How Christians Are Changing the Soul of American Politics* (New York: Free Press, 1996).

4 This is the thesis of my book *The Culture of Disbelief.*

5 Richard John Neuhaus, "A New Order of Religious Freedom," in *The Essential Neo-Conservative Reader,* ed. Mark Gerson (Reading, Mass.: Addison-Wesley, 1996), p. 386.

6 See *Roberts v. Madigan,* 921 F. 2d 1047 (10th Cir. 1990).

7 A particular critic of the Third World bishops was the Right Reverend Frederick Borsch, head of the Episcopal Diocese of Los Angeles, who presented his attack at the diocesan convention in 1999. But there were many others, equally harsh.

8 George Weigel, "Christian Conviction and Democratic Etiquette," in Mark Gerson, ed., *The Essential Neoconservative Reader* (Reading, Mass.: Addison-Wesley, 1996), pp. 395, 408.

INDEX

ABOUT THE AUTHOR

Stephen L. Carter, the William Nelson Cromwell Professor of Law at Yale, is the author of several acclaimed books, including *The Culture of Disbelief*, *Integrity*, and *Civility*. The *New York Times Book Review* has called him one of the nation's leading public intellectuals, and *Time* magazine identified him as one of fifty leaders for the next century. He lives with his family near New Haven, Connecticut.